Shakespeare's Caliban examines *The Tempest*'s "savage and deformed slave" as a fascinating but ambiguous literary creation with a remarkably diverse history in criticism and on stage, in art, poetry, and film, and, during the twentieth century, in sociopolitical writings, especially by Caribbean and African authors. This book, by a historian and a Shakespearean, explores the cultural background of Caliban's creation in 1611 and his disparate metamorphoses in the following three and three-quarter centuries. Drawing on a wide range of literary and historical sources, *Shakespeare's Caliban* reflects current interests in the "reception" of artistic works, while explaining how and why Caliban was so flexible and useful a cultural signifier.

Shakespeare's Caliban

Shakespeare's Caliban
A Cultural History

ALDEN T. VAUGHAN
and
VIRGINIA MASON VAUGHAN

CAMBRIDGE
UNIVERSITY PRESS

Published by the Press Syndicate of the University of Cambridge
The Pitt Building, Trumpington Street, Cambridge CB2 1RP
40 West 20th Street, New York, NY 10011-4211, USA
10 Stamford Road, Oakleigh, Melbourne 3166, Australia

© Cambridge University Press 1991

First published 1991
First paperback edition 1993
Reprinted 1993, 1994, 1996

Printed in the United States of America

Library of Congress Cataloging-in-Publication Data is available.

A catalogue record for this book is available from the British Library.

ISBN 0-521-40305-7 hardback
ISBN 0-521-45817-X paperback

For
Mabel Gouldman Mason
and in memory of
Muriel True Vaughan

Contents

Preface

We were driving across Canada in July 1983, en route to the Stratford Festival, when Alden (a historian who specializes in early American race relations) asked Virginia (a Shakespearean who had worked mostly on the history plays), "Do you think Caliban was Shakespeare's representation of an American Indian?" "Probably not," Virginia replied, "but I haven't given it much thought." A hundred miles later we had decided to collaborate on a close examination of Caliban. Our initial goal was to investigate Shakespeare's possible models for Prospero's slave in *The Tempest*, but increasingly we became intrigued by a broader and timelier concern: the myriad uses to which Caliban has been put – by actors, artists, and almost every category of writers – in the nearly four centuries since Shakespeare fashioned him for the Jacobean stage. As we discovered an ever more complex and fascinating Caliban, we shared our tentative thoughts in lectures to laypeople, professional Shakespeareans, American-culture specialists, and, not least, a freshman class of several hundred students in the humanities. We also published several articles in scholarly journals on aspects of Caliban interpretation and appropriation. We had become, in student parlance, Caliban groupies.

This book is the fruition of our joint effort to track Caliban's eventful odyssey from Shakespeare's time to the present. It shows how and, wherever possible, why each age has appropriated and reshaped him to suit its needs and assumptions, for Caliban's image has been incredibly flexible, ranging from an aquatic beast to a noble savage, with innumerable intermediate manifestations. Caliban has for several centuries been a durable cultural signifier

Preface

for poets, playwrights, novelists, artists, and social commentators. Writers as diverse as John Milton, Harriet Beecher Stowe, T. S. Eliot, W. H. Auden, Rubén Darío, Edward Kamau Brathwaite, and Ngugi Wa Thiong'o were inspired by *The Tempest* and its savage slave; so were artists as diverse as William Hogarth, Henry Fuseli, and John Gilbert; and if no great composer set the play to music (Verdi intended to), at least Henry Purcell and some less prominent musicians tried their hands.[1] Caliban is not limited to high culture, however; he can also be found in popular novels, comic books, and children's stories.[2] This book documents *The Tempest*'s, and especially Caliban's, influence on a host of authors, actors, and artists throughout the world.

1 In "List, List, O List . . . Of Films and Videotapes of Shakespearean Operas," Sy Isenberg lists Attenberg, Fibich, Gatty, Gibbs, Halevy, Lattuada, Martin, Purcell, Reichardt, Smith, Zumsteeg, and Sutermeister as composers of operas based on *The Tempest* in *Shakespeare on Film Newsletter*, XIV, No. 2 (1990): 5. He overlooked British composer Michael Tippett's three-act opera *The Knot Garden*, which was performed at the Royal Opera House in 1973. See also O. F. Babler, "Shakespeare's *Tempest* as an Opera," *Notes and Queries*, CLXXXVI (1951): 30–31. A radically different invocation of *The Tempest* metaphor in musicology is Wilfred Mellers, *Caliban Reborn: Renewal in Twentieth-Century Music* (New York: Harper & Row, 1967).

2 Caliban is a character in the Marvel comic book, "An Age Undreamed Of," from February 1985; he also appears in Mark Lewis's children's story, "Kaliban's Christmas" (1987). For more information on Caliban in children's literature, see Antoinette I. Teplitz, "Caliban Through the Ages" (unpublished M. A. thesis, De Paul University, Chicago, 1989). Twentieth-century novelists have also adapted *The Tempest*'s themes and characters for a variety of purposes; we cite a few examples here. John Fowles's *The Magus*, rev. ed. (New York: Dell Publishing, 1978), is perhaps the most famous appropriation; Fowles presents a Prospero figure on a Greek island who manipulates the narrator into changing his values and behavior. Novels with "Caliban" in the title include John Ginger's *Caliban on Thursday* (London: London Magazine Editions, 1976), set in an English public school; Paul West's *Caliban's Filibuster* (New York: Doubleday, 1971), which portrays Cal, a failed novelist who plays with language; and, more recently, Stephen Popkes's *Caliban Landing* (New York: Congden & Weed, 1987), a science-fiction "thriller" based on the theme of "first contact" with a new world of strange creatures. Caliban also is frequently alluded to within novels; for example, Thomas Wolfe entitled the first chapter of *The Web and the Rock* "The Child Caliban," which describes the birth and upbringing of George Webber (Garden City, N.Y.: Sun Dial Press, 1940), pp. 1–12. Most recently, Cudjoe, the hero of John Edgar Wideman's *Philadelphia Fire* (New York: Henry Holt, 1990), explicitly identifies himself with Caliban. For surveys of Calibanic figures in Canadian literature, see Chantal Zabus, "A Calibanic Tempest in Anglophone & Francophone New World

Preface

The reinscription of a text – or a character like Caliban – is, of course, nothing new; in today's poststructuralist era, almost everyone takes for granted the text's indeterminism. But reinscription is not a random process, isolated from broader intellectual, social, and political concerns. The changes in Caliban through 375 years of interpretation reflect specific intellectual concerns, of course, but they also suggest something larger, more reflective of society in general than simply the individual scholar's or actor's or artist's immediate preference. Their preferences are products of their times. Thus, Caliban's history is cultural history, or at least a significant strand of it, in microcosm. Changing interpretations of Caliban provide a window on cultural trends, just as those trends simultaneously determine Caliban's changing characteristics.

I

While our joint exploration of Caliban was in its final stages, we discovered that several other Shakespearean scholars were delving into what Germans call *Rezeptionsästhetik* (loosely translated as the aesthetics of reception), partly, perhaps, in response to Hans Robert Jauss's work on reception and canon formation.[3] It may therefore be useful here to suggest how our study relates to some of the recent works and especially how it differs from them in its scope and focus.

The most provocative of the recent studies on reception and canon formation is Gary Taylor's *Reinventing Shakespeare: A Cultural History from the Restoration to the Present*. Given Taylor's subject (all of Shakespeare) and chronology (from the Restoration to 1989), his analysis is perforce general. He addresses basic questions: "When did people decide that Shakespeare was the greatest English dramatist? . . . Who did the deciding? . . . And once Shakespeare's hegemony was achieved, how was it maintained?"[4] The answers to these questions required broad historical surveys of dramatic

Writing," *Canadian Literature*, No. 104 (Spring 1985): 35–50; and Diana Brydon, "Re-writing *The Tempest*," *World Literature Written in English*, XXIII (1984): 75–88.
3 See Hans Robert Jauss, *Toward an Aesthetic of Reception*, trans. Timothy Bahti (Minneapolis: University of Minnesota Press, 1982).
4 Gary Taylor, *Reinventing Shakespeare: A Cultural History from the Restoration to the Present* (New York: Weidenfeld & Nicolson, 1989), p. 5.

practices in the Restoration, editing procedures in the eighteenth century, bardolatry in the nineteenth century, and the establishment of the academic Shakespeare industry in the twentieth century.

Michael Bristol's *Shakespeare's America, America's Shakespeare* is also a comprehensive study of the institutions that have fostered and controlled the production of Shakespeare in the United States. Bristol argues that "the interpretation of Shakespeare and the interpretation of American political culture are mutually determining practices."[5] His book eschews analysis of specific Shakespearean texts; rather, his concern is the institutions that shaped Shakespeare in the United States: H. H. Furness's variorum editions in the nineteenth century, the establishment of the Folger Shakespeare Library in the early twentieth century, the institutionalization of Shakespeare in the classroom, and the influence of particular academicians on interpretation.

Unlike Taylor's and Bristol's surveys, Jonathan Bate's *Shakespearean Constitutions: Politics, Theatre, Criticism, 1730–1830* is chronologically limited. Still, it keeps the entire Shakespeare canon within its purview. Bate uses eighteenth- and nineteenth-century political cartoons, caricatures, and parodies to show how English political discourse appropriated Shakespeare.[6] He argues that despite the impression left by many Marxist analyses of Shakespeare, the dramatist is not always used as an instrument of cultural containment; Shakespeare, as Bate amply demonstrates, has repeatedly been a weapon of the oppressed as well as the oppressor.

Shakespeare's Caliban can be seen as the next logical step in Shakespeare reception studies: the analysis of one character from his inception to the present. A reader might well ask, Isn't the evolution of a single literary figure too narrow and idiosyncratic to reveal much about cultural significations? We once harbored such suspicions, we confess, but no longer. Consider for a moment how innumerable cultural figures – literary, religious, mythological – have experienced frequent and often profound changes in the public's perception that reflect broader cultural contexts. Eve, Mary, and

5 Michael D. Bristol, *Shakespeare's America, America's Shakespeare* (New York: Routledge, 1990), p. 3.
6 Jonathan Bate, *Shakespearean Constitutions: Politics, Theatre, Criticism, 1730–1830* (Oxford: Clarendon Press, 1989), p. 3.

Satan are obvious examples of religious characters whose profound metamorphoses have recently been recounted.[7] Secular historical figures, too, are reevaluated from era to era, their stock rising and falling in response to evolving political and social concerns. Cleopatra and Joan of Arc come quickly to mind.[8] Among Americans, the abolitionist John Brown is an apt example. He has been viewed in some times and places as a violent psychopath, in others as a noble visionary; the contrasting interpretations have reflected divergent cultural contexts.[9] In fact, all historical (and fictional) figures are texts, subject to changing perceptions and assessments. Studies of the interpretive changes and the forces that fostered them tell much about the texts themselves and much too about the societies that reinterpret an earlier era's received wisdom. The same holds for Caliban.

II

If the study of one historical personage or one literary character is indeed a fruitful focus of inquiry, a reader still might wonder why we picked Caliban. Surely he is not unique in his changeability. Through the years, most of Shakespeare's major characters have weathered drastic reinterpretive shifts. Images of Shylock, Cleopatra, and *The Taming of the Shrew*'s Kate are cases in point: All have recently received more sympathetic treatment than before, largely because alterations in critical perspective allow us to see them afresh.[10] Similarly, Hamlet, Macbeth, and Othello have endured

---

7 Changing interpretations of these three figures – among the many that could be cited – have recently been described in J. A. Phillips, *Eve: The History of an Idea* (New York: Harper & Row, 1984); Marina Warner, *Alone of All Her Sex: The Myth and the Cult of the Virgin* (New York: Random House, 1976); and Jeffrey Burton Russell, *The Prince of Darkness: Radical Evil and the Power of Good in History* (Ithaca, N.Y.: Cornell University Press, 1988).

8 Lucy Hughes-Hallett, *Cleopatra: Histories, Dreams and Distortions* (New York: Harper & Row, 1990); Marina Warner, *Joan of Arc: The Image of Female Heroism* (New York: Knopf, 1981).

9 Stephen B. Oates, *To Purge This Land of Blood: A Biography of John Brown* (New York: Harper & Row, 1970). For the story of another American changeling, see Michael A. Lofaro and Joe Cummings, eds., *Crockett at Two Hundred: New Perspectives on the Man and the Myth* (Knoxville: University of Tennessee Press, 1989).

10 See, for example, Irene Dash's review of changing images of Kate in *Wooing*,

diverse interpretations on stage and in scholarly criticism, often in response to changing societal perspectives.[11] But none of these characters, nor any other in Shakespeare's canon, has undergone the extreme range of metamorphoses that have marked Caliban's tumultuous career.[12] He has in various eras been seen as a tortoise, a giant fish, a grotesque monster, a primitive everyman, an anthropoid missing link, and – especially nowadays – an American Indian or a Caribbean slave of African or mestizo ancestry. And unlike other Shakespearean characters, Caliban's identification as a beast has been applied literally rather than figuratively. Also unlike most other Shakespearean characters, Caliban has had a large life beyond the stage and study: Since the last quarter of the nineteenth century, and especially in recent decades, Caliban has been a major sociopolitical emblem throughout the world. Writers of diverse genres (journalists, poets, political pamphleteers) and numerous nationalities (French, Cuban, Nicaraguan, Barbadian, Canadian, Ghanian, and Zambian, to name a few) have invoked Caliban in support of various – often contradictory – sociopolitical causes.

Caliban has been a particularly sensitive barometer of intellectual and social change, partly, no doubt, because Shakespeare's characters are so universally recognized and so often reflective of the human predicament. Shakespeare has, accordingly, been read throughout the world (as, of course, have other great writers, regardless of their nationality) for the beauty and power of his imagery. But Shakespeare has also been widely read because, as an instrument of

Wedding, and Power: Shakespeare's Women (New York: Columbia University Press, 1981), pp. 33–64.

11 In the nineteenth century, for example, critics argued that it was inconceivable that Othello could be black. Now it is unusual to find him played by anyone but a black actor. Hamlet has varied from Laurence Olivier's oedipally conflicted man "who couldn't make up his mind" to Mel Gibson's man of action. Postwar interpretations of Lear have evolved from a benign, befuddled old man to much starker views, as in Peter Brook's film based on Jan Kott, *Shakespeare Our Contemporary* (Garden City, N.Y.: Anchor Books, 1966), pp. 127–68.

12 In *Shakespeare's Mercutio: His History and Drama* (Chapel Hill: University of North Carolina Press, 1988), Joseph A. Porter has analyzed the figure of Mercury in western culture, culminating in Shakespeare's fiery character. The focus is primarily on literary analogues before 1595 and Shakespeare's exploitation of the Mercury figure in crafting *Romeo and Juliet*. Porter allows only 26 pages to adaptation and appropriation since 1595. Just as Mercutio differs greatly from Caliban, so Porter's study differs from ours.

British cultural imperialism, his plays entered perforce the curricula of nations around the world when British language and literature followed the British flag.[13] The canon, one might say, succeeded the cannon. Thus *The Tempest*, *Hamlet*, *Macbeth*, and other Shakespearean plays were read by children and adults from Sydney to Singapore, Quebec to Cape Town, Bridgetown to Bombay. When the British Empire dissolved in the aftermath of World War II, Shakespearean motifs became handy weapons in the accompanying clash of words.

The Tempest's anti-imperialist overtones proved especially apt in this context, and Caliban – the quintessential colonial victim – seized center stage. Thus Caliban rests at the core of many recent interpretations of *The Tempest*. And as we approach the quincentennial of Columbus's arrival in the New World, it seems particularly appropriate to understand how Prospero's slave got there too. His Americanization, in fact, is relatively recent. A century ago, Sidney Lee identified Caliban with the natives of the Western Hemisphere, thereby inviting an association between Shakespeare's savage and colonized peoples. Not until Octave Mannoni's vivid application of the Caliban–Prospero metaphor to Madagascar half a century later did its profound implications for western imperialism emerge. Ever since, Caliban has been widely appropriated by sociopolitical causes, with worldwide implications.

Perhaps, too, on a more philosophical level, Caliban fascinates because he violates the order of things. In Shakespeare's drama, Prospero represents western European hierarchy and the primacy of language. Caliban has learned this language but only to curse what it signifies. Caliban appeals to rebellious instincts because he challenges a dominant culture. His very opposition to Prospero's hegemony helps to define the appropriator's assumptions and values.

As an opposing force, the "other" onto whom the dominant culture projects its fears of disorder, Caliban thus becomes a powerful symbol of resistance and transgression. Kenneth Burke's comments on symbolic figures could apply to Caliban: Such symbols provide "a terminology of thoughts, actions, emotions, attitudes, for codify-

13 See especially Ania Loomba, *Gender, Race, Renaissance Drama* (Manchester, U.K.: Manchester University Press, 1989), ch. 1.

ing a pattern of experience."[14] This pattern of resistance and transgression varies from culture to culture, but it generally focuses on
issues of hierarchy, dominance, freedom, control, and sexuality.
We propose that Caliban's rebellion against Prospero's control – in
whatever form it is represented – embodies issues fundamental to
a culture's ideology. (Burke defines "ideology" as "the nodes of
beliefs and judgment which the artist can exploit for his effects. It
varies from one person to another, but in so far as its general
acceptance and its stability are more stressed than its particular
variations from person to person and from age to age, an ideology
is a culture."[15]) Ideology is never a single static viewpoint but is
instead a variable range of attitudes. Or, in Stephen Greenblatt's
words, "the work of art is the product of a negotiation between a
creator or class of creators, equipped with a complex, communally
shared repertoire of conventions, and the institutions and practices
of society."[16] Negotiations, of course, do not stop at the moment of
production; they continue as a text is studied, enacted, adapted,
and appropriated at discrete cultural moments – *epistemes*, to use
Foucault's term – when institutions, practices, and ideologies have
undergone radical change. Because Caliban has repeatedly been
represented as a figure opposed to dominant ideologies, whatever
those ideologies may be, he provides a spectrum of interpretations
seldom matched in the history of western literature.

Shakespeare's Caliban differs significantly, then, from the more
generalized work of Taylor, Bristol, and Bate in its focus on a single
character over his entire life span, from the moment of creation to
the eve of our publication. But if our subject is narrower in its focus
on a single character, it is broader in its concern with the text's
moment of production as well as its subsequent reception. *The
Tempest*, unlike many Shakespearean plays, has long attracted
analyses of Shakespeare's intentions at the time of creation, and
Caliban often is pivotal to those interpretations. Moreover, subsequent interpretations, appropriations, and adaptations of Caliban

14 Kenneth Burke, *Counter-Statement* (Berkeley: University of California Press, 1931),
   p. 154.
15 Burke, *Counter-Statement*, p. 161.
16 Stephen Greenblatt, "Towards a Poetics of Culture," in *The New Historicism*, ed.
   H. Aram Veeser (New York: Routledge, 1989), pp. 1–14; quotation on p. 12.

usually depend, explictly or implicitly, on the interpreters' assumptions about his meaning in the original text. Representations of Caliban as fish or ape or Indian or African imply, in most instances, a faithful rendering of Shakespeare's text, even if Shakespeare's original audience missed the meaning.

III

Our methodology (to use a slightly pompous term) in the pages that follow meshes our respective training in history and literary criticism; in the truest sense, this is an interdisciplinary and collaborative study, combining syncretic textual analysis with diachronic change. Accordingly, we view *The Tempest* as both an aesthetic creation and a vehicle of cultural history.

The term "cultural history" concisely summarizes our approach to Caliban. By "culture," the more ambiguous half of the label, we mean, in anthropologist Clifford Geertz's definition, "the framework of beliefs, expressive symbols, and values in terms of which individuals define their world, express their feelings, and make their judgments." Like Geertz, we believe that societies use "ordered clusters of significant symbols" to make sense of their world. Cultures, in turn, appropriate literary texts, among other sorts of texts, in accord with their values and ideologies. On a broad level, "the study of culture, the accumulated totality of such patterns, is the study of the machinery individuals and groups of individuals employ to orient themselves in a world otherwise opaque."[17] Through nearly four centuries of human history, as knowledge of Shakespeare's texts has spread worldwide, the varied uses to which succeeding generations and disparate cultures have put Caliban reveal a great deal about their changing attitudes toward – among other concerns – hierarchy, slavery, social progress, license, appetite, control, order, and power. We see Shakespeare's monster as an important "expressive symbol," a cultural signifier that changes through space and time, geography and chronology. In the pages that follow, we examine how and why Caliban changed as he did. In this sense, our study is both cultural and historical.

17 Clifford Geertz, *The Interpretation of Cultures* (New York: Basic Books, 1973), pp. 144–45, 363.

Preface

As cultural historians, we find many sorts of evidence appropriate for our examination. We do not privilege traditional canonical literary critics like Dryden and Johnson, but we do not ignore them either. In our survey of Caliban's history, we use anecdotes, poems, treatises – the stuff of Geertz's "thick description."[18] But we also try to establish a larger, global framework of world events and revolutionary ideas.[19] We hope our eclectic, interdisciplinary approach will appeal not only to readers well versed in Shakespeare but also, perhaps especially, to readers concerned with changing patterns of cultural perception.

This book opens with a chapter that reminds readers of Caliban's place in the earliest surviving text of *The Tempest* (1623) and sorts out some of the problems of Caliban's appearance and character. The chapter is purposefully elementary and introductory, designed to review the basic evidence of *The Tempest*'s earliest productions and Caliban's place in the First Folio text. Readers who have not recently seen or read *The Tempest* may want to refresh their memories; we recommend the 1987 Oxford Shakespeare edition (our text for quotations) or a facsimile of the First Folio, but any good edition will do.

The first major section of this book, Part II, entitled "Origins," reconstructs what is known of Caliban's genesis at the moment of production. It outlines the direct and indirect influences on Shakespeare's thought: historical events and political circumstances, etymological roots, literary models, popular customs, and folklore – in short, the sources and analogues that are likely to have shaped Caliban in the dramatist's mind.

The "Origins" section assumes that Shakespeare's genius lay partly in his ability to plumb literary traditions, historical events, and his own fertile imagination for dynamic stage characters.

18 Geertz explains "thick description" on pages 6–7 and 9–10 of *Interpretation of Cultures*. Louis A. Montrose appropriates this term for "new historicist" critics, claiming that, like Geertz, they construe *"all* of culture as the domain of literary criticism – a text to be perpetually interpreted, an inexhaustible collection of stories from which curiosities may be culled and cleverly retold." See "The Poetics and Politics of Culture," in *The New Historicism*, pp. 15–36, esp. p. 19.
19 For a critique of Geertz's methodology, especially his use of "local knowledge" to analyze political events in Indochina during 1965, see Vincent P. Pecora, "The Limits of Local Knowledge," in *The New Historicism*, pp. 243–76.

Preface

Sometimes, of course, Shakespeare modeled his major characterizations on specific individuals, most notably in the history plays, where various kings and noblemen – Julius Caesar, the Henrys, and King John, for example – are portrayed more or less as history recorded them, subject to substantial poetic license. In other instances Shakespeare drew on generic models – types rather than individuals – the Machiavellian villain for *Richard III*, the "pantaloon" for *Taming of the Shrew*'s Gremio, the fool for *Twelfth Night*'s Feste. But in some cases, notably Caliban's, Shakespeare's prototypes are at best enigmatic. Most of the suggested models are plausible, a few are probable, none are provable. The search for evidence goes on, however, because legions of scholars, readers, and viewers want to know, for the sake of knowing, what Shakespeare meant his characters to be.

An argument has often been made that Shakespeare's intentions are irrelevant, that only his text matters, and that it can be interpreted however the reader chooses; all readings are valid. For several decades this "semantic autonomy" of literary works, Shakespeare's included, appealed to critics who held with T. S. Eliot that an author's interpretive authority ends when his words emerge in print or sound; henceforth the reader or listener determines their meaning. That theory had gained considerable popularity in the mid-1940s with the publication of W. K. Wimsatt and Monroe Beardsley's essay on the "Intentional Fallacy," which argued against accepting an author's assessment of his or her *stylistic* purpose.[20] Wimsatt and Beardsley did not, however, advocate thematic anarchy; on matters of character and plot they held the traditional position that the author's intentions are essential to a full analysis, however ineffectively those intentions may have been executed. Nonetheless, some zealous devotees of the "new criticism" distorted the "intentional fallacy" to mean that Caliban or any other literary characterization is *only* what the reader or viewer wants him to

---

20 T. S. Eliot, "Tradition and the Individual Talent," in *Selected Essays* (New York: Harcourt, Brace & World, 1932); William K. Wimsatt and Monroe Beardsley, "The Intentional Fallacy," *Sewanee Review*, LIV (1946): 468–88. For an assessment of "the intentional fallacy," see E. D. Hirsch, Jr., *Validity in Interpretation* (New Haven, Conn.: Yale University Press, 1967), esp. pp. 10–27.

Preface

be; with *The Tempest's* first production or its first publication, Shakespeare's intentions ceased to matter.

This book conforms to the current view of artistic creativity that blends the best features of both theories: First, an actor or director or reader may take whatever liberties he or she wishes with any of Shakespeare's texts; they are, after all, in the public domain, and alterations or interpretations may be artistic contributions in their own right. Second, the playwright's intentions do matter. He (in this instance) created a story that he wanted his readers or viewers to understand; he embedded in that story signifiers central to his own culture; and he created characters to represent those messages through words and actions. It is therefore reasonable and relevant to find out, as best we can, what the author intended. As Geoffrey Bullough argues in the Preface to his *Narrative and Dramatic Sources of Shakespeare* (1957–75), scholars and dramatists have for centuries wanted "to explore the workings of Shakespeare's mind." That is not to say that everything in the plays has an identifiable source or that every possible source is significant. "I have been told," Dr. Samuel Johnson observed sarcastically, "that when Caliban, after a pleasing dream, says, *I cry'd to sleep again*, the author imitates Anacreon," when, in fact, everyone has the same reaction.[21] There are limits to the usefulness of intentionalism.

In any event, scholars have wrangled over Caliban's genesis since at least the middle of the eighteenth century. What did Shakespeare intend when he fashioned his puppy-headed monster? Was his paradigm the American Indian, for example, or an African perhaps, or Europe's mythical wodewose? And if he had American Indians in mind, were they Montaigne's noble savages or their ignoble opposites or a combination of both? Or, on the other hand, did the playwright shun obvious exemplars and contrive instead a creature unrelated to existing figures or types? The answer, of course, is elusive and endlessly debatable. With no Shakespeare letters or notebooks to offer insights and no autobiography to rummage for clues, all evidence must come from the play itself, augmented by Shakespeare's other writings and by the context of his times.

21 *The Plays of William Shakespeare . . .*, 2nd ed., 10 vols., Vol. I, ed. Samuel Johnson and George Steevens (London: Printed for C. Bathurst et al., 1778), p. 32.

But that context is itself incredibly complex: all the ideas to which Shakespeare was exposed, all the events of which he was even subliminally aware, and all the people with whom he had the slightest contact. We have tried to survey all probable sources and to suggest the milieus that may have influenced Shakespeare's thinking. We have, in sum, tried to provide a sense of the literary and historical contexts within which *The Tempest* was conceived. Accordingly, we begin Caliban's story at its true beginning, however murky, before we proceed to the more extensive – and, happily, more identifiable – record of the monster's progress since his conception.

Our much longer Part III, "Receptions," reconstructs Caliban's story from 1611 to the present. It is partly a story of shifting *interpretations* within a general adherence to Shakespeare's original: Differing ways of seeing *The Tempest* and Caliban as new literary and historical contexts encourage new readings of the play and the person. It is also a story of changing *appropriations*. As a Canadian scholar recently put the case, "*The Tempest* is a Masque, an art form strongly dependent on symbolism," which allows us to "come out with applications appropriate for a present cultural dilemma."[22] And finally, receptions are sometimes *adaptations* – borrowings that owe much to the spirit or characters of Shakespeare's play but very little to its text. The lines between interpretation, appropriation, and adaptation are not rigid, of course; our point is that Caliban's odyssey often strays from literary criticism of the play or its performance into artistic inventions or sociopolitical issues that have little to do, at least directly, with Shakespeare's play. Caliban, over the centuries, has served many masters, not all of whom, one suspects, have read *The Tempest* or care to. Caliban, in short, is a cultural icon as well as a literary figure.

The immense variety of Caliban interpretations, appropriations, and adaptations makes his three-and-three-quarter-century odyssey a bit like his much briefer drunken caper with Trinculo and Stephano: Not every step can be charted, and the path is erratic at best, but we can detect a general progression across the stage. We can also

22 Max Dorsinville, *Caliban without Prospero: Essays on Quebec and Black Literature* (Erin, Ontario: Press Porcépic, 1974), p. 12.

discern some larger patterns of interpretation. The late seventeenth century – to summarize broadly – deemed Caliban a pure monster, with emphasis on his vices, deformities, crudities, and beastly qualities, in keeping with the era's concern with basic distinctions between savagery and civility. The eighteenth century continued to view him as the personification of various vices, but here and there a hint of potential virtue crept in. With the romantic movement of the early nineteenth century, Caliban became more docile, and his "natural" qualities were newly appreciated; later in the nineteenth century he was often portrayed as the missing link – part beast, part human, and wholly Darwinian. Although the catalysts for shifting interpretations are admittedly oversimplified by terms such as "romantic" and "Darwinian," we hold them to be essentially valid and widely understood and have not therefore elaborated on these useful labels; to do them full justice in the light of contemporary scholarship would require a separate volume in itself.

The situation is different, we believe, for twentieth-century interpretations and adaptations. They have been less thoroughly studied and are generally more diffusely motivated than their eighteenth- and nineteenth-century precursors. We have accordingly gone to greater lengths to explain why in the twentieth century Caliban is, for many interpreters, Shakespeare's prototype of the New World native – a "noble savage" or, oppositely, Stuart England's dim view of "natural man." Other recent critics, for quite different reasons, see Caliban from starkly altered perspectives: Within the past few decades these have included Caliban as Caribbean, Caliban as South American, Caliban as African, even Caliban as Quebecois. In short, Shakespeare's orphaned slave has been adopted by a remarkable assortment of foster parents, who have embraced him for their own intellectual, social, and political reasons. Although to some literary critics he is still a monster or benevolent wild man, he now most frequently symbolizes the exploited native – of whatever continent and whatever color – who struggles for freedom, dignity, and self-determination from European and American Prosperos. Shakespeare would, no doubt, find these interpretations quite remarkable. Yet he would also, we suspect, find them justifiable, for he too might consider the varied receptions of Caliban a fascinating sign of humanity's continuing concern with the order of things and with the acceptable boundaries of "we" and "they."

We admit that we write within our own *episteme*, a time of rapid global change and, closer to home, of transition in the academic world. Undoubtedly, current ideological concerns influence us and our book in ways we scarcely suspect. In the late 1980s and early 1990s, global issues have penetrated the groves of academe until political and literary theories often seem the same. We received our formal training before poststructuralism invaded the academy, yet we continue to absorb valuable ideas from today's scholarly world. Accordingly, we embrace the indeterminacy of the text; we try not to privilege one interpretive school over another; and we entertain simultaneously a wide assortment of readings of *The Tempest* as legitimate and intellectually stimulating. At the same time, because we were trained in an era that valued analytic research and jargon-free writing, this study, we hope, blends the best of old and new academic values.

Acknowledgments

During our lengthy pursuit of Caliban we have encountered a wonderful array of kind and knowledgeable listeners, critics, supporters, and helpers. We have also incurred innumerable intellectual and moral debts. The lists of institutions and individuals in the next few paragraphs undoubtedly and regrettably fail to mention many who lent us a hand along the way. In some cases we never learned the names of people who asked questions from the audience or "talked Caliban" with us in seminar discussions or casual conversations. We hope they will nonetheless take some pleasure in seeing the finished product of our mutual ruminations.

Most of the research for this book was conducted at the Folger Shakespeare Library in Washington, D.C., our home away from home, whose staff has been unfailingly generous in sharing its considerable expertise, always with courtesy and frequently with enthusiasm. Especially helpful during our many visits to the Folger were Nati Kravatsi, Jean Miller, Barbara Mowat, Elizabeth Niemyer, Betsy Walsh, and Julie Ainsworth.

We also made productive forays to other research libraries: the American Antiquarian Society in Worcester, Massachusetts; the Newberry Library in Chicago; the Huntington Library in San Marino, California; the Furness Library in Philadelphia; the Library of Congress (often) in Washington; and the British Library in London. Closer to home, we made frequent demands on the staffs and resources of the Columbia University libraries in New York City and the Robert Hutchings Goddard Library at Clark University in Worcester, Massachusetts. At the latter, Susan Baughman and Mary Hartman were wonderfully supportive. We are grateful to the librarians of these great facilities.

Acknowledgments

Several scholars – some close friends, others known to us only through correspondence – provided valuable critiques. For constructive reviews of the entire manuscript we are forever indebted to Andrew Gurr, Peter Hulme, and Gary Taylor; their suggestions are now embedded in the book in countless places, large and small. We are deeply grateful, too, for readings of separate chapters at earlier stages of their evolution: Chapter 5 by James Axtell, James P. Ronda, and Wilcomb E. Washburn; Chapter 6 by Carol D'Lugo, Marvin D'Lugo, and Lemuel A. Johnson; Chapter 7 by Charles H. Shattuck; Chapter 8 by Kenneth S. Rothwell; Chapter 9 by William Pressly; and Chapter 10 by Ejner J. Jensen. In addition, several scholars gave us expert advice or essential help on specific matters: John F. Andrews, Ingeborg Boltz, Thomas Berninghausen, Peter Blaney, John J. Conron, Robert D. Crassweller, Howard Felperin, SunHee Kim Gertz, Brian Gibbons, Arthur M. Kinney, Irvin Leigh Matus, David Harris Sacks, Winfried Schleiner, Stanley Sultan, Kurt Tetzeli von Rosador, and John W. Velz. We appreciate, too, the editors of *Shakespeare Quarterly* and *The Massachusetts Review* for permission to incorporate the articles that appeared in their pages; in revised and expanded form they are now Chapters 5–7.

We acknowledge with gratitude the several individuals and libraries that have kindly provided us with illustrations and granted us permission to reproduce them in this book: for photographs from the art collection of the Folger Shakespeare Library, with permission to reproduce them (Figures 1–4, 6–9, 13–32); for photographs from the Staatliche Museen Preussischer Kulturbesitz, Kunstbibliothek, Berlin (Figures 34 and 35); for a photograph and permission to reproduce it from the Library of Congress (Figure 5); for a photograph and permission to use it from Joe Cocks Studio, Stratford-upon-Avon (Figure 10); for a photograph from the Courtauld Institute of Art, London, with permission to reproduce it from Lord St. Oswald and the National Trust (Figure 12); for a photograph from *Forbidden Planet* from Photographics Unlimited, and permission to reproduce it from Turner Entertainment Co. (Figure 11); for a photograph and permission to reproduce it from László Lakner (Figure 36).

Poets and publishers have been generous with permission to quote poems, in whole or in part, that invoke Caliban. Our thanks to Theodore Weiss for "Caliban Remembers," from his *From Princeton*

Acknowledgments

One Afternoon; Oxford University Press and Faber & Faber, Ltd., for Edwin Muir's "Sick Caliban," from his *Collected Poems*; Taban lo Liyong for "An Excerpt from an Essay on Uneven Ribs" and "Uncle Tom's Black Humour," from his *Frantz Fanon's Uneven Ribs*; Harcourt Brace Jovanovich Inc., for Louis Untermeyer's "Caliban in the Coal Mines," from his *Selected Poems*; Arthur H. Stockwell, Ltd., for Raphael E. G. Armattoe, *Deep down the Blackman's Mind*; Oxford University Press for Edward Kamau Brathwaite's "Caliban" and "Glossary," from his *Islands*, and for Robert and William Brough, *The Enchanted Isle*, ed. Michael R. Booth; Michael Hamburger for "The Tempest: An Alternative," from his *Collected Poems, 1941–1983*; Texas Tech University Press for Walter McDonald's "Caliban on Spinning" and "Caliban in Blue," from his *Caliban in Blue and Other Poems*; Lemuel A. Johnson for "Calypso for Caliban," from his *Highlife for Caliban*; Donald Davie for "Shakespeare in the Atlantic," from *Poems for Shakespeare, 6*, ed. Roger Pringle; Random House, Inc., for W. H. Auden's "The Sea and the Mirror," from his *Collected Poems*; and George Braziller, Inc., for Norman Rosten's "My Caliban Creature," from his *Selected Poems*.

We also express our thanks to the individuals and institutions that gave us financial support at various stages of our project. We both held fellowships at the Folger Library – Virginia in 1986–87 as an O. B. Hardison, Jr., Fellow, and Alden in 1989 as a Weinmann Fellow. Columbia University and Clark University also helped to underwrite part of our expenses through sabbaticals and research funds. Without such support we would still be talking about Caliban rather than pursuing him in print.

Finally, we are grateful for each other's patience and zest. Coauthorship has been, like Prospero's/Caliban's island, a "brave new world" for us.

Note on editions

All quotations from *The Tempest* in this book are from the recent Oxford edition, edited by Stephen Orgel (Oxford University Press, 1987), except when we address particular cruxes in the Folio; in such cases we quote Charlton Hinman's *The Norton Facsimile of the First Folio of Shakespeare* (New York: W. W. Norton, 1968). Quotations from the latter are identified by the traditional "through line number" (TLN) that is assigned consecutively to every line in the text rather than (as in most editions) by act and scene.

Choosing a text for our quotations from *The Tempest* proved more difficult than we anticipated. We were tempted to use the Folio throughout, partly for its unquestioned authority and partly because we quote other Tudor-Stuart texts, wherever feasible, in their original published versions. Yet the difficulties of obsolete orthography, punctuation, and even letter forms (e.g., the long *s*) might annoy many readers, and the Norton facsimile is unwieldy and expensive. Accordingly, we sought a "user-friendly" edition that also had impeccable scholarly credentials. At the same time, we wanted our study of Caliban to lead readers to their own consideration of *The Tempest*; thus, we preferred a readily accessible edition. Although we are greatly indebted – as our notes indicate – to Frank Kermode's Arden edition of *The Tempest* (London, 1954), we decided on the Oxford edition, available in hardcover and paperback, as the most recent and most reliable modern text. We vary from it only in our use of Roman numerals, rather than Arabic, to indicate acts and scenes, because we think they are thereby more easily identifiable.

Quotations from other Shakespearean plays are taken from the most widely used one-volume edition, *The Riverside Shakespeare*, ed. G. Blakemore Evans (Boston: Houghton Mifflin, 1974).

Part I
Introduction

Chapter 1
Caliban's debut

Caliban, a salvage and deformed slave.
The Tempest (names of the actors, 1623 Folio)

Caliban is the core of the play.
Frank Kermode (1954).

Caliban. In modern poetry he is a recurring symbol for the victimization of Third World peoples. In the theatre he can be anything the director imagines, from amphibian to punk rocker to black militant. Contemporary film shows him as the id: In *Forbidden Planet* he is Dr. Morbius's (Walter Pidgeon's) destructive impulse, ready to kill rather than be suppressed; in Paul Mazursky's adaptation *Tempest*, he (Raul Julia) is a libidinous Peeping Tom, ogling Miranda from fake foliage and blaring "New York, New York" on his clarinet. Caliban can even play two roles at once: The protagonist in *Mrs. Caliban*, a recent novel by Rachel Ingalls, is a six-foot seven-inch human amphibian of insatiable sexual appetite and simultaneously a fetus; both are figments of the heroine's starved libido.[1] Such bizarre characters, inspired by Shakespeare's Caliban, attest to the monster's integral place in our cultural heritage, a symbol that can be endlessly transformed yet is always recognizable.

Caliban in the late twentieth century is, of course, far removed in both time and interpretation from the character Shakespeare created

1 Rachel Ingalls, *Mrs. Caliban* (London: Faber & Faber, 1983).

3

in 1611. This chapter goes back to the beginning of Caliban's meta-phorical odyssey to examine Shakespeare's text in detail, for Caliban as Shakespeare portrayed him (or, rather, as he first appears in print in the Folio edition) sets a necessary background to the discussion that follows.

We have hewed as closely as possible to the printed text, but we caution readers that any understanding of the play inevitably involves judgments about words and contexts that are in themselves interpretive. Similarly, it is a matter of textual interpretation to accept or reject the characters' "accuracy" in reporting "events," as in Prospero's charge that Caliban tried to rape Miranda or that Caliban is the issue of a witch and the devil. On these and other matters, did Shakespeare want us to take Prospero literally? How a reader answers that question largely determines his or her inter-pretation of Caliban and the broader conception of the play.

I

Records from the early seventeenth century show that *The Tempest* was performed at the court of King James I on 1 November 1611 and was repeated (possibly with alterations) in the winter of 1612–13 at the wedding celebrations for Princess Elizabeth and Frederick, elector of Palatine.[2] There may have been other, unrecorded show-ings – and revisions – before Shakespeare's death in 1616. No texts survive before 1623. Why John Heminges and Henry Condell placed it first in their Folio edition is open to speculation, as is the text's possible evolution from 1611 to 1623.[3]

The general context in which Shakespeare composed *The Tempest* is less ambiguous. By 1610, James had substantially stabilized his regime; England enjoyed an uneasy peace with her traditional enemies France and Spain, and the religious squabbles within the Anglican church that had marked Elizabeth's later and James's early years had largely subsided. Royal marriages commanded consid-erable attention, as did England's precarious footholds in North

2 For the bare facts of *The Tempest*'s early performances, see E. K. Chambers, *William Shakespeare*, Vol. I (Oxford: Clarendon Press, 1930), p. 491.
3 For a concise printing history of *The Tempest*, see Orgel's edition (Oxford University Press, 1987), pp. 56–62.

America. It seems likely that Shakespeare was well aware of current news; his contacts were numerous and notable, especially among investors in the Virginia Company of London. Several topical references in *The Tempest* – Indians, a fortuitous shipwreck, Bermuda – attest to the dramatist's awareness of New World events. But other events, both foreign and domestic, may have exerted equal or greater influence, as, no doubt, did literary and theatrical concerns that were the warp and woof of Shakespeare's livelihood.

The Tempest was an appropriate play to stage before Princess Elizabeth and her fiancé. A major plot of the play – the dynastic marriage of a duke's daughter to a king's son – no doubt had topical appeal for a royal audience celebrating an equally political and dynastic marriage. David M. Bergeron argues, in fact, that "James and his family are re-presented in *The Tempest* through the issues of peaceful succession, royal genealogy, interpretation, and the union of the kingdoms."[4] The union of Naples and Milan through Miranda's marriage may have been a projection of James's continuing concern for the peaceful union of his native Scotland with England. It could also suggest the union of Protestant England and Germany embodied in the marriage between Elizabeth and Frederick.

But *The Tempest* seems to have sparked special attention from the author. It was the last drama Shakespeare wrote without a collaborator and may have been the last of his plays staged by the King's Men before he retired to Stratford. Significantly, perhaps, *The Tempest* depicts a magician absorbed in his art, the power to craft illusions, who, at the drama's conclusion, deliberately renounces his gift, drowns his book, and returns to a life of responsibility rather than creativity. Although modern critics resist overt biographical readings of Shakespeare's dramas, *The Tempest* remains implicitly autobiographical. By 1611, Shakespeare, like James, was concerned about the marriage of his daughters and what inheritance he could leave them;[5] Shakespeare died only five years after the probable date of

---

4 David M. Bergeron, *Shakespeare's Romances and the Royal Family* (Lawrence: University of Kansas Press, 1985), p. 181.
5 Susannah married Dr. John Hall in 1608; Judith married Thomas Quiney in 1616. S[amuel] Schoenbaum, *William Shakespeare: A Compact Documentary Life* (Oxford University Press, 1977), pp. 286–93.

the play's composition. No wonder Prospero's farewell to his art is often taken for the author's retirement declaration.[6]

As a member of the King's Men, Shakespeare crafted a play that had more than topical appeal. To suit the royal palate, he included within his play an elaborate masque of gods and goddesses, similar in many respects to the spectacles designed by Inigo Jones for James and Queen Anne. Shakespeare arranged his play so that it would roughly fit the "unity of time" (four hours) and the "unity of place" (a small island) – classical protocols he never bothered with else-where, except in the early and Plautine *Comedy of Errors*. He also focused his plot on issues of royal concern: Conspiracy and possible usurpation must have appealed to the monarch who had escaped annihilation during the Gunpowder Plot of 1605.[7] As a king who styled himself the "father of his people," James surely had some interest in issues of government and authority. The play's super-natural elements may also have intrigued him; in 1597 he had pub-lished a treatise on demonology, and throughout his life he remained interested in witchcraft and magic.[8] Duke Prospero, a ruler who lost power by devoting himself to his studies, could have been a surrogate for a king who preferred hunting and collecting rare animals to governing. And Caliban, perhaps, represented (as anti-masque) the unruly forces of English society – rowdies and mal-contents who undermined the ideal unity and harmony of James's body politic. That the king saw Shakespeare's drama as a mirror image of his own court and country is unlikely. But the parallels

6 Thomas Campbell, ed., *The Dramatic Works of William Shakspeare, with a Life by Thomas Campbell* (London: Edward Moxon, 1838), pp. lxiii–lxiv. Shakespeare collaborated on two, perhaps three, subsequent plays: *Henry VIII, The Two Noble Kinsmen*, and *Cardenio* (no text survives). *The Tempest*, however, marks the end of his phenomenal productivity and thorough commitment to the stage.
7 Glynne Wickham suggests that Caliban's plot to murder Prospero may be a direct reference to "the Gunpowder treason." See "Masque and Anti-Masque in 'The Tempest'," in *Essays and Studies 1975*, ed. Robert Ellrodt (London: John Murray, 1975), pp. 1–14, esp. p. 12.
8 Jacqueline E. M. Latham argues that *The Tempest* was directly influenced by Shakespeare's reading of James's *Daemonologie* and that Caliban's parentage (born of a devil and a witch) would have sparked particular interest in the monarch. See "'The Tempest' and King James's 'Daemonologie'," *Shakespeare Survey*, XXVIII (1975): 117–23.

are evident in hindsight and could not have been wholly lost on *The Tempest*'s early audiences.

II

It should be apparent from this brief introduction that Caliban is not the most important character in *The Tempest*, though he is, as most critics and directors make clear, essential. As Frank Kermode observed in his influential introduction to the second Arden edition, "Caliban is the ground of the play."[9] He has a scant 177 lines of text (compare Prospero's 653 lines), and he appears in only five of the nine scenes, yet Caliban is central to *The Tempest*'s plot and structure and to its dialogue. He speaks more words than any character except Prospero, though barely more than Stephano or Ariel. (The exact proportions, meticulously measured by Marvin Spevack, are Prospero 29.309%, Caliban 8.393%, Stephano 8.137%, and Ariel 7.888%; each of the other characters has less than 7.5% of the text's words.[10]) Not that a character's importance can be quantified. Surely Caliban is qualitatively more important to the play's dynamics than anyone but Prospero, regardless of the number of his words. Almost as important as his own lines, of course, are the volume and significance of the words spoken to him or about him; by this measure Caliban is clearly, next to Prospero, *The Tempest*'s predominant character. But our principal concern is Caliban's ambiguity rather than his importance: Of all the characters in *The Tempest*, Caliban is the most enigmatic and the most susceptible to drastic fluctuations in interpretation. He is Shakespeare's changeling.

The Folio edition of 1623 simply describes Caliban in the cast of characters as "a salvage and deformed slave." (The *l* in "salvage" was probably silent, as in "calm."[11]) Each of the operative words

9 *The Tempest*, ed. Frank Kermode, "The Arden Shakespeare," 6th ed. (London: Methuen, 1958), p. xxv.

10 Marvin Spevack, *A Complete and Systematic Concordance to the Works of Shakespeare*, 9 vols. (Hildesheim, Germany: Georg Olms, 1968–80), Vol. I, pp. 36–62. The other characters' percentages, according to Spevack, are Gonzalo 7.221, Miranda 6.242, Antonio 6.167, Ferdinand 6.098, and Trinculo 5.088.

11 On the pronunciation of "salvage," see Richard Grant White, ed., *The Works of William Shakespeare*, Vol. II (Boston: Little, Brown, 1875), p. 94, which asserts that

illuminates Caliban's character. His savagery, for example, attests to his crudeness and lack of qualities that Englishmen in the early seventeenth century considered essential to human progress.[12] In Shakespeare's day, "savage" meant wild, barbarous, uneducated, undomesticated – in short, *uncivilized* by upper-class European standards.[13] The supposed shortcomings of savage people often were enumerated in long lists of negatives: They had no religion, no written language, no established laws, no hierarchical government, no refined (again, by upper-class European standards) habits of dress, speech, and eating.[14] "Savage" was thus shorthand for someone culturally inferior to the smug observer. Englishmen lavished the label on the Irish and on the American Indians, the ethnic

the word was pronounced both ways in Shakespeare's time because it entered English through both the French *sauvage* and the Italian *salvaggio*. We contend, however, that Shakespeare probably did not pronounce the *l*, because that spelling appears only twice in the canon: in *The Tempest*'s list of characters, which may have been added by the First Folio's editors, and in "salvages and men of Inde" ("savages" in Orgel's edition [II.ii.57]); the only other use of the word in *The Tempest* omits the *l* (I.ii.354). The more than forty other uses (including the variants "savagely," "savageness," and "savagery") in more than twenty other Shakespearean plays do not include *l*. See Marvin Spevack, *The Harvard Concordance to Shakespeare* (Cambridge, Mass.: Harvard University Press, 1973), pp. 1081, 1083; and Horace Howard Furness, comp., *Notes on Studies of The Tempest. Minutes of the Shakspere Society of Philadelphia for 1864–65* (Philadelphia: The Shakspere Society, 1866), p. 33. See also Helge Kökeritz, *Shakespeare's Pronunciation* (New Haven, Ct.: Yale University Press, 1953), pp. 310–11.

12 In the text of the play, Caliban is called "savage" only once – by an angry Miranda (I.ii.354). But the inclusion of the word in the cast of characters suggests (unless it was inserted by the Folio's editors) that it was central to Shakespeare's conception of Caliban.

13 The *Oxford English Dictionary* (*OED*) lists thirteen definitions of "civility." Among those that were current in the sixteenth century are (1) "connected with citizenship, and civil polity"; (6) "Good polity . . . social order, as distinct from anarchy and disorder"; (10) "The state of being civilized; freedom from barbarity"; (11) "Polite or liberal education; training in the 'humanities', good breeding; culture, refinement"; and (12) "Behaviour proper to the intercourse of civilized people; ordinary courtesy."

14 Among the many modern studies of early English notions of savagery, see Margaret T. Hodgen, *Early Anthropology in the Sixteenth and Seventeenth Centuries* (Philadelphia: University of Pennsylvania Press, 1964), esp. ch. 9; and Bernard Sheehan, *Savagism and Civility: Indians and Englishmen in Colonial Virginia* (Cambridge University Press, 1980), ch. 1–3. For an example from Shakespeare's day, see [Thomas Palmer], *An Essay of the Meanes how to Make our Trauailes, into Forraine Countries the More Profitable and Honourable* (London: Printed for Mathew Lownes, 1606), esp. pp. 60–68.

groups most newsworthy in Tudor-Stuart times, and also on a host of other peoples in Africa, Asia, and even Europe. Shakespeare used variants of "savage" – as noun, adjective, or adverb – in a score of plays, without exhibiting any pattern of ethnic or geographic preference. Savagery could exist anywhere, even in England, especially (in the eyes of the upper classes) among vagabonds, gypsies, and "sturdy beggars." Accordingly, "savage" tells us much about Caliban's cultural condition (as perceived by Prospero and Miranda) but nothing about his physical appearance or moral attributes.

Caliban's social condition is clear too. Prospero repeatedly calls him a slave – "Caliban, my slave," "What ho, slave!" "poisonous slave," "most lying slave." Miranda chides the "Abhorred slave," though the line may be Prospero's, in which case only he explicitly labels Caliban a slave.[15] Ariel, too, is called a slave, but, unlike Caliban, he is promised his freedom after a few more hours of servitude. In any event, Caliban himself admits and laments his bondage, complaining to Stephano and Trinculo that he is "subject to a tyrant" (III.ii.40). Most important, Prospero treats him as a slave throughout the play, ordering him about and punishing his indolence or recalcitrance ("If thou neglect'st, or dost unwillingly" [I.ii.367]) with cramps, stitches, and stings. Caliban's slavery begins before the play's action opens and lasts a bit past the final curtain, when he will regain his liberty and his island.[16]

Whereas The Tempest is precise about Caliban's slavery, it is annoyingly imprecise about his deformity. Morton Luce's lament is initially tempting: "If all the suggestions as to Caliban's form and feature and endowments that are thrown out in the play are collected, it will be found that the one half renders the other half im-

---

15 For a summary of the debate over the proper assignment of the "abhorred slave" speech, see The Tempest, ed. Horace Howard Furness, "A New Variorum Edition of Shakespeare," Vol. IX (1892; repr. New York: American Scholar Publications, 1966), pp. 73–74; Furness, Notes on Studies of The Tempest, pp. 18–19; The Tempest, ed. Orgel, p. 17.
16 Caliban's age is never mentioned in the text; his behavior implies young adulthood. Clues in the text suggest that he is approximately 24 years old: Prospero and Miranda have been on the island for 12 years, and Caliban was about age 12 when they arrived. See The Tempest, ed. Morton Luce (the first Arden edition) (London: Methuen, 1901), p. xxxiv; The Tempest, ed. Orgel, p. 28 (n. 1).

possible."[17] Yet when the clues are arranged in some semblance of order and context, Luce's complaint is palpably overstated. Of principal importance – though misread by Luce and many others – is the Folio's assertion that Caliban has a *human* form, however misshapen. Before Caliban appears on stage, Prospero tells Ariel that when Caliban's mother Sycorax confined Ariel in a cloven pine,

> ... Then was this Island
> (Saue for the Son that [s]he did littour heere,
> A frekelld whelpe, hag-borne) not honour'd with
> A humane shape.
>
> (TLN 408–11; Orgel ed. I.ii.281–84)[18]

If the final two lines of that passage are wrenched from context, as they have often been, they are easily misinterpreted; they seem to deny rather than affirm Caliban's human stature.[19] That impression is unintentionally encouraged by the new Arden and Folger Library editions, where the penultimate line of the crucial passage begins a new page, thus visually distorting the syntax. The new Arden and Oxford editions, moreover, substitute dashes for the First Folio's parentheses, which is especially misleading if the last two lines are read independently of their essential precursors.[20] When the passage is read intact, including the First Folio's parentheses, it clearly establishes Caliban as the only human-shaped creature on the island before Prospero and Miranda arrived. Ariel, though necessarily

17 *The Tempest*, ed. Luce, p. xxxv.
18 Lines from the 1623 Folio are taken from *The Norton Facsimile of the First Folio of Shakespeare*, ed. Charlton Hinman (New York: Norton, 1968). Nicholas Rowe's edition (London: Jacob Tonson, 1709) was the first to emend the Folio's "he" to "she."
19 *Shakespeare's Comedy, The Tempest, as Arranged for the Stage by Herbert Beerbohm Tree* (London: J. Miles, 1904), pp. x–xi, presented one of the early arguments for Caliban's human shape. Some commentators follow suit, but many, including some of the most prominent scholars, continue to misread the passage. *The Oxford Companion to English Literature*, ed. Margaret Drabble (London: Guild Publishing, 1985), p. 159, asserts that Caliban "is only semi-human," a fairly frequent assumption of literary critics and stage directors.
20 *The Tempest*, ed. Kermode (Arden edition), p. 28; *The Tempest*, ed. Louis B. Wright, (Folger edition) (New York: Washington Square Press, 1961), p. 16; *The Tempest*, ed. Orgel (Oxford edition), p. 116.

Caliban's debut

appearing on stage as a human, takes any form Prospero desires.[21]
Any doubt about Caliban's physical humanity is removed, temporarily at least, when Miranda exclaims on her first glimpse of
Ferdinand: "This / Is the third man that e'er I saw, the first / That
e'er I sigh'd for" (I.ii.445–47); Prospero and Caliban must be the
others, for she has already denied any memory of her life before
arrival on the island. A few lines later, Prospero indirectly corro-
borates Miranda when he chides her for unseemly excitement over
Ferdinand: "Thou think'st there is no more such shapes as he, /
Having seen but him and Caliban" (I.ii.479–80). Because Miranda
has surely seen a wide assortment of beasts and fish, these lines
strongly suggest that the only "shapes" under consideration are
human. (We assume that Prospero has excluded himself. As Miranda's
father, he would not suggest himself as a possible object of her am-
orous affections.) On the other hand, in Act III Miranda implicitly
contradicts her earlier testimony. She tells Ferdinand that her own
is the only female face she's seen (in a looking glass)

> . . . nor have I seen
> More than I may call men than you, good friend,
> And my dear father. . . .
>
> (III.i.50–52)

Does she not consider Caliban a man? In the context of her passion
for Ferdinand, Caliban is apparently beneath consideration, whatever his biological status.

Adding to the certainty that Caliban is human are the efforts
Prospero and Miranda take to educate and civilize him. They have
attempted what can be done only to a human; there is no hint that
they tried to teach language and astronomy to an animal or a fish.
Caliban proved, in their judgment, impervious to nurture, but he
did learn their language, and he continues to serve them in wholly
human ways. "We cannot miss [i.e., do without] him," Prospero
reminds his daughter: "He does make our fire, / Fetch in our wood,
and serves in offices / That profit us" (I.ii.311–13). Although Caliban
is a "savage" and therefore potentially educable, he is not, in Pros-

21 As Stephen Orgel points out (Oxford edition, p. 27), Ariel appears in the text as a
male and yet is assigned essentially "female" tasks.

11

pero's or Miranda's eyes, either admirable or an acceptable suitor. But that he is biologically capable of impregnating Miranda, and hence probably human, is clear enough from Prospero's charge that Caliban tried to violate her honor and Caliban's retort that had Prospero not prevented him, "I had peopled else / This isle with Calibans" (I.ii.349–50).

Despite the overwhelming evidence of Caliban's basic physiology, several passages suggest that he is barely – to Prospero, Miranda, and the others (but not necessarily to Shakespeare) – on the human side of the animal kingdom. A partial list of the epithets Prospero flings at Caliban includes "earth," "filth," "hag-seed," "beast," "misshapen knave," and "a bastard one." He is, Prospero insists, "as disproportioned in his manners / As in his shape" (V.i.290–91). Miranda almost matches her father's venom, if the disputed passage in the First Folio is hers, for she calls Caliban "A thing most brutish" and condemns his "vile race" (I.ii.356–57). And in lines that are unquestionably hers, Miranda tells her father that Caliban is "a villain, sir, / I do not love to look on" (I.ii.309–10). Caliban, in sum, earns no laurels from father or daughter, yet on balance they both affirm his human shape, however physically and psychologically distorted he may be.

Trinculo and Stephano, the besotted idlers, are no more flattering and no clearer on Caliban's shape, but they too affirm his humanity. Trinculo initially calls Caliban a "fish," based on his smell: "What have we here – a man or a fish?... he smells like a fish; a very ancient and fish-like smell" (II.ii.24–26). Trinculo then sees that the creature is "Legged like a man, and his fins like arms!" (II.ii.32–33). (Trinculo's description of Caliban's upper limbs as "fins like arms" indicates that the presumed [by smell] fish has, in fact, arms, yet Caliban is often portrayed on stage and in illustrations with arms made to look like fins, thus reversing the import of Trinculo's observation.) At this point, Caliban is hiding under a gaberdine, his head and torso not clearly visible. Trinculo examines him further and concludes that "this is no fish, but an islander that hath lately suffered by a thunderbolt" (II.ii.34–35) – in sum, a human inhabitant. Later, Trinculo reverts to aquatic imagery (of which he has almost a monopoly in the play), again probably for olfactory reasons; he labels Caliban "debosh'd Fish" (TLN 1376; "debauched fish" in

Orgel, III.ii.26) and "half a fish and half a monster" (III.ii.28–29), but these are epithets rather than descriptions. Trinculo surely categorizes Caliban as human when he tells him and Stephano, ". . . there's but five upon this isle: we are three of them" (III.ii.5).

Two uses of aquatic imagery do not come from Trinculo. Near the end of the play, Antonio calls Caliban "a plain fish" (V.i.266), which could refer to either appearance or odor; the conspirators have recently been chin-deep in a "foul lake" (IV.i.183). More significant – and controversial – is Prospero's "thou tortoise" (I.ii.316). At first glance this might imply a tortoiselike body, but when read in context, and especially in view of the word that follows "tortoise," the epithet unquestionably refers to Caliban's dilatoriness. (In I.ii.315–16, Caliban fails to respond when called; Prospero demands "Come forth, I say; there's other business for thee. / Come, thou tortoise, when?") By Shakespeare's day, an abundance of fables, beginning with Aesop's, and numerous zoological treatises emphasized the tortoise's leisurely pace; the metaphor would have been obvious to a Jacobean audience.[22] Some illustrators and critics have nonetheless avidly seized the tortoise image. In the nineteenth century, for example, one scholar proposed that "Caliban is . . . a kind of tortoise, the paddles expanding in arms and hands, legs and feet." Another commentator saw Caliban as a dwarf in stature, with the legs and forefins of a turtle, and, "if the hardly human face were fashioned after that of a tortoise . . . the eyes would be 'deepset' by nature as well as by drink . . . and he would be 'dim-eyed' and 'beetle-browed,'" his body covered with patches of "loathsome leprosy." More recently and more temperately, two American critics have argued that "'Come, thou tortoise' tended to give a vague approximation of the shape of the deformity."[23] More often, Caliban

22 See, for example, John Leo [Leo Africanus], *A Geographical History of Africa*, trans. John Pory (London: George Bishop, 1600), p. 951; and Edward Topsell, *The Historie of Serpents* (London: Printed for William Jaggard, 1608), p. 282r.

23 Joseph Hunter, *A Disquisition on the Scene, Origin, Date, Etc. of Shakespeare's Tempest* (London: Printed by L. Whittingham, 1839), p. 123; Brinsley Nicholson, "Shakespeare Illustrated by Massinger," *Notes and Queries*, 4th ser., I (1868): 289–91; Barry Gaines and Michael Lofaro, "What Did Caliban Look Like?" *Mississippi Folklore Register*, X (1976): 175–86. All three works implicitly or explicitly misread the lines about Caliban's human shape. Gaines and Lofaro further contend (p. 178) that "tortoise" did not imply slowness until the late seventeenth

has been portrayed with fish rather than turtle attributes – scales, fins, and shiny skin – which reflect the critic's or artist's or actor's fixation on offhand epithets rather than the overwhelming evidence of Caliban's essentially human form. By contrast, Frank Kermode insists (correctly, we believe) that Caliban is occasionally called a fish "largely because of his oddity, and there should be no fishiness about his appearance."[24]

"Monster" is Caliban's most frequent sobriquet, but it comes only from Trinculo and Stephano and may therefore be less descriptive than simply pejorative – attempts by a jester and a butler to assert a modicum of superiority over their self-proclaimed "foot-licker." In any event, "monster" appears in the text some forty times, usually with a pejorative adjective: "shallow," "weak," "credulous," "most perfidious and drunken," "puppy-headed," "scurvy," "abominable," "ridiculous," "howling," "ignorant," and "lost." Only "brave," used twice, might be a favorable modifier, and it is almost certainly meant sarcastically. More neutral are "servant-monster," "man-monster," "lieutenant-monster," and "poor monster." To the extent that "monster" implies physical deformity, as it did generally but not exclusively in Shakespeare's time, these abundant reminders strengthen the notion of Caliban as grotesque.[25] They do nothing, however, to specify the deformity. Nor does Alonso's quip that "This is a strange thing as e'er I looked on" (V.i.289). The text tells us that Caliban had long nails to dig pignuts (II.ii.162); otherwise his physical deformities are unspecified.

Other references to Caliban are little help. Several times he is called "mooncalf," suggesting stupidity and an amorphous shape.

century, and hence Prospero must have referred to Caliban's appearance. They base that judgment on the OED, in which the earliest citation of one meaning of the word is 1670, yet overlook a 1589 usage ("Venus standeth on the Tortoys, as shewing that Loue creepeth on by degrees") that clearly equates the animal with dilatoriness. Aesop's Fables was first published in English in 1485; more than a dozen editions followed before 1611.

24 The Tempest, ed. Kermode, p. 62. Cf. Willard Farnham, for example, who insists that Caliban's body "is part primitive man and part crude fish": The Shakespearean Grotesque (Oxford: Clarendon Press, 1971), p. 166. For artistic portrayals of Caliban as an aquatic animal, see Chapter 9 herein.
25 The OED's basic definitions all stress abnormality, usually (but not always) manifested in outsized proportions.

Caliban's debut

Pliny's *Natural History*, translated into English in 1601, described a mooncalf as "a lumpe of flesh without shape, without life, . . . Howbeit, a kind of moving it hath."[26] Prospero once dubs Caliban "this thing of darkness" (V.i.275), possibly implying a dusky skin, though more likely a faulty character. Similarly, Prospero's "thou earth" (I.ii.314) hints at darkness or dirt or, more likely, baseness of character. Stephano once calls Caliban "cat" (II.ii.70), but the text itself and contemporaneous proverbs clearly link the epithet to alcohol's purported ability to make even a cat speak.[27]

Several times Caliban's parentage – his mother, Prospero tells us, was an Algerian witch, his father the devil – is invoked, as in "demi-devil" and "a born devil"; such lineage may imply a less-than-human shape, for unions with the devil, especially by a witch, often brought forth – according to conventional wisdom – all sorts of grotesque births.[28] The charge of devilish parentage may be Prospero's hyperbole.[29] In light of the other evidence in the text that Caliban is essentially human, the attribution of satanic parentage, if such it was, more likely testifies to Caliban's inherently warped character. And the progeny of a witch and the devil *could* have been human – again, according to conventional wisdom – in fundamental shape, though inwardly and outwardly deformed. As George Steevens observed in his 1793 edition of *The Tempest*, "It is not easy to determine the shape which our author designed to bestow on his monster. That he has hands, legs, etc. we gather from the remarks of Trinculo, and other circumstances in the play. . . . Perhaps Shakespeare himself had no settled ideas concerning the form of *Caliban*."[30] In any event, the confusion of epithets that abounds in *The Tempest* encourages artists, actors, and readers to see Caliban however they wish. For three centuries they have enthusiastically accepted the invitation.

26 Caius Plinius Secundus, *The Historie of the World*, trans. Philemon Holland (London: A. Islip, 1601), p. 163.
27 See Kermode's note, *The Tempest*, p. 65.
28 Gaines and Lofaro, "What Did Caliban Look Like?" pp. 179–88.
29 *The Tempest*, ed. Orgel, p. 25.
30 *The Plays of William Shakspeare*, 4th ed., 15 vols., Vol. III, ed. George Steevens and Samuel Johnson (London: Printed for T. Longman, 1793), p. 158.

III

Aside from its specific language, the text also provides clues to Caliban's role, and to some extent his nature, through the structure of the plot. He is a pivotal character who, by means of parallels and contrasts, frequently elucidates the ways one views the other characters. His first appearance, for example, is sandwiched between Prospero's opening interview with Ariel and his first encounter with Ferdinand. Caliban manifests significant similarities with, and differences from, both of these characters – parallels and contrasts highlighted by juxtapositions in the text. Caliban, of course, is unaware of these contrasts and parallels because he never appears on stage with either Ariel or Ferdinand. He presumably does not know of Ferdinand at all, and he may be oblivious to Ariel's existence. He suffers the pinches caused by Ariel, but he assigns such bodily punishments to Prospero's magic. Caliban insists to Stephano that to thwart Prospero and succeed in their conspiracy, they must begin by stealing the magician's books.

Caliban first crawls from his cave in a scene of exposition that follows the audience's initial view of Ariel. The airy spirit had asked for freedom from Prospero's domination; after reviewing Ariel's history, Prospero threatens his spirit-servant with a return to the cloven pine, then promises freedom as a reward for a bit more service. Ariel, though often in fear of Prospero, gladly agrees. Despite Prospero's irascibility, there clearly is affection between them.

Caliban is in many ways Ariel's opposite, although their situations are somewhat similar. Both were on the island when Prospero and Miranda arrived. Both are now servants. Both are afraid of the magician's powers. But Ariel is a spirit; he enters from above, flies aloft, and can make himself invisible. Caliban is earthy and earth-bound. He crawls from a cave; his deformity may keep him hunched over, close to the ground. And his earthiness – a near-bestiality (Prospero insists) that prevents him from assimilating civility and morality – makes his relationship with Prospero differ sharply from Ariel's. The spirit-servant had originally been imprisoned in a cloven pine because he would not enact Sycorax's "earthy and abhorred commands" (I.ii.273). Nonhuman spirit though he is, Ariel understands right from wrong. Human though he is,

16

Caliban's debut

Caliban lacks moral perception. He responds chiefly to appetite. The principles of parallelism and contrast equally govern Caliban's position vis-à-vis Ferdinand, who is introduced directly after Caliban's first appearance. Both men apprehend the music of the isle, yet it affects them differently. Music, "with its sweet air," allays Ferdinand's passion and leads him to Miranda. She assumes at first that Ferdinand is a spirit, but Prospero assures her that "it eats and sleeps and hath such senses / As we have" (I.ii.413–14). Ferdinand's courtship of Miranda is chaste, its purpose honorable marriage. Caliban, who hears the same music, is also attracted to Miranda, but he has no "nurture" – no moral awareness – to allay his passions. He had lodged in Prospero's cell until he tried to rape Miranda, and he wishes his attack had succeeded: "O ho, O ho! Would't had been done!" (I.ii.348).

The parallels between Caliban and Ferdinand are conveyed visually as well as verbally. Caliban enters (in II.ii) with a "burden of wood"; his task is to carry logs for Prospero. That is also Ferdinand's task: In the scene immediately following Caliban's wood-fetching assignment, Ferdinand enters "bearing a log." Unlike Caliban, he delights in his labor because he is inspired by love of Miranda. Thus, both Caliban and Ferdinand are human creatures with appetites who must perform tiresome labor, but whereas the prince is civilized and controls his appetites and even enjoys his work, the mooncalf has no higher aspirations than to overthrow Prospero and is enslaved by his own desires.

Caliban's situation on the island also parallels Miranda's. At a young age both were isolated from their peers and educated by Prospero. Such limited experience makes them vulnerable and naive. Caliban has seen only one woman besides his mother, and she (Miranda) "as far surpasseth Sycorax / As great'st does least" (III.ii.100–01). Because Miranda has seen no men besides her father and Caliban, she assumes that Ferdinand is a spirit, until her father exclaims

> Thou think'st there is no more such shape as he,
> Having seen but him and Caliban. Foolish wench,
> To th' most of men this is a Caliban,
> And they to him are angels.

(I.ii.479–82)

17

Similarly, Caliban mistakes Stephano and Trinculo for gods; Miranda admires Antonio and Sebastian as part of a "brave new world." Both the beast and the beauty misjudge the basic characters of those they initially admire.

Prospero prides himself on Miranda's education. He boasts that on the island

> Have I, thy schoolmaster, made thee more profit
> Than other princes can that have more time
> For vainer hours, and tutors not so careful.
>
> (I.ii.172–74)

He has not been so successful with Caliban. The monster first learned language: how to name "the bigger light and how the less, / That burn by day and night" (I.ii.335–37). But Caliban would not retain "any print of goodness," Miranda charges, and instead is "capable of all ill!" (I.ii.351–52)

> . . . I pitied thee, [she chides him],
> Took pains to make thee speak, taught thee each hour
> One thing or other. When thou didst not, savage,
> Know thine own meaning, but wouldst gabble like
> A thing most brutish, I endowed thy purposes
> With words that made them known. But thy vile race –
> Though thou didst learn – had that in't which good natures
> Could not abide to be with. . . .
>
> (I.ii.352–59)

For all Miranda's and Prospero's efforts, Caliban remains (to them, at least) "a born devil, on whose nature / Nurture can never stick" (IV.i.188–89). His bestiality and stubbornness contrast starkly with Miranda's beauty and obedience.

Juxtaposed to Antonio's and Sebastian's brutal plot against Alonso is Caliban's conspiracy to murder Prospero. Stephano's "celestial liquor" is a comic parallel to Prospero's magic. Like Sebastian, Stephano aspires to become a king; both men seek total power through murder. Prospero interrupts their schemes by spectacles: A banquet that suddenly disappears confounds the Italian nobles, while Prospero's rich garments, hanging on a line near the entrance

18

to his cave, distract Stephano and Trinculo – despite Caliban's warnings – into a comic parade of "borrowed robes."

There remains an important contrast, however, between the several conspirators. Alonso, the intended victim of Antonio's most recent scheming, repents his past and reconciles himself to Prospero. Antonio has no lines in the conclusion, and most commentators consider him unrepentant and unlikely to change. Raised with the benefits of "civilization," Antonio knowingly chooses the path of evil. By contrast, Caliban seems to learn from his mistakes, especially his misguided adoration of Stephano and Trinculo. In his final speech he promises that

> I'll be wise hereafter,
> And seek for grace. What a thrice-double ass
> Was I to take this drunkard for a god,
> And worship this dull fool!
>
> (V.i.294–97)

Though Caliban remains "natural" man in contrast to "civilized" Antonio, the monster's desire for grace underlines the civilized world's debasement and, once again, emphasizes Caliban's ultimate humanity.[31]

The play ends soon after this speech. Prospero and the nobles will return to Italy the next morning, their ship and sailors suddenly as good as new. Ariel will be free to soar, and Caliban will reinherit his island. The play's conclusion says nothing about Caliban's fate or how he feels about Prospero's and Miranda's departure. Perhaps this is why so many sequels to *The Tempest* have been written, most of them concerning Caliban's subsequent career. Caliban is a loose end; for centuries readers and playgoers have wanted to tie him up. He captures their fancy, and they, unlike Prospero, are reluctant to abandon him.

This introduction to Caliban's long career has focused on the raw materials Shakespeare left us: verbal signifiers indicating a man-monster whose shape and character are ambiguous, and structural

31 Deborah Willis's "Shakespeare's *Tempest* and the Discourse of Colonialism," *Studies in English Literature*, XXIX (1989): 277–89, argues that "the play's true threatening 'other' is not Caliban, but Antonio" (p. 280).

19

signifiers indicating his importance to the play's major themes. But from what experience, traditions, and sources did Shakespeare draw such ideas? What are Caliban's plausible origins in the life and literature of Shakespeare's time? The next two chapters explore some of the answers offered by critics in several disciplines during more than three centuries of "Caliban watching."

Part II
Origins

Chapter 2
Historical contexts

[W]hat's past is prologue.

The Tempest (II.i.251)

[W]e tend not to appreciate the extent to which some themes, situations, incidents, and even phrases in *The Tempest* were part of the common coin of Shakespeare's day.

Charles Frey (1979)

Geoffrey Bullough's massive *Narrative and Dramatic Sources of Shakespeare* is more than a scholar's magnum opus.[1] It is also a testament to the endless search for the historical and literary documents that Shakespeare used, or may have used, in crafting nearly two-score dramas. Bullough, of course, is only the latest and most ambitious of the compilers: Charlotte Ramsay Lennox began the quest in the middle of the eighteenth century; John Payne Collier and W. C. Hazlitt, among others, followed in the nineteenth century; and the editors of individual plays have often, on a smaller scale, identified and reprinted key "sources."[2] The compilers and editors assume,

1 Geoffrey Bullough, *Narrative and Dramatic Sources of Shakespeare*, 8 vols. (London: Routledge & Kegan Paul, 1957–75).
2 Charlotte Ramsay Lennox, *Shakespeare Illustrated: or The Novels and Histories, on Which the Plays of Shakespeare Are Founded . . .* , 3 vols. (London: A. Millar, 1753–54); John Payne Collier, ed., *Shakespeare's Library: A Collection of the Ancient Novels, Romances, Legends, Poems, and Histories, Used by Shakespeare as the Foundation of His*

reasonably enough, that even the redoubtable Shakespeare did not fashion dramas wholly from his own imagination.

Pinpointing Shakespeare's borrowings for plots, characters, and phrases is usually problematic. The major sources for a few plays are, of course, indisputable: *Richard III*'s reliance, directly or indirectly, on Raphael Holinshed, Edward Hall, and Thomas More and *Romeo and Juliet*'s dependence on Arthur Brooke's version of a story by Bandello are obvious examples.³ *The Tempest*'s sources are notoriously less certain. Most of its modern annotators discuss a variety of contemporaneous texts, and editors often reprint extracts from several documents that, judging from similarities of plot or language, probably influenced Shakespeare. Frank Kermode appends to the Arden edition portions of William Strachey's "True Reportory" (1610), Silvester Jourdain's *Discovery of the Barmudas* (1610), an anonymous Virginia Company pamphlet (also 1610), Montaigne's essay on cannibals (John Florio's edition of 1603), and Ovid's *Metamorphoses* (both in Latin and in Arthur Golding's translation of 1567). Bullough prints all of these except the Montaigne essay (omitted because of its length rather than doubt about its relevance) and adds extracts from Ben Jonson's *Hymenaei*, Erasmus's *Colloquia*, and half a dozen "analogues." For Bullough, Strachey's account of a shipwreck on Bermuda and Ovid's *Metamorphoses* are certain sources; several others he deems "probable" or "possible."⁴ Although some Shakespearean scholars may question Bullough's designations, he

Dramas, 2 vols. (London: T. Rodd, 1850); William Carew Hazlitt, ed., *Shakespeare's Library: A collection of the Plays, Romances, Novels, Poems, and Histories Employed by Shakespeare in the Composition of His Works*, 2nd ed., 6 vols. (London: Reeves & Turner, 1875). The latter work is, as the similarity of its title implies, an updated and expanded version of Collier's collection. See also Hazlitt, ed., *Shakespeare Jest-Books: Reprints of the Early and Very Rare Jest-Books Supposed to Have Been Used by Shakespeare*, 3 vols. (London: Willis & Sotheran, 1864). Kenneth Muir, *Shakespeare's Sources, I: Comedies and Tragedies* (London: Methuen, 1957), provides an analysis rather than a collection; it gives slight attention to *The Tempest* (perhaps reserving it for a planned second volume that has not appeared), but see pages 3–4, 257, 260–61.
3 Bullough, *Narrative and Dramatic Sources*, Vol. III, pp. 221–301; Vol. I, pp. 269–363.
4 *The Tempest*, ed. Frank Kermode, "The Arden Shakespeare," 6th ed. (London: Methuen, 1958), pp. 135–41, 145–50; Bullough, *Narrative and Dramatic Sources*, Vol. VIII, pp. 237–340. *The Tempest*, ed. Stephen Orgel, "The Oxford Shakespeare" (Oxford University Press, 1987), contains extracts from Strachey, Montaigne, and Ovid (pp. 209–19, 227–41).

seems to have included most of *The Tempest's* plausible literary antecedents.

There is far less agreement about Caliban's sources. A few scholars have posited a single prototype, based not on one document but on a cluster of historical texts or ideas. A prime example is the relatively recent assumption that Shakespeare's savage represented America's Indians (discussed at length in Chapter 5), and there are other, less popular theories. An authority on Elizabethan politics proposes that *The Tempest* is, on one level at least, a reflection of Jacobean political intrigue: Caliban represents the deformed "flatterer and toadier" Robert Cecil.[5] Another explanation is that Caliban emblemizes the mobs of Caesar's Rome and Elizabeth's England; still another that he "personifies the paganization of Christianity," especially the fanaticism of the Inquisition.[6] Such monocausal interpretations are relatively rare. More common is the assumption that Shakespeare drew on a variety of existing historical and literary models and his own perspicacity to form a wholly new character. Morton Luce, a prominent editor of the early twentieth century, for example, saw in Caliban "a compound of three typical ideas" – monster, African slave, and dispossessed Indian. The editors of the new Arden, Oxford, and Pelican editions of *The Tempest* are comparably eclectic, if less tripartite.[7] Such multifaceted explanations of Caliban's origins of course add a new frustration. If Caliban is multigeneric, the several prototypes and their sources should not only be identified but also be weighed for relative influence if Shakespeare's intentions are to be fathomed. Precision in this matter is obviously impossible

5 E. P. Kuhl, "Shakespeare and the Founders of America: *The Tempest*," *Philological Quarterly*, XLI (1962): 129–32, esp. p. 132.
6 Paul A. Jorgensen, "Shakespeare's Brave New World," in Fredi Chiappelli et al., eds., *First Images of America: The Impact of the New World on the Old*, 2 vols., Vol. I, (Berkeley: University of California Press, 1976), pp. 83–90, esp. p. 85. Emma Brockway Wagner, *Shakespeare's The Tempest: An Allegorical Interpretation*, ed. Hugh Robert Orr (Yellow Spring, Oh.: Antioch Press, 1933), pp. 72, 78–79. Jorgensen modifies his characterization later (p. 87) by cautioning that "one [cannot] overlook the special closeness between the problems of Caliban and those of the Indian."
7 *The Tempest*, ed. Morton Luce (first Arden edition) (London: Methuen, 1901), pp. xxxii–xxxiv, esp. p. xxxii; *The Tempest*, ed. Kermode, pp. xxxiii, xxxviii–xxxix, lxii–lxiii, 67 (n. 148); *The Tempest*, ed. Orgel, pp. 7, 11, 19, 23–28, 37; *The Tempest*, ed. Northrop Frye, "The Pelican Shakespeare," rev. ed. (Baltimore: Penguin Books, 1970), pp. 15–24.

(some would say irrelevant), but the historical sources that have been touted as likely influences on Shakespeare's conceptualization of Caliban deserve – as an essential background to his subsequent journey – a general description and assessment here.

I

Caliban's name may reveal Shakespeare's intentions. "Caliban," critics generally agree, cannot be meaningless; it is too distinctive to be indifferently chosen, too important to be misleading. Shakespeare must have meant it to signify, however subtly, Caliban's geographic or symbolic roots or, more likely, the essence of his character. The comedies, after all, are littered with characters whose names reflect their natures. The constables Dogberry (*Much Ado*) and Dull (*Love's Labour's Lost*) come quickly to mind, as do Mercutio and Benvolio (*Romeo and Juliet*), Malvolio (*Twelfth Night*), and Perdita (*Winter's Tale*). In *The Tempest*, "Prospero" probably is a derivative of the Latin *prospere* (to succeed or make fortunate), and Miranda surely reflects "wonder."[8] The etymology in such cases is highly plausible if not certain. Caliban's etymology, by contrast, is obscure and contentious. Even critics who insist that Shakespeare meant to convey a meaning in "Caliban" cannot agree on what it is; they merely share the assumption that he seized upon some word – a descriptive or ethnic label, or a place name, or a foreign term – to signify Prospero's "savage and deformed slave."

Since the late eighteenth century, the most popular explanation has been that "Caliban" is an intentional anagram of "can[n]ibal." The case, briefly stated, is that the consonants *l*, *n*, and *r* are virtually interchangeable in European transliterations of the unwritten Caribbean Indian languages; thus, "calib" is tantamount to "carib" or "canib," and the latter is the acknowledged linguistic source of "cannibal." A simple rearrangement of the letters – an anagram or its close linguistic counterpart, a metathesis – produces "Caliban."[9]

---

8 For conjectures on the names of these and other *Tempest* characters, see *The Tempest*, ed. Horace Howard Furness, "A New Variorum Edition of Shakespeare," Vol. IX (1892; repr. New York: American Scholar Publications, 1966), pp. 4–7; *The Tempest*, ed. Luce, pp. 177–79.
9 There are several minor variations of this explanation. Kermode (Arden edition, p.

Historical contexts

(The fabrication of anagrams must have been sparse before spelling became standardized, but a few anagrammatical Renaissance poems survive, and Ben Jonson in 1609 used the phrase "anagramatize our names," which suggests that the practice existed among poets and playwrights.[10]) Shakespeare's nominal choice thereby reveals, some argue, that the dramatist's model was an American Indian of the most unsavory sort.[11] A close alternative explanation is that "Caliban," as an extended anagram of "Carib," suggests that Shakespeare meant the monster to be a New World native but not necessarily a man-eater.[12]

Both versions are plausible, for in Shakespeare's day "Carib" and "cannibal" were widely used in English and Continental publications and, no doubt, in conversation, at least among the literati. Both words had entered European languages soon after 1492, when friendly natives told Columbus that some of their enemies were "canibales"; other Indians later referred to the same natives as "Caribes."[13] Because the Caribs, or Canibs, ate human flesh (so their

xxxviii), for example, says that "Caliban" usually is considered "some form of the word 'Carib,' meaning a savage inhabitant of the New World; 'cannibal' derives from this, which implies that Caliban was named for the Caribs more than for the cannibals." *The Oxford Companion to English Literature*, ed. Margaret Drabble (London: Guild Publishing, 1985), p. 159, suggests that "His name probably derives either from 'Carib' or 'cannibal.'" The most perceptive and suggestive discussion of cannibalism and Europe's "discovery" of America, and of their connections to *The Tempest*, is by Peter Hulme, *Colonial Encounters: Europe and the Native Caribbean, 1492–1797* (London: Methuen, 1986), ch. 1–3. See also François Laroque, "Cannibalism in Shakespeare's Imagery," *Cahiers Elisabéthain*, XIX (1981): 27–37; and Stephen Orgel, "Shakespeare and the Cannibals," in Marjorie Garber, ed., *Cannibals, Witches, and Divorce: Estranging the Renaissance* (Baltimore: Johns Hopkins University Press, 1987), pp. 40–66.

10 *OED*, s.v. "anagram."

11 The question remains whether an audience at *The Tempest* would have recognized Shakespeare's ploy if he intended "Caliban" as an anagram. For a discussion of the American Indian as a possible prototype for Caliban, see Chapter 5.

12 *The Tempest*, ed. Kermode, p. xxxviii. Charles Mills Gayley, *Shakespeare and the Founders of Liberty in America* (New York: Macmillan, 1917) p. 62, asserts that *Calibana* was the Italian word for the land of the Caribbean Indians; the Italian dictionaries we have consulted give the word as *Caraibi* or *Caraibico*. The Oxford *Dictionary of English Etymology*, ed. C. T. Onions (Oxford: Clarendon Press, 1966), traces *cannibal* from *Cariba*, which meant "brave" or "daring" in the native language.

13 Samuel Eliot Morison, trans. and ed., *Journals and Other Documents on the Life and Voyages of Christopher Columbus* (New York: Limited Editions Club, 1963), p. 186; J.

27

enemies said; the evidence is less certain today than it seemed in Columbus's time), "cannibal" gradually became the European word for man-eaters, the most depraved, beastly type of human.[14] Prior to Columbus's return to Spain in 1493, Europeans had described man-eating humans and semihuman creatures with similar appetites as "anthropophagi." The European term remained common in early travel accounts but soon shared popularity with the Americanism; by the early seventeenth century, "cannibal" had largely replaced the older but less mellifluous word. Whether Shakespeare contrived "Caliban" as an anagram of "cannibal" to suggest the savage's moral degradation or his ignoble American origins, the essential component is the anagram: Shakespeare used it, many critics insist, to signify "Carib" or "cannibal" or perhaps both.

The first of those possibilities – that Shakespeare intended his savage to be a Carib but not a cannibal – gains tangential support from late-sixteenth-century cartography: "Caribana" almost invariably appears in bold type across the northern part of South America. If Shakespeare's eye caught that designation, his Caliban may have been intended as a New World native, though not necessarily an islander. And because many of the maps sported vignettes of cannibals, sometimes nearby the geographic label, "Caribana" might well suggest anthropophagism as well. By 1611, in any event, "Caribana" was a common enough cartographic term (Figure 1) to offer the playwright a handy source – *if* he wanted to give his savage an anagrammed American place name.[15]

H. Trumbull, "Cannibal," *Notes and Queries*, 5th ser., IV (1875): 171–72; Douglas Taylor, "Carib, Caliban, Cannibal," *International Journal of American Linguistics*, XXIV (1958): 156–57; Pedro Henríques Ureña, "Caribe," in *Obras Completas, 1938–1939–1940*, Vol. VIII, ed. Juan Jacobo de Lara (Santo Domingo: Universidad National Pedro Henríques Ureña, 1979), pp. 9–16.

14 A lively debate among anthropologists and historians concerns the charge that the Caribs (and other "primitive" peoples) regularly – or ever – ate human flesh as part of their diet. See especially Michael Harner, "The Ecological Basis for Aztec Sacrifice," *American Ethnologist*, IV (1977): 117–35; Marvin Harris, *Cannibals and Kings: The Origins of Cultures* (New York: Random House, 1977); W[illiam] Arens, *The Man-Eating Myth: Anthropology and Anthropophagy* (Oxford University Press, 1979); Thomas S. Abler, "Iroquois Cannibalism: Fact not Fiction," *Ethnohistory*, XXVII (1980): 309–16.

15 See, for example, the map in Richard Hakluyt, *The Principall Navigations, Voiages and Discoveries of the English Nation . . .* (London: Printed by George Bishop and Ralph Newberrie, 1589), foldout map preceding p. 1 (a reprint from A. Ortelius,

1. Europe, Africa, and the Americas – with "Caribana" prominently labeled – from Theodor de Bry, *Americae pars VIII* (1599).

The persuasiveness of the "cannibal" anagram is dampened by the word's specificity and universality in Shakespeare's day. Originally, of course, "cannibal" was an exclusively Caribbean referent, but by the late sixteenth century it had become synonymous

Theatrum Orbis Terrarum [Antwerp, 1570]). Although Gustav H. Blanke, "Early English Images of North America and Shakespeare's 'The Tempest'," in Horst Arndt and Franz-Rudolf Weller, eds., *Landeskunde und Fremdsprachenunterricht* (Frankfurt: Dietserweg, 1978), p. 81 (n. 31), reports that a Mercator map of 1569 "uses the name 'Caliban' for Guiana," the label, in fact, is "Carib."

with man-eating in any time or place. Roughly half the uses of "cannibal" in English publications before 1611 neither state nor imply a connection to the Western Hemisphere.[16] Thus, if Shakespeare intended "Caliban" as an anagram of "cannibal," presumably he intended also to suggest anthropophagism, for Shakespeare's pre-1611 references to cannibals all imply man-eating: "hungry cannibals," "bloody cannibals" (3 Henry VI, I.iv.152; V.iv.61); "Cannibals that each [other] eat / The Anthropophagi" (Othello, I.iii.143–44); and "he had been cannibally given, he might have boiled and eaten him too" (Coriolanus, IV.v.188–9). Would Shakespeare have chosen an anagram of "cannibal" for a savage who did not practice what his name preached?

Another stumbling block to the acceptance of the "cannibal" explanation is its late emergence in print. It can be dated quite precisely to the 1778 edition of Samuel Johnson and George Steevens's annotated Tempest, which included – as did their previous and later editions (1773, 1785) – notes by several prominent scholars in addition to their own. Among the frequent annotators was the Reverend Richard Farmer, master of Emmanuel College, Cambridge, principal librarian of Cambridge University, and author of an Essay on the Learning of Shakespeare (1767). Johnson and Steevens's edition of 1773 had carried a few annotations about Caliban's character, but none about his name; the 1778 and subsequent editions stated bluntly that "The metathesis in Caliban from Canibal is evident. FARMER."[17] Although that statement did not appear in the 1787 compendium of Johnson-Steevens criticism, it resurfaced in their later editions as revised by Isaac Reed (1803 et seq.), again without additional comment. Readers of the standard early-nineteenth-century editions of The Tempest were thus introduced to Farmer's explanation of Caliban's name and, inferentially, to Caliban's possible American roots. By 1821, when the third variorum – largely the work of Edmond Malone – appeared, Caliban's etymology was well established:

16 For example, see Robert Baker, "The Second Voyage to Guinie" (1563) in Hakluyt, Principall Navigations, p. 139.
17 The Plays of William Shakespeare . . . , 2nd ed., 10 vols., Vol. I, ed. Samuel Johnson and George Steevens (London: Printed for C. Bathurst et al., 1778), p. 32 (2nd pagination). Farmer's An Essay on the Learning of Shakespeare Addressed to Joseph Cradock, Esq. (Cambridge, England: For W. Thurlbourn and J. Woodyer, 1767) does not mention Caliban's etymology, nor do any of its subsequent editions.

"Caliban, as was long since observed by Dr. Farmer, is merely the metathesis of Canibal."[18] The Farmer-Malone explanation of Caliban's etymology has flourished ever since. It has also attracted a few skeptics. In 1892, H. H. Furness summarized the situation in his variorum edition: "Dr. FARMER'S derivation of this name as a metathesis of Cannibal has generally been accepted." Furness himself, however, dissented. "Is it likely," he scoffed,

that, when *The Tempest* was acted before the motley audience of the Globe Theatre, there was a single auditor who, on hearing Prospero speak of Caliban, bethought him of the Caribbean Sea, and instantly surmised that the name was a metathesis of Cannibal? Under this impression, the appearance of the monster without a trace of his bloodthirsty characteristic must have been disappointing.[19]

Furness did not undermine the anagram explanation. Morton Luce's 1901 introduction to *The Tempest* accepted Caliban as "an obvious transposition" of "cannibal" and insisted that "no name could have been more suggestive or more attractive to an audience of that day." Luce objected, implicitly, to Furness's literalness. Caliban, Luce insisted, "takes this title only as being a *type*; we must not expect to see him devouring human flesh on the stage."[20] Luce's, rather than Furness's, assumption has carried the day: most commentators on *The Tempest* assert, usually without a hint of doubt, that "Caliban" is simply an anagram of "cannibal." The tacit corollary often is that Caliban's name thus demonstrates America's influence on *The Tempest*'s plot and persona and Shakespeare's intention to portray Caliban as at least partly a New World native.[21] Yet no conclusive

18 *The Plays and Poems of William Shakespeare . . . ,* Vol. XV, ed. Edmond Malone (London: Printed for F. C. and J. Rivington et al., 1821), p. 15. Half a century later, the metathesis was "indisputable," according to Adolphus William Ward, *A History of English Dramatic Literature to the Death of Queen Anne,* 2 vols., Vol. I (London: Macmillan, 1875), p. 442.
19 *The Tempest,* ed. Furness, p. 5 (n. 10).
20 *The Tempest,* ed. Luce, pp. xxxiii, xxxviii.
21 E.g., *The Comedies of Shakespeare,* ed. W. J. Craig (Oxford University Press, 1924), p. 3; Hulme, *Colonial Encounters,* p. 3. If Shakespeare did adapt "cannibal" for his savage's name, he may have been inspired by Montaigne's essay on Brazilian cannibals, which he surely read. Montaigne's essay gives little attention to the

31

or even circumstantial evidence has connected Prospero's slave to eaters of human flesh. The geographic link – "Caliban" as a variant of the name for a New World region connoting mystery and incivility – seems to us more plausible than the cannibal connection, but is equally unproven.

II

Other etymological explanations of Caliban have had enthusiastic advocates, though fewer by far than the "Carib/cannibal" possibilities. In 1889 Theodor Elze proposed that *The Tempest*'s island was Pantalaria, between Tunis and Italy, an alternate site to Joseph Hunter's earlier but almost completely ignored suggestion of neighboring Lampedusa and William Bell's of Corcyra (Corfu, Kerkira), off the western coast of Greece.[22] Elze contended that Pantalaria could readily have been reached by a drifting Prospero and Miranda after their exile from Milan – assuming that they left from Genoa, the nearest port – and by Alonzo's windblown ship en route from Tunis to Naples. Pantalaria also boasts the right topology: fresh springs, brine pits, barren and fertile places, and almost everything else in *The Tempest*'s description of Prospero's island. And on the nearby African coast, the town of Calibia offered Shakespeare a linguistic prototype for the son of an Algerian witch. "[W]hy should Shakespeare," Elze wondered, "who, forsooth, connected Tunis with Carthage and Widow Dido, have to devise, out of an American word, a name that all the while lay ready to his hand?" Maps of the Mediterranean, Elze noted, had shown Calibia since 1529.[23] (Elze

cannibalistic customs of the Indians he praised; on the other hand, there is little in the essay to suggest Caliban's character. For more on Montaigne, see Section IV in this chapter.
22 Theodor Elze, "Die Insel der Sycorax," *Shakespeare Jahrbuch*, XV (1880): 251–3 (an English version of Elze is available in the Furness variorum, p. 3); Joseph Hunter, *A Disquisition on the Scene, Origin, Date, etc. of Shakespeare's Tempest* (London: Printed by C. Whittingham, 1839), p. 18. Cf. J. Payne Collier, ed., *The Works of William Shakespeare*, 8 vols. (London: Whittaker & Co., 1842–44), Vol. I, p. 6; William Bell, *Shakespeare's Puck, and His Folklore*, Vol. II (London: Printed for the author, 1861), p. 308.
23 *The Tempest*, ed. Furness, pp. 1–4, discusses the various Mediterranean islands that have been advocated; Furness casts his vote on p. 5 (n. 10). See also Hunter,

neglected to mention that Calibia also appeared in a book of 1603 that Shakespeare mined for *Othello*.[24]) But Elze converted few Shakespearean scholars to the Calibia explanation. Furness was a rare exception.

Another possible but equally unproven source of Caliban's name, offered by a few nineteenth-century critics, is *kalebôn*, an Arabic word for "vile dog." The assumption underlying this derivation is that *kalebôn* appeared often enough in the popular literature of Tudor-Stuart England for Shakespeare to have adopted it, consciously or unconsciously, as a pejorative name for a North African creature.[25] Although the argument is reasonable, the absence of additional evidence has been fatal – almost no one endorses the Arabic derivative. A similar lack of enthusiasm greeted a suggestion that Shakespeare adapted "Caliban" from the Hindu *Kalee-ban*, a "satyr of Kalee, the Hindoo Proserpine."[26] Even less support adheres to the possibility that Shakespeare transliterated the German *kabliau* (codfish) or borrowed the Greek word for a drinking cup or, finally, that "Caliban" might be "among the many names by which the Three Magi are known in different countries of Europe."[27]

Slightly more support adheres to another explanation, launched in 1895 by Albert Kluyver, a Dutch scholar, who rejected the "cannibal" explanation because "it is improbable that Shakespeare should have known *Caliban* as an English name for a cannibal." Rather, Kluyver proposed, Shakespeare must have been familiar with the gypsy language, which had flourished in England for a century before 1611. *Cauliban* (or *kaliban*) meant "black" or things associated

Disquisition on Shakespeare's Tempest, p. 18; and "Ivica and Formentera," in G. F. Sargent, *Shakespeare Illustrated* (London: How & Parsons, 1842), n.p.

24 Richard Knolles, *The Generall Historie of the Turkes . . .* (London: Printed by Adam Islip, 1603), p. 705.

25 *The Tempest*, ed. J. Surtees Phillpotts, "The Rugby Edition" (London: Rivington's, 1876), p. xviii; *The Tempest*, ed. Furness, p. 5 (n. 10).

26 *The Tempest*, ed. Furness, p. 5 (n. 10); *Notes and Queries*, 3d ser., VI (1864): 202.

27 *The Tempest*, ed. Furness, p. 5 (n. 10); *Notes and Queries*, 4th ser., VII (1871): 56; Bell, *Shakespeare's Puck*, Vol. II, p. 307; Hunter, *Disquisition on Shakespeare's Tempest*, pp. 124–25. For a lengthy discussion of several other etymological explanations, see Roger Toumson, *Trois Calibans* (Habana: Casa de las Américas, 1981), pp. 201–99. Still another suggestion, "*Kali* (beauty) + *ban* or *bane*" is in Harry Berger, Jr., "Miraculous Harp: A Reading of Shakespeare's *Tempest*," *Shakespeare Studies*, V (1969): 259.

with blackness. "Prospero does not consider Caliban as a person, for he addresses him as *earth* and *filth*, i.e., *mud, dirt.*"[28] Kluyver's solution to the Caliban conundrum received little support among Shakespeareans, although E. K. Chambers in 1931 stated without further comment that "Caliban appears to be derived from the Gypsy *cauliban* 'blackness.'"[29] A few scholars, including Kermode and Bullough, have recently briefly noted the Romany word and its possible connection to Caliban.[30] Most modern critics ignore it.

Although the similarity of spellings and the pejorative meaning of *cauliban* have justified its occasional mention, the plausibility of the gypsy word as a Caliban source depends as much on historical as on linguistic evidence. Were gypsies (and a gypsy word) familiar and appropriate signifiers for Shakespeare and his audiences? The historical context is, in fact, more suggestive than critics have acknowledged. Documents of various kinds – laws, royal decrees, dramas, sermons, poetry – attest that gypsies were a lively and disturbing issue in Tudor-Stuart England and give plausibility to *cauliban* as a Caliban etymology.

Crown and Parliament considered gypsies a menace. The first major proscription appeared in 1530, when the government prohibited further immigration of these European vagabonds who were commonly styled Egyptians but in fact had originally come from northern India. Part of the government's concern was the gypsies themselves: They were widely suspected of thievery and idleness. England feared them too as a magnet for her own vagabonds, who joined the wandering gypsy tribes because the life-style attracted "counterfeit Egyptians." (As Dale Randall observes, all gypsies were counterfeit; none, the evidence suggests, were in fact Egyptian.[31]) In

28 Albert Kluyver, "Kalis and Caliban," trans. A. E. H. Swaen, *Englische Studien*, XXI (1895): 326–28; John Holland, *A Historical Survey of the Customs, Habits, and Present State of the Gypsies* (London: Printed for the author, 1816), p. 148; B. C. Smart and H. T. Crofton, eds., *The Dialect of the English Gypsies*, 2nd ed. (London: Asher, 1875), p. 92.

29 E. K. Chambers,.*William Shakespeare: A Study of Facts and Problems*, 2 vols., Vol. I (Oxford: Clarendon Press, 1930), p. 494. Chambers did not mention "cannibals," "Caribs," or other possible Caliban etymologies.

30 *The Tempest*, ed. Kermode, p. xxxviii (n. 2); Bullough, *Narrative and Dramatic Sources*, Vol. VIII, p. 258.

31 Dale B. J. Randall, *Jonson's Gypsies Unmasked: Background and Theme of the Gypsies Metamorphos'd* (Durham, N.C.: Duke University Press, 1975), p. 51.

Historical contexts

1562, a law imposed new burdens on gypsies, because, in a reversal
of roles, many of them had begun to pose as English vagabonds to
escape the more severe legislation against gypsies. The already
confusing distinction between gypsies and English vagabonds thus
was further blurred, though in any event it was a distinction with
little functional difference: English officials considered both categories
of landless and jobless people threats to the social order and frequently curbed their liberties. Yet gypsies, because they were less
likely to be of English birth and language than homegrown vagabonds, often were targets of special discrimination. Laws, tracts,
and sermons increasingly lamented their baneful influence. The 1597
act authorized heavy penalties for people "pretending themselves
to be Egipcyans, or wandering in the Habbite Forme or Attyre of
counterfayte Egipcians." In 1603, James I, in his first campaign for
social order, demanded rigorous enforcement of the existing laws
against gypsies. They remained a conspicuous subdivision of
England's lower class for nearly a century more.[32]

England's contempt for gypsies and fear of their disruptive influence infused Renaissance literature. Thomas Dekker's *Lanthorne
and Candle-light*, which enjoyed several editions between 1608 and
1620, berated gypsies as "a people more scattered then the Jewes,
and more hated: beggerly in apparell, barbarous in condition, beastly
in behavior: and bloudy if they meete advantage."[33] Ben Jonson's
Volpone (1607) castigated them more briefly but as unflatteringly, as
did a host of other writings before 1611 that addressed the gypsy
menace.[34] (Jonson's *The Gypsie Metamorphos'd* was not produced

32 Randall, *Jonson's Gypsies Unmasked*, pp. 47–53. See also Frank Aydelotte,
Elizabethan Rogues and Vagabonds (Oxford: Clarendon Press, 1913), pp. 17–20;
A. L. Beier, *Masterless Men: The Vagrancy Problem in England, 1560–1640* (London:
Methuen, 1985), esp. pp. 58–62; R. H. Tawney and Eileen Power, eds., *Tudor
Economic Documents*, Vol. II (London: Longmans Green, 1924), p. 355.
33 Thomas Dekker, *Lanthorne and Candle-light* ... (London: Printed for Iohn Busbie,
1608), sig. [G4].
34 [Benjamin Ionson], *Ben: Jonson his Volpone, or the Foxe* (London: Printed for Thomas
Thorppe, 1607), sig. [C4v]. For other pre-*Tempest* chastisements of gypsies, see,
for example, [George Abbot], *A Briefe Description of the Whole Worlde* (London:
Printed for John Browne, 1605), sig. K4r–K4v; John Cowell, *The Interpreter: or,
Booke Containing the Signification of Words* ... (Cambridge: John Legate, 1607),
sig. Bb1; and S[amuel] R[id], *Martin Mark-All, Beadle of Bridewell* ... (London:
Printed for Iohn Budge, 1610), sig. [G4r–H1v].

35

until 1621 and was not published until 1625, but its title and subject poignantly underline the gypsies' prominence in Jacobean thought.) Shakespeare wrote gypsies into four plays. The brief mention in *As You Like It* (V.iii.14–15) is innocuous, but *Romeo and Juliet* has a clearly pejorative reference to a gypsy (II.iv.41); *Antony and Cleopatra* (the latter, of course, *was* Egyptian) refers to "a gypsy's lust" (I.i.10); in *Othello*, Desdemona's handkerchief is initially a gift to Othello's mother from "an Egyptian . . . a charmer [who] could almost read / The thoughts of people . . ." (III.iv.56–58). Not damning statements, to be sure, but hardly favorable.

None of this points directly to gypsies as Shakespeare's model for Caliban. Rather, the historical and literary evidence shows clearly that they were a current topic in 1611 and suggests that Shakespeare, influenced by tales of gypsies (who often blackened their faces) and by the king's proscription of these alien vagabonds, might have chosen a gypsy word for his "thing of darkness." Caliban exhibits a good many – but by no means all – of the characteristics attributed to gypsies: slovenly appearance, "savage" behavior, deceitful character, and (until taught by Miranda) a language unintelligible to the island's dominant population. And like gypsies and other vagrants, Caliban is associated with the spread of diseases ("the red plague rid you" [I.ii.366]), with raucous dancing, and with social disorder in general. Perhaps Shakespeare's audiences saw in Caliban a satirical yet occasionally sympathetic portrayal of the "counterfeit kinde of roagues" who epitomized to Jacobeans the dark and dangerous side of human nature.[35]

III

Whatever the origins of Caliban's name, Shakespeare may have drawn the broader context of his role and character from a wealth of contemporaneous historical texts. Several documents of the sixteenth and early seventeenth centuries were almost certainly known to Shakespeare and are widely acknowledged to have in-

35 Paul Slack, *The Impact of the Plague in Tudor and Stuart England* (London: Routledge & Kegan Paul, 1985), pp. 303–10; Cowell, *The Interpreter*, sig. Bb1. Another possible connection between gypsies and Caliban is that the latter were sometimes called "Moone-men"; Caliban was a "mooncalf."

luenced the play. Most of those documents relate in some way o Europe's "discovery" of the Western Hemisphere and thus suggest connections between *The Tempest* and the unfolding drama of England's overseas empire. Simultaneously, the documents hint at Caliban – if one is disposed to read them that way – as Shakespeare's emblemization of New World natives.

The earliest views of America that could have suggested to Shakespeare an American context and an Indian Caliban are, of course, Columbus's accounts of his first transatlantic voyage. We have already discussed the possible implications of "Carib" and 'cannibal"; the same documents that introduced those words to European vocabularies – and the flood of texts that followed in the era of European reconnaissance – may also have shaped Shakespeare's sense of the "brave new world" and its inhabitants. The earliest document to influence *The Tempest* appears to have been Antonio Pigafetta's account of Ferdinand Magellan's "voyage or navigation made about the world" in 1519–22. (After Magellan was killed in the Philippines, Juan Elcano brought home the crucial reports.) Pigafetta's narrative was first published in French around 1526 and frequently thereafter in several languages. Shakespeare could have read either or both of Richard Eden's translations (1555, 1577) of an Italian version in *The Decades of the Newe World or West India*, by Pietro Martire d'Anghiera, to which Eden appended Pigafetta's narrative.

Pigafetta recorded that Magellan's expedition wintered for two months near Antarctica,

all which tyme they sawe no man except that one daye by chaunce they espyed a man the stature of a giante, who came to the haven daunsyng and syngynge, and shortly after seemed to cast dust over his heade.... This giante was so bygge, that the heade of one of owr men of a meane stature, came but to his waste. He was of good corporature and well made in all partes of his bodie, with a large vysage paynted with dyvers coloures, but for the most parte yelowe. Uppon his cheekes were paynted two hartes, and redde circles abowt his eyes. The heare of his headde was coloured whyte, and his apparell was the skynne of a beaste sowde togyther.[36]

36 Pietro Martire d'Anghiera, *The Decades of the Newe Worlde or West India . . .* , trans. Rycharde Eden (London: William Powell, 1555), pp. 218v–19r. Eden and Richard

(Some years after Shakespeare's death, an English writer would debunk the story, claiming that Patagonians were large but "nothing so monstrous, or Giant-like as they were reported; . . . the Spaniards did not thinke, that ever any English man would come thither, to reprove them; and thereupon might presume the more boldly to lie. . . ."[37]) Pigafetta had also reported that the voyagers seized two of the giants "by a deceypte" and shackled them. "[W]hen they sawe how they were deceaved they rored lyke bulles and cryed uppon theyr greate deuile Setebos to helpe them. . . . The Capitayne named these people Patagoni."[38]

Shakespearean scholars since the late eighteenth century have been virtually unanimous in attributing the name of Sycorax's god Setebos to Pigafetta's narrative. Other affinities have also been noticed between Pigafetta's relation and The Tempest, including a description of St. Elmo's fire, the miraculous escape of all aboard a ship presumed to be lost at sea, and – perhaps relevant to Caliban – a reference to cannibali. Recently a good case has been made for Francis Fletcher's narrative of Sir Francis Drake's circumnavigation of 1577–80 as an alternative or additional source to Pigafetta's: Fletcher mentioned "Settaboth," "a most dreadful tempest," a native drunk on European liquor, and other parallels to Shakespeare's play.[39]

Forty years after Richard Farmer first suggested The Tempest's indebtedness to Pigafetta, Edmond Malone pointed out an even greater affinity between the play and several accounts of Sea Ven-

Willes (who completed the volume on Eden's death) included a condensed version of this account in The History of Travayle in the West and East Indies . . . (London: Richard Jugge, 1577), p. 433v. On Pigafetta and his "relation," see Antonio Pigafetta, Magellan's Voyage: A Narrative Account of the First Circumnavigation, trans. and ed. R. A. Skelton, 2 vols., Vol. I (New Haven, Conn.: Yale University Press, 1969), pp. 1–28, 183; for a modern translation of Pigafetta's description of the giant (from a French manuscript version), see pp. 46–47.

37 Francis Fletcher et al., The World Encompassed by Sir Francis Drake (London: For Nicholas Bourne, 1635), p. 22.

38 d'Anghiera, Decades of the Newe Worlde, p. 219v.

39 Farmer's discussion of Setebos is in Plays of William Shakespeare, ed. Johnson and Steevens, Vol. I, pp. 31–32 (2nd pagination). See also Sidney Lee, A Life of William Shakespeare (London: Smith, Elder, 1898), p. 253; Craig, ed., Comedies of Shakespeare, p. 3; Charles Frey, "The Tempest and the New World," Shakespeare Quarterly, XXX (1979): 29–41, esp. pp. 33–37; Skelton, ed., Magellan's Voyage, Vol. I, pp. 41–50.

Historical contexts

ure's wreck on Bermuda in 1609. That June, a major relief expedition had departed England for the struggling outpost at Jamestown, Virginia; near the West Indies a hurricane battered the nine vessels, sinking one and scattering the others along the Atlantic seaboard. Most of the surviving ships eventually straggled into Virginia's James River. But the storm drove *Sea Venture*, with Admiral Sir George Somers and governor-designate of Virginia Sir Thomas Gates on board, into a rocky outcropping of the Bermuda Islands. Despite the pounding waves and fierce winds, everyone on board – more than 150 men, women, and children – reached shore safely before the sea demolished the ship. During the next nine months, Somers directed the construction of two small vessels from salvaged rigging and fresh-hewn cedar planks to carry the whole company to Virginia. In the meantime, Bermuda refuted its reputation as "the ile of divels." It was paradise: balmy weather, luxurious foliage, convenient timber, and abundant fish, fowl, and wild pigs. In late May 1610 all of the survivors (a few had died on the island) reached Jamestown, except two fugitives from justice who remained at large. By September, Governor Gates was back in England to report the miraculous event and to recruit further relief for the Virginia colony.[40]

For Shakespeareans, Gates's most significant cargo was an epistolary description of the Bermuda episode by William Strachey, one of its survivors, to an anonymous "Excellent Lady" – probably Sarah, wife of Sir Thomas Smythe, treasurer of the Virginia Company. "A True Reportory of the Wracke, and Redemption of Sir Thomas Gates, Knight...," dated 15 July 1610, told in graphic

40 William Strachey, "A True Reportory of the Wracke, and Redemption of Sir Thomas Gates, Knight; upon, and from the Ilands of the Bermudas...," in Samuel Purchas, *Hakluytus Posthumous or Purchas is Pilgrimes*, 4 vols. (London: For H. Fetherstone, 1625; repr. 20 vols., Glasgow: J. MacLehose & Sons, 1905–07), Vol. XIX, pp. 5–72; Silvester Jourdain, *A Discovery of the Barmudas, Otherwise Called the Ile of Divels* (London: Printed by John Windet, 1610). Both pamphlets are readily available in Louis B. Wright, ed., *A Voyage to Virginia in 1609: Two Narratives* (Charlottesville: University Press of Virginia, 1964). Also relevant are the pamphlets cited in footnote 45 and two collections edited by Philip L. Barbour: *The Complete Works of Captain John Smith (1580–1631)*, 3 vols., Vol. II (Chapel Hill: University of North Carolina Press, 1986), pp. 345–51; and *The Jamestown Voyages under the First Charter, 1606–1609*, 2 vols., Vol. II (Cambridge, U.K.: Hakluyt Society, 1969), pp. 280–89.

39

Shakespeare's Caliban

detail the horrors of the storm, the miraculous landing on Bermuda, the tribulations of the sojourn there, and the state of the Jamestown colony when the Somers/Gates party finally reached its destination. Although Strachey's account was not published until 1625, scholars since 1892 have argued that Shakespeare must have read it in manuscript or possibly in a now-lost published version.[41] Shakespeare knew most of the major promoters of the Virginia enterprise, and their principal topic that fall must have been *Sea Venture's* "wracke and redemption." Strachey himself returned to London in the fall of 1611; as a prominent scholar and sudden celebrity, he very likely talked with Shakespeare before *The Tempest's* performance on the first of November.[42] In any event, Strachey's influence on Shakespeare is now largely taken for granted. In 1964, Louis B. Wright, director of the Folger Shakespeare Library and editor of a modern version of Strachey's manuscript, could have been speaking for most of his professional colleagues when he claimed that "It was this letter that Shakespeare had obviously read before writing *The Tempest*"; Strachey's narrative "inspired one of Shakespeare's most fascinating plays." Passages by Strachey that echo in *The Tempest* include "A most dreadfull Tempest," a description of St. Elmo's fire, names similar to Gonzalo and Ferdinand, and several other details.[43]

41 Because Strachey's "True Reportory" probably was unpublished until 1625, when it appeared in Samuel Purchas's *Purchas his Pilgrimes*, Malone and others overlooked its influence on *The Tempest*. Furness (variorum, pp. 312–15) discovered the similarity of certain passages, but he assumed that Shakespeare could not have seen the document until it was "possibly, printed in 1612." Furness accordingly dated the play's first performance as 1613. For subsequent examinations of the Bermuda-Virginia documents, see Gayley, *Shakespeare and the Founders of Liberty*, pp. 40–76, 225–30; and Robert Ralston Cawley, "Shakspere's Use of the Voyagers in *The Tempest*," *Publications of the Modern Language Association* (hence-forth *PMLA*), XLI (1926): 688–726.

42 S. G. Culliford, *William Strachey, 1572–1621* (Charlottesville: University Press of Virginia, 1965), pp. 126, 151–54. See also the suggestive discussion of the Strachey/*Tempest* affinities in Stephen Greenblatt, *Shakespearean Negotiations: The Circulation of Social Energy in Renaissance England* (Berkeley: University of California Press, 1988), pp. 147–58.

43 Specific parallels between Strachey's account and *The Tempest* are noted in Wright, ed., *Two Voyages*, pp. x, xviii, 6, 7, 18, 24, 31; and especially in Bullough, *Narrative and Dramatic Sources*, Vol. VIII, pp. 275–94. For a pre-1609 commentary on the Bermudas that alludes to tempests, devils, evil spirits, and strange noises, see [Thomas Tymme], *A Silver Watch-bell* (London: Printed for William Cotton, 1605), pp. 81–82.

Even if Shakespeare somehow missed Strachey's narrative, he had at his disposal two other accounts of the Bermuda adventure, both drawn from firsthand experience and both published in London in 1610: Silvester Jourdain's *A Discovery of the Barmudas, otherwise Called the Ile of Divels*, and Richard Rich's *Newes from Virginia: The Lost Flocke Triumphant*. Jourdain's slim narrative contained a few details not in Strachey (the resort to strong drink by some of the passengers, for example), whereas Rich's brief tetrameter verse description spelled Bermuda "Bermoothawes" (close to the First Folio's orthography), and some of Rich's phrases sound to credulous ears similar to lines by Gonzalo and Prospero.[44]

Three other tracts, none primarily concerned with the shipwreck but all available before 1611, may have influenced Shakespeare more broadly. Captain John Smith's *A True Relation of Such Occurrences and Accidents of Noate as Hath Hapned in Virginia since the First Planting of that Collony* (1608) told just what its title promised, though probably with less candor than Smith's original version, sent from Virginia at the end of the colony's first year, which Shakespeare may have read. Smith wrote before *Sea Venture* sailed onto the scene, of course, but his account of the first year of England's outpost at Jamestown has some *Tempest* overtones. Of slightly later vintage, *A True and Sincere Declaration of the Purpose and Ends of the Plantation Begun in Virginia* (1609), written by Sir Thomas Smythe or under his direction, appeared in London after it was known that the fleet had encountered a hurricane but before news of the shipwrecked party's survival reached England. The tract refers several times to "the Tempest" and blames it for most of the Virginia colony's troubles. A slightly later publication, *A True Declaration of the Estate of the Colonie in Virginia* (1610), was an attempt by the Virginia Company to revive its sagging reputation. The pamphlet puts a bright face on the dispersal of the Somers fleet and the survival of *Sea Venture*'s passengers. Moreover, it calls the settlers' dissensions at Jamestown "this tragicall Comaedie," perhaps hinting that the colony's bizarre career was fit for the stage. *A True Declaration* also refers to the

---

44 Jourdain, *Discovery of the Barmudas*, p. 5; Rich's poem was printed in London by Edward Allde and is conveniently reprinted in Alexander Brown, *The Genesis of the United States*, 2 vols. (1890; repr. New York: Russell & Russell, 1964), Vol. I, pp. 420–26.

Jamestown colonists' "tempest of dissension."[45] (Not much should be made of the word "tempest," of course; it was the common term for storm, and Shakespeare had used it often in earlier plays.) From these varied accounts of *Sea Venture*'s wreck and the Virginia colony's woes, scholars generally agree, came Shakespeare's inspiration for the island setting, the tempest and St. Elmo's fire, the shipwreck survived by all hands, the pastoral Eden, the contentious factions, the stern but kindly leader, and a variety of nuances in plot, characters, and dialogue.[46] Implicit in the assumption that the several tracts influenced *The Tempest* is Shakespeare's conflation of the events and people on the island with those on the mainland: the whole of British America, rather than Bermuda alone, thus becomes the play's inspiration, and the whole corpus of American travel literature becomes Shakespeare's basic source.[47]

At the very least, *The Tempest* has several direct allusions to America almost certainly drawn from the writings of 1609–10 and earlier British and Continental travel accounts. "The still-vexed Bermoothes" are the Bermuda islands (they *could* be a disreputable section of London, or conceivably both localities at once[48]); Setebos is the

45 Smith's tract is best consulted in Barbour, ed., *Works of Captain John Smith*, Vol. I, pp. 3–117. *A True and Sincere Declaration* was printed for J. Stepneth and shows a title-page date of 1610 but was issued in December 1609. It is reprinted with introductory remarks in Brown, *Genesis of the United States*, Vol. I, pp. 337–53. *A True Declaration*, printed in 1610 for William Barret, is reprinted in Peter Force, comp., *Tracts and Other Papers Relating to the . . . Colonies in North America*, 4 vols. (1844; repr. Gloucester, Mass.: Peter Smith, 1963), Vol. III, #1.

46 See, for example, Gayley, *Shakespeare and the Founders of Liberty*, pp. 53–76; Cawley, "Shakspere's Use of the Voyagers," pp. 689–99 and passim; Wright, ed., *Two Voyages*, pp. 6, 7, 18, 24, 31; and Bullough, *Narrative and Dramatic Sources*, Vol. VIII, pp. 240, 271–73, 275–99.

47 See especially the perceptive essay by John Gillies, "Shakespeare's Virginian Masque," *ELH*, III (1986): 673–707, esp. pp. 676–83.

48 *The Tempest*, ed. Kermode, p. 24; Eric Partridge, *A Dictionary of Slang and Unconventional English*, 5th ed., 2 vols. (London: Routledge & Kegan Paul, 1961), Vol. I, p. 48; Robert Nares, *A Glossary . . .* (London: Printed for Robert Triphook, 1822), p. 39. Because 1616 is the earliest date assigned in the dictionaries to the London district's identification as "Bermuda" or "Bermoothes," the name apparently stemmed from the practice of English debtors escaping to the island, which engendered a local parallel in escaping to an unpoliced part of London. Settlement of the island began in 1612; *The Tempest*'s reference is therefore almost certainly to the island rather than the neighborhood, unless it is a post-1616 addition to the text.

Patagonian god mentioned by Pigafetta; "salvages and men of Ind" probably refers to American Indians (East Indians are possible too); and surely Trinculo alludes to American natives when he laments that Englishmen "will not give a doit to relieve a lame beggar [but] will lay out ten to see a dead Indian" (II.ii.32–34). Thus *The Tempest* reflects Shakespeare's familiarity with England's varied and voluminous literature on New World discovery.

IV

But where in this Anglo-American outpouring is Caliban? There were no natives on Bermuda, so the shipwrecked party's experience and the several accounts of it cannot be direct sources.[49] Yet most of the narratives that reported *Sea Venture*'s escapade, including Strachey's "True Reportory," tell also of the complex contact between natives and newcomers in early Virginia. Perhaps Caliban's plot with Stephano and Trinculo to murder Prospero echoes not (or not only) the Bermuda conspiracies to overthrow Admiral Somers but instead the Indians' hostility toward the Jamestown settlement or earlier against the Roanoke colonists.[50] Thus, Caliban may signify not a specific Indian but a generalized view of the Indians in Britain's area of culture contact. A more specific historical source for Caliban might be Captain John Smith's first account (1608) of the Virginia colony: He describes Pocahontas as Chief Powhatan's "only Nonpariel" (the label Prospero gave to Miranda [III.ii.98]), and an Indian messenger, Rawhunt, who was "much exceeding in deformitie of person, but of a subtill wit and crafty understanding." As a possible progenitor of Caliban, Rawhunt has generated little enthusiasm,

49 The firsthand accounts make clear that there were no Indians on the islands. See, for example, Wright, ed., *Two Voyages*, p. 108. Cf. Barbour, ed., *Works of Captain John Smith*, Vol. II, p. 350, which implies that *Sea Venture* had two Indians aboard when it crashed on Bermuda and that one of them murdered the other there. Even if Smith is right (and the absence of corroboration in the eyewitness accounts makes it unlikely), those Indians would hardly have been prototypes for Caliban, who was, of course, the only human inhabitant of the island when the Europeans arrived and remained there when they left.
50 Gayley, *Shakespeare and the Founders of Liberty*, pp. 61–69; Cawley, "Shakspere's Use of the Voyagers," pp. 712–21.

and "to identify Miranda with Pocahontas," Bullough warns, "is a tempting fancy which must be sternly repressed."[51]

It is no fancy, however, that by 1611 Shakespeare had access to scores of verbal and pictorial accounts of American natives and their interaction with European explorers and settlers that could have reinforced whatever signals he received from the Bermuda and Virginia tracts.[52] As an apparently avid reader of histories and travel accounts, Shakespeare must have relished Richard Hakluyt the younger's great compendia (1582, 1589, 1598–1600), and he probably also read many of the separately printed exploration tracts, including Thomas Hariot's report (1588) of the English outpost on Roanoke Island, with its detailed description of the neighboring Indians. Hariot's pamphlet reappeared in 1590, with engravings by Theodor de Bry of John White's vivid and generally accurate paintings of American Indians.[53] Shakespeare's contemporaries – indeed Shakespeare himself – must have lingered over those depictions. And because kidnapped Indians were London showpieces in the late sixteenth and early seventeenth centuries, Shakespeare may have seen, conceivably have talked with, real Indians.[54] From this welter of material he could have fashioned a wholly or partly Indian Caliban. And he need not have had specific texts or illustrations

51 Barbour, ed., *Works of Captain John Smith*, Vol. I, p. 93; Bullough, *Narrative and Dramatic Sources*, Vol. VIII, p. 241.
52 On early English travel literature, see especially John Parker, *Books to Build an Empire: A Bibliographical History of English Overseas Interests to 1620* (Amsterdam: N. Israel, 1965). On documents that may especially have influenced *The Tempest*, see Gayley, *Shakespeare and the Founders of Liberty*, pp. 225–30; Cawley, "Shakspere's Use of the Voyagers," passim; Bullough, *Narrative and Dramatic Sources*, Vol. VIII, pp. 237–74; and Frey, "*The Tempest* and the New World."
53 Although de Bry's versions of White's paintings are heavily stylized in accordance with European conventions, they nonetheless retain a general faithfulness. For good reproductions of the original watercolors, see Paul Hulton and David B. Quinn, *The American Drawings of John White, 1577–1580*, 2 vols. (Chapel Hill: University of North Carolina Press, 1964). For an analysis of the de Brys's (father and sons) other illustrations of Indians, see Bernadette Bucher, *Icon and Conquest: A Structural Analysis of the Illustrations of de Bry's Great Voyages*, trans. Basia Miller Gulati (Paris: 1977; repr. University of Chicago Press, 1981).
54 Sidney Lee, "Caliban's Visits to England," *Cornhill Magazine*, n.s., XXXIV (1913): 333–45; Carolyn T. Foreman, *Indians Abroad, 1492–1938* (Norman: University of Oklahoma Press, 1943), pp. 14–19. For an eighteenth-century instance of London's continuing curiosity about Indians, see Richmond P. Bond, *Queen Anne's American Kings* (Oxford University Press, 1952), ch. 1.

or firsthand observations in mind: The temper of the times was enough. As Charles Frey reminds us,

we tend not to appreciate the extent to which some themes, situations, incidents, and even phrases in *The Tempest* were part of the common coin of Shakespeare's day. . . . We need to read the voyage literature, therefore, not necessarily to find out what Shakespeare read, but to ascertain what Shakespeare and his audience together would have been likely to know.[55]

It is more than likely that by 1611 American natives were part of every English man and woman's common coinage.

The Tempest aside, half a dozen allusions to Indians pepper the Shakespeare canon. Some are innocuous: Indian sun worship in *All's Well That Ends Well* (I.iii.204–07), for example, and the queen's "lovely boy, stolen from an Indian king," in *A Midsummer Night's Dream* (II.i.22), unless, as is remotely possible, the latter is an East Indian potentate. Other references to American natives are mildly pejorative, like *Othello*'s – if one accepts the First Quarto reading – "base Indian [who] threw a pearl away / Richer than his tribe" (V.ii.347),[56] or the bawdy account in *Henry VIII* of "some strange Indian with the great tool come to court, the women so besiege us" (V.iii.34–35). In sum, Shakespeare's Indian allusions were vague or inconsequential, as indeed they are in *The Tempest*, where the only direct reference is Trinculo's jibe at dead Indians on display (II.ii.32–34) and perhaps Stephano's suspicion of "savages and men of Ind" (II.ii.57). Shakespeare's texts thus offer few clues to his perception and opinion of New World natives. Most of the evidence for Caliban as Indian must come from indirect connections between Prospero's slave and the prevailing image of Indians in the texts and iconography of the sixteenth and early seventeenth centuries.

55 Frey, "*The Tempest* and the New World," pp. 38, 34 (we have reversed the sequence of Frey's statements without, we believe, distorting his meaning). For similar sentiments, see Bullough, *Narrative and Dramatic Sources*, Vol. VIII, p. 240; *The Tempest*, ed. Furness, pp. 312–13.

56 For a lengthy discussion of "Indian" versus "Iudean," see *Othello*, ed. Horace Howard Furness, "A New Variorum Edition of Shakespeare" (Philadelphia: Lippincott, 1886), pp. 327–31; see also the several newer analyses listed in Margaret Lael Mikesell and Virginia Mason Vaughan, comps., *Othello: An Annotated Bibliography* (New York: Garland Publishing, 1990).

The Indians portrayed in discovery literature and other contemporaneous literary and artistic media ran an incredible gamut from near-beast to almost-noble savage, with innumerable intermediate positions.[57] Shakespeare might, for example, have drawn on French explorer/historian André Thevet's *New Found Worlde* (1568). Although some of Thevet's comments on the Indians were favorable, or at least neutral, some were viciously derogatory. In an especially critical passage he derided inhabitants of America as "wild and brutish people, without Fayth, without Lawe, without Religion, and without any civilitie: but living like brute beasts, . . . eating herbes and rootes, being always naked as well women as men." A decade later, prominent Elizabethan explorer George Best described the natives of northeastern Canada:

They live in Caves of the Earth, and hunte for their dinners or praye [prey], even as the Beare, or other wilde beastes do. They eate raw fleshe and fishe, and refuse no meate, howsoever it be stincking. They are desparate in their fighte, sullen of nature, and ravenous in their manner of feeding.[58]

---

57 On early English images of the Indians, see Bernard Sheehan, *Savagism and Civility: Indians and Englishmen in Colonial Virginia* (Cambridge University Press, 1980); Karen Ordahl Kupperman, *Settling with the Indians: The Meeting of English and Indian Cultures in America* (Totowa, N.J.: Rowan & Allenheld, 1980); Robert Berkhofer, *The White Man's Indian: Images of the American Indian from Columbus to the Present* (New York: Knopf, 1978), passim; Loren E. Pennington, "The Amerindian in English Promotional Literature," in K. R. Andrews, N. P. Canny, and P. E. Hair, eds., *The Westward Enterprise: English Activities in Ireland, the Atlantic, and America, 1480–1650* (Detroit: Wayne State University Press, 1979); and Alfred H. Cave, "Richard Hakluyt's Savages: The Influence of 16th Century Travel Narratives on English Indian Policy in North America," *International Social Science Review*, LX (1985): 3–24. There is a wealth of undigested information in H. C. Porter, *The Inconstant Savage: England and the North American Indian, 1500–1660* (London: Gerald Duckworth, 1979). For a recent brief but essentially sound correlation of pre-1611 literary images of Indians with Caliban, see Meredith Anne Skura, "Discourse and the Individual: The Case of Colonialism in *The Tempest*," *Shakespeare Quarterly*, XL (1989): 53–57.
58 André Thevet, *The New Found Worlde, or Antarctike*, trans. T. Hacket (London: Henrie Bynneman for T. Hacket, 1568), p. 36; Roger Schlesinger and Arthur P. Stabler, eds., *André Thevet's North America: A Sixteenth-Century View* (Montreal: McGill-Queen's University, 1986), passim; George Best, *A True Discourse of the Late Voyages of Discoverie . . .* (London: Henry Bynneman, 1578), p. 62. See also the bestial view of Indians in most of the de Bry volumes published before 1611 and the analysis of them in Bucher, *Icon and Conquest*, passim.

These passages might have been in Shakespeare's mind when he had Caliban inhabit a cave, act brutishly, and be sullen toward Prospero. Perhaps counteracting the largely negative Indian image – if, indeed, it was Caliban's prototype – was Michel de Montaigne's relatively sympathetic treatment of New World natives in his essay "Of the Caniballes." In striking contrast to prevailing notions of Indian societies, the French philosopher's cultural relativism found much to praise in cannibalistic Indians (but not in cannibalism), while mocking his own nation's – and western civilization's – vanity and corruptions. Brazilian cannibals, Montaigne asserted with acerbic irony, are more virtuous than their French contemporaries: The former live sensibly and humanely for the most part; their guide is natural law; they uphold standards of honor, valor, and decency; they wreak their vengeance on the dead rather than on the living. As Northrop Frye wisely wrote, Montaigne "is saying that, despite their unconventional way of getting their proteins, cannibals have many virtues we have not. . . . They are not models for imitation; they are children of nature who can show us what is unnatural in our own lives."[59]

Shakespearean scholars recognized as early as 1780 that Gonzalo's utopian speech owes much to John Florio's translation (1603) of Montaigne's essay.[60] (A copy in the British Library bears a signature that may be Shakespeare's.[61]) The similarities of expression between the speech and the essay are, Shakespeareans largely agree, too close to be coincidental. Even Margaret Hodgen, who marshals impressive evidence that Montaigne's description of a barbarian/utopian society "fell back on a tradition that is as old as the hills in England and France," admits that "the lines in The Tempest are still

59 Michel de Montaigne, The Essayes: or Morall, Politike and Millitarie Discourses, trans. John Florio (London: For Edward Blount, 1603), pp. 100–07; The Tempest, ed. Frye, p. 17.
60 In 1780, Edward Capell first pointed out Montaigne's influence, according to George C. Taylor, "The Date of Edward Capell's Notes and Various Readings to Shakespeare," Review of English Studies, V (1929): 319.
61 S[amuel] Schoenbaum, William Shakespeare: Records and Images (Oxford University Press, 1981), pp. 102–04, discusses the British Library copy's signature and concludes that its authenticity is dubious.

more like those in *Of the Caniballes* than any other formulation."[62] As for Caliban, he bears little resemblance to Montaigne's Brazilians, but he may have been Shakespeare's ironic parody of them.[63] Or maybe not: An alternative possibility is that Montaigne's benign attitude toward the Brazilians softened Shakespeare's portrayal of Caliban, adding a touch of dignity and sensitivity to the monster's characteristics.[64] In any event, Shakespeare almost certainly gleaned from Montaigne's essay some of Gonzalo's phrases and perhaps borrowed, anagrammatically, Caliban's name.[65]

Whatever Shakespeare's personal perception of the New World natives may have been, *The Tempest* surely portrays Caliban as an ignoble savage – though not necessarily an *American* savage. No kind words come his way. He is accused of ignorance, ingratitude, and lechery. His purported crime is to attempt, as Prospero delicately puts it, "to violate / The honour of my child." Caliban later encourages Stephano, with bumbling assistance from Trinculo, to murder Prospero and seize Miranda and the island for himself. Their plot fails, largely because the two European rogues prove less astute than Caliban. But he has already contributed to the fiasco by succumbing to their "celestial liquor." Here, in stark but suggestive terms, some critics say, Shakespeare summarized a popular European view of the Indians as lewd, rebellious, and intoxicated.[66]

There is an opposite way to read Caliban's role in *The Tempest*.

62 Margaret T. Hodgen, "Montaigne and Shakespeare Again," *The Huntington Library Quarterly*, XVI (1952–53): 23–42, quotations on pp. 29, 39. See also Elizabeth Robbins Hooker, "The Relation of Shakespeare to Montaigne," *PMLA*, XVII (1902): 312–66, esp. pp. 344–47, 366; Robert Ralston Cawley, "Shakspere's Use of the Voyagers in *The Tempest*," *PMLA*, XLI (1926): 703–06.

63 Ward, *History of English Dramatic Literature*, Vol. I, p. 442. See also Bullough, *Narrative and Dramatic Sources*, Vol. VIII, pp. 253–55.

64 Montaigne's influence on Caliban's formation is variously interpreted by, for example, Sidney Lee, "The American Indian in England," in Sidney Lee, *Elizabethan and Other Essays*, ed. Frederick S. Boas (Oxford: Clarendon Press, 1929), pp. 294–96; Cawley, "Shakspere's Use of the Voyagers," pp. 714–21; and *The Tempest*, ed. Kermode, pp. xxxiv–xxxviii.

65 For representative assertions that Caliban's name came from Montaigne's essay, see *The Tempest*, ed. Luce, p. xxii; A. H. Gilbert, "Montaigne and *The Tempest*," *Romanic Review*, V (1914): 363; and Annabel Patterson, *Shakespeare and the Popular Voice* (Oxford: Basil Blackwell, 1989), p. 155.

66 For example, Leslie Fiedler, *The Stranger in Shakespeare* (New York: Stein & Day, 1972), p. 237. For further discussion of this motif, see Chapter 5 herein.

48

Historical contexts

"This island's mine by Sycorax my mother, / Which thou tak'st from
me," Caliban laments early in the play (I.ii.331–32). The obvious
parallel between dispossessed Caliban and dispossessed Indians has
led numerous readers, especially in recent decades, to see Caliban as
a noble and deeply wronged native. As Walter Cohen succinctly
encapsulates the argument, "*The Tempest* uncovers, perhaps despite
itself, the racist and imperialist bases of English nationalism."[67]
Advocates of this view cite a variety of possible parallels – or, rather,
parallels that surely exist by hindsight but that only *might* have been
perceived by Shakespeare – between Caliban and the American
Indians. Like the Indians, he is generous to the early invaders of
his land. As Caliban laments to Prospero and Miranda, at first

> . . . I loved thee,
> And showed thee all the qualities o' th' isle,
> The fresh springs, brine pits, barren place and fertile –
> (I.ii.336–38)

Prospero and Miranda reward Caliban's guilelessness by enslaving
and despising him. Later in the play, Caliban tries again to befriend
new aliens. In his inebriated infatuation with Trinculo and Stephano
he offers an extended refrain of his earlier speech to Prospero and
Miranda:

> I'll show thee every fertile inch o' th' island – . . .
> I'll show thee the best springs; I'll pluck thee berries;
> I'll fish for thee, and get thee wood enough.
> . . . .
> I prithee let me bring thee where crabs grow,
> And I with my long nails will dig thee pig-nuts,
> Show thee a jay's nest, and instruct thee how
> To snare the nimble marmoset. I'll bring thee
> To clust'ring filberts, and sometimes I'll get thee
> Young scamels from the rock.
> (II.ii.142–66)

67 Walter Cohen, *Drama of a Nation: Public Theater in England and Spain* (Ithaca, N.Y.:
Cornell University Press, 1985), p. 401. For further discussion of the anticolonial
interpretation, see Chapter 6 herein.

Caliban's kindness to the feckless pair is, to be sure, primarily for his own advantage, but in part it is also a mark of native generosity toward strangers who initially seem godlike: "Hast thou not dropped from heaven? . . . I will kiss thy foot. I prithee be my god" (II.ii.131, 143). Once again Caliban is betrayed, for Stephano and Trinculo are no more his real friends than were Prospero and Miranda. All Europeans, from the deposed duke to the drunken butler, are at heart imperialists whose only interest in the native is in what he can do for them. They exploit him at every turn; they appropriate his land and his labor; they abuse him verbally and physically. Their principal legacies to Caliban are a language in which to curse and a liquor in which to drown his sorrows.

Between Caliban as the beastly savage and the noble but vanquished savage, American or otherwise, are more complex possibilities. Several of the most vigorous proponents of Caliban's Indian origins assert a mixed view: Shakespeare fused a variety of reports about the American natives into a single ambiguous paradigm, one that was faithful to the tenor of the sources. Caliban is human but has beastly qualities; he is savage but potentially redeemable; he resists European efforts at education and "civilitie" but – despite Prospero's insistence that nurture will never stick on him – he learns a European language and is remarkably articulate in it. In short, Caliban melds Europe's accounts of the Indian: a bit of Thevet's "brute beast," some of Montaigne's noble Brazilians, but mostly the more ambivalent Indians that abound in the collections of Richard Eden and Richard Hakluyt and in the numerous pamphlets, letters, and sermons by Shakespeare's contemporaries.[68] So say a host of Shakespearean scholars, either explicitly or implicitly, when they conjecture that Caliban was Shakespeare's image of the American Indian.[69]

[68] The mixed view described here melds the interpretations of, especially, Sidney Lee, "The Call of the West," and his many other publications (for citations see Chapter 5); Cawley, "Shakspere's Use of the Voyagers," and Robert Ralston Cawley, The Voyagers and Elizabethan Drama (Boston: Heath, 1938), esp. pp. 344–94. Many critics combine this amalgamated Indian image with other influences, such as monsters, wild men, or inanimate forces of nature.
[69] For further discussion of Caliban as Indian, see Chapter 5.

V

In light of the historical conjunction of *The Tempest* and England's
abundant literature of imperialism, the attempts to find American
links are not surprising. What is surprising is the infrequency of
attempts to link *The Tempest*, and especially Caliban, with Africa.
The principal reason is perhaps the relative paucity of English literature about Africa in the years just before 1611 and, within the
relevant literature, the scarcity of plausible *Tempest* associations.
And yet the works of Leo Africanus and others, mostly in the second half of the sixteenth century, and the accounts of travel to
Africa incorporated in Eden's and Hakluyt's anthologies, offered a
corpus of material that Shakespeare may have tapped for Caliban.[70]

The Tempest has several specific references to Africa, of course.
Most voluminous is the discussion of Claribel's marriage to the king
of Tunis (II.i.67–125), with its strong implications that the African
coast is culturally if not geographically distant from Europe and that
marriage to an African king is somehow degrading, whatever its
diplomatic advantages. More significant for Caliban are the clear
indications that his mother, Sycorax, was an Algerian before her
banishment to the island and his birth (I.ii.257–71). (He was "got,"
snarls Prospero, "by the devil himself," but given Prospero's malice
toward Caliban, the parental attribute may be more bombast than
biology.) In any event, few commentators have extracted from the
island's proximity to the Tunisian coast and Sycorax's Algerian
ancestry an African Caliban. Theodor Elze, previously mentioned,
saw an etymological connection in the town of Calibia. J. S. Phillpotts
preferred the Arabic *kalebôn* (vile dog) as the likely origin of Caliban's
name and posited as well an African genesis. "Little notice," he
complained, "has been taken by commentators of CALIBAN's being
African by birth, his mother, SYCORAX, having come from Algiers.

70 John Leo [Leo Africanus], *A Geographical Historie of Africa*, trans. John Pory (London:
George Bishop, 1600); Richard Hakluyt, *The Principal Navigations Voyages Traffiques
& Discoveries of the English Nation*, 12 vols. (London: 1598–1600; repr. Glasgow:
James MacLehose & Sons, 1903–05), esp. Vol. VI. See also Lois Whitney, "Did
Shakespeare Know 'Leo Africanus'?" *PMLA*, XXXVII (1922): 470–83; and Rosalind
Johnson, "African Presence in Shakespearean Drama: Parallels between Othello
and the Historical Leo Africanus," *African Presence in Early Europe* (*Journal of
African Civilizations*, VII [1985]): 276–87.

We seem to catch in him an echo of tales told by prisoners on their return from that Algerine captivity which overtook so many a seafarer of the time."[71] In the twentieth century, Morton Luce's influential Arden edition of *The Tempest* proposed a multigeneric Caliban who was partly "an African of some kind," particularly "a (negro) slave." But Robert Cawley dismissed Luce's reasoning, especially his assumption that "this thing of darkness" had anything to do with pigmentation. More recently, Bullough has alluded, without further comment, to "the American and African 'savages' to whom his [Caliban's] character owes much," but most commentators on *The Tempest* say nothing about Caliban's possible African roots, except to note, almost casually, Sycorax's Algerian past.[72]

VI

Looking abroad for *Tempest* and Caliban models may be unnecessary. Events in the British Isles, and the discourses they generated, offer a host of suggestive texts and contexts on which Shakespeare may have drawn for a play about (among other things) absolutism, property, rebellion, and subjection. Especially in the hands of "new historicists," *The Tempest* resonates the social and political issues of Elizabethan and early Jacobean England.

Gary Schmidgall, for example, sees *The Tempest* as political allegory. It was written, he argues, for James I in accord with what Schmidgall terms "the courtly aesthetic" – a theatrical mode of "spectacular, decorative, and romantic courtly fashion." At the heart of *The Tempest* is a preoccupation with the ruler and the ruled, in which Caliban symbolizes the antithesis of order and degree. He also reflects the abundant Tudor homilies on disobedience – propagandistic state sermons that preached the evil of rebellion. Caliban, Schmidgall contends, "lives" in *The Exhortation* (1547) and the *Homily against Disobedience and Willful Rebellion* (1571):

the sermons clarify Caliban's relation to Prospero and the efficacy of the power the latter exerts over him. . . . Prospero's powers rise to the angelic,

---

71 *The Tempest*, ed. Phillpotts, p. xvii.
72 *The Tempest*, ed. Furness, p. 3; *The Tempest*, ed. Luce, p. xxxv; Cawley, "Shakspere's Use of the Voyagers," p. 719 (n. 21); Bullough, *Narrative and Dramatic Sources*, Vol. VIII, p. 250.

while Caliban's are deteriorated, animalistic, of the earth and earthy. He is "filth," "earth," "a thing of darkness," and thus is "deservedly confin'd into this rock." The obedience Caliban owes to Prospero is then like that of a man to God, man to king, and beast to man.[73]

Caliban's deformity, in Schmidgall's analysis, symbolizes his ignorance and sensuality, and his supine groveling indicates his immorality. In sum, Caliban embodies the destructive forces of rebellion that Prospero (surrogate for King James) is duty-bound to repress and punish.[74] Curt Breight is more precise about those rebellious forces. "Caliban's conspiracy," he proposes, "appears to present a précis of Elizabethan fears regarding masterless men, and the drunkenness of the conspirators enforces specific official beliefs that subversion sprang from the local alehouse." Prospero allows himself to be vulnerable to Caliban's conspiracy – much as Elizabeth and James had publicly lamented their own vulnerability to foreign and domestic enemies – less from any true dangers than from the rhetoric's validation of harsh repression. Prospero, like James, committed an act of political excision: the rooting out of real but exaggerated conspirators, traitors, and unruly elements in his quest for an obedient and orderly reign.[75]

A wider and still more specific set of sociopolitical *Tempest* contexts has recently been argued by Donna Hamilton. Prospero, she writes, as

a ruler with magical and thus transcendent powers, stands in homologous relationship to King James and his concerns about his rights to a certain amount of power and to be served (and supplied) properly. Ariel and Caliban, who are in bondage and who continually express their longing for freedom, are homologous to the metaphors, idioms, and rhetoric used in

73 Gary Schmidgall, *Shakespeare and the Courtly Aesthetic* (Berkeley: University of California Press, 1981), esp. pp. 43, 191.
74 Schmidgall, *Shakespeare and the Courtly Aesthetic*, pp. 186–202. An earlier interpretation of Caliban based on English political contexts is in Kuhl, "Shakespeare and the Founders of America," pp. 129–32. See also Richard Marienstras, *New Perspectives on the Shakespearean World*, trans. Janet Lloyd (Cambridge University Press, 1981), pp. 176–77.
75 Curt Breight, "'Treason doth never prosper': *The Tempest* and the Discourse of Treason," *Shakespeare Quarterly*, XLI (1990): 1–28, esp. pp. 17, 27–28. See also Jorgensen, "Shakespeare's Brave New World," p. 85.

the Commons to express the subjects' right to liberty and freedom, their right to present grievances or to "complain," and their fears of "restraint" and loss of property.[76]

Caliban's role in Hamilton's reconstruction of *The Tempest*'s historical context is to represent not only "the English fear of being made 'slaves' in their own land" but also (as others have suggested) the dispossessed natives of America and (as only a few have suggested) of Ireland. "Caliban's compulsion to raise a rebellion is . . . as analogous to the native Irish inclined to call again for Tyrone [to oust the English] as to the English Parliament refusing to grant supply [to the king] when so few of their grievances had been addressed." Similarly, the Indians in Virginia resented and resisted the imposition of English authority. In the English context, then, Caliban "is an exaggerated representation of that debased and deformed state that some parliamentarians claimed they would be reduced to were subjects to lose their rights"; in the colonial contexts (Virginian and Irish) he was the image of the exploited but resistant native. Thus Hamilton blends two current interpretive concerns – Jacobean politics and colonial discourse – into a multifaceted historical explanation of Caliban's roots and thereby heralds, perhaps, a renewed eclecticism in *Tempest* analysis.[77]

VII

To report Caliban's various etymological and historical contexts is not, obviously, to resolve them. The diversity of opinion among Shakespeareans regarding Caliban's etymology and history and the ambiguity of the sources preclude consensus. Yet even if one subscribes, as we do, to the conviction that Shakespeare's intentions and the play's exact sources can never be resolved and are not, in any event, the most important intellectual issues, we hold, too, that to understand fully the ways Caliban has been interpreted, appropriated, and adapted over the centuries requires an understanding

76 Donna B. Hamilton, *Virgil and The Tempest: The Politics of Imitation* (Columbus: Ohio State University Press, 1990), p. 48.
77 Hamilton, *Virgil and The Tempest*, pp. 53, 64, 114. See also Greenblatt, *Shakespearean Negotiations*, pp. 152–58.

of the common literary coin of 1611. We have stressed in this chapter the relevant historical literature (broadly defined), but perhaps more important to the author and early audiences of *The Tempest*, as well as to Caliban's genesis, were several literary sources.

Chapter 3
Literary contexts

Me, poor man, my library / Was dukedom large
enough.

The Tempest (I.ii.109–10)

Caliban's monstrosity is rich in traditional resonances.

Gary Schmidgall (1981)

Poetry, drama, civic pageantry, and folklore probably influenced Shakespeare's eclectic imagination when he created Caliban. The grammar school curriculum at Stratford must have introduced Shakespeare to a wide range of classical materials, several of which could have shaped Prospero's enchanted island; and his membership in the cosmopolitan world of the London stage surely exposed him to events, writings, and conversations that in their own right constituted a liberal education. Accordingly, many of Shakespeare's plays owe unmistakable debts to classical and contemporaneous literary texts, and *The Tempest* is no exception. But, similar to the historical texts on which Shakespeare could have drawn, his sources for Caliban are not easily discerned or universally acknowledged. Robert Graves demonstrates how eclectic the search for prototypes can be when he claims that

Caliban is partly Afagddu in the *Romance of Taliesin*; partly Ravaillac, the Jesuit-prompted murderer of Henry IV; partly an Adriatic devil in Calahorra's romance; partly a sea monster, "in shape like a man", seen off Bermuda

56

during Admiral Sommers' stay there; partly Shakespeare's own *malus angelus*.[1]

Although it is not plausible that Shakespeare exploited *all* the literary analogues that critics have suggested, Caliban may well have been derived from one or from several. We can do no more here than to identify the "nonhistorical" texts – both written and oral – that Shakespeare may have plumbed for Caliban's creation.

Whether or not Shakespeare borrowed directly from the texts described here, each was embedded within the culture he inherited, readily available for reinterpretation. Admittedly, these texts are not equal in importance or merit; some are less probable or less significant sources than others. Because of its wide range of significations – many of them contradictory – the wild man, a figure from popular folklore, civic pageantry, and sixteenth-century drama, receives greater attention than other literary analogues. This legendary figure was appropriated at the end of the sixteenth century for allegorical purposes by Edmund Spenser, who included two "salvage men" in his *Faerie Queene*. But the wild man's earliest roots, as Hayden White has shown, were in Hebraic lore and in the classical legends of Greece and Rome.[2] Our survey begins, accordingly, with the classical texts Shakespeare must have known.

I

In the process of acquiring what Ben Jonson termed the dramatist's "less Greek," Shakespeare likely read Homer's *Odyssey*, perhaps at the King's School in Stratford. That classic story includes Odysseus' encounter with the Cyclops, a barbaric people who have

no counsels there,
Nor counsellers, nor lawes, but all men beare
Their heads aloft on mountaines, and those steepe,

---

1 Robert Graves, *The White Goddess: A Historical Grammar of Poetic Myth* (New York: Farrar, Straus & Giroux, 1966), p. 426n.
2 Hayden White, "The Forms of Wildness: Archaeology of an Idea," in *The Wild Man Within: An Image in Western Thought from the Renaissance to Romanticism*, ed. Edward Dudley and Maximillian E. Novak (University of Pittsburgh Press, 1972), pp. 3–38.

And on their tops too; and there houses keepe
In vaultie Caves, their housholds governd all
By each man's law, imposde in severall;
Nor wife, nor child awd, but as he thinks good,
None for another caring.[3]

When Odysseus and his men enter the cave of Polyphemus, son of Poseidon, they discover that he is a cannibal. After boasting that "We Cyclops care not for your Goat-fed Jove / Nor other Blest ones; we are better farre. / To Jove himself dare I bid open war" (IX.384–86), Polyphemus seizes several of Odysseus' followers, dashes their heads against the floor, and tears them to pieces to make his meal; he "laps up all their gore / Gusht from thie torne-up bodies" (IX.402–03), never pausing until they are entirely consumed. Odysseus counters with a special wine that fuddles the one-eyed giant's wits; Polyphemus terms it divine, "Of Nectar and Ambrosia" (IX.495). It is unlike anything he knows, and he quickly becomes falling-down drunk. While the giant is in a besotted stupor, Odysseus blinds him and escapes. Polyphemus is a prototype of the wild man; he lives apart from civilized society and embodies barbaric qualities in opposition to the *polis*.

Although Caliban does not share Polyphemus's taste for human flesh, he lives in a cave, is morally blind, and succumbs to Stephano's "celestial" liquor. And Caliban's monstrosity, though never specified, is stressed throughout *The Tempest*. In these respects, Shakespeare may have borrowed from Homer's one-eyed giant.

A more likely literary source for *The Tempest* is Virgil's *Aeneid*. Recent commentators have seen profound similarities between Virgil's epic and Shakespeare's play, not just in specific lines and scenes but in structure and theme. Jan Kott contends, for example, that

The Tempest repeats the sequence of the first four books of the *Aeneid*: the sinking of the royal ship, the saving of the shipwrecked men, the attack by

3 Cited from *Chapman's Homer*, 2 vols., ed. Allardyce Nicoll (New York: Bollingen Series XLI, 1956), Vol. II, 154, Book IX, lines 174–81. Cited henceforth by book and line numbers within the text. Chapman's translation of Homer's *Iliad* was first published in 1611, the *Odyssey* in 1614, but Shakespeare could have seen either in manuscript as he composed *The Tempest*.

the Harpies, the ordeal of hunger and thirst, the interrupted wedding pageantry. The Virgilian code becomes the theater of Prospero's art.[4]

John Pitcher sees additional parallels in the masque of Ceres; it recapitulates Dido's tragic history but in transcendent form. Because Ferdinand and Miranda's union is lawful, their history – unlike Dido's – will bring happiness to succeeding generations.[5]

Specific allusions to the *Aeneid* abound in Shakespeare's text: Sebastian, Antonio, and Gonzalo repeatedly refer in Act II, scene i, to "Widow Dido." Prospero's island seems to be located somewhere near Tunis, which Gonzalo argues is the same as Virgil's Carthage. Ariel's harpies are much like those in Virgil's Book III: "flying things / with young girls' faces, but foul ooze below, / Talons for hands, pale famished nightmare mouths." When Aeneas and his men sit down to a "savory feast," the Harpies attack "With deafening beat of wings" and destroy the repast.[6] And Prospero, like Aeneas, is cast out from his homeland and concerned to build a dynasty.

Despite this evidence of Virgil's influence on Shakespeare, the *Aeneid* contains no direct literary analogues to Caliban. The Cyclops and Polyphemus are mentioned only briefly. In Book VII, Allecto assumes the shape of an old woman: "So she became Calybe, thrall in age / To Juno, and a priestess of her temple." As a Fury, Allecto represents intense anger, but Calybe seems a far cry from Shakespeare's Caliban.[7]

Donna B. Hamilton's political reading of *The Tempest*, discussed in Chapter 2, is based on the premise that Shakespeare deliberately imitated Virgil's *Aeneid*, but instead of searching for specific inspirations for Caliban, she sees him as the coalescence of several Virgilian themes. Caliban, she argues, "combines both the Troy conspiracy patterns and the debased Aeneas figure."[8] His plot against Prospero

4 Jan Kott, "The *Aeneid* and *The Tempest*," *Arion*, III (1976): 424–51; quotation on p. 440.
5 John Pitcher, "A Theatre of the Future: *The Aeneid* and *The Tempest*," *Essays in Criticism*, XXXIV (1984): 193–215, esp. pp. 204–05.
6 Virgil, *The Aeneid*, trans. Robert Fitzgerald (New York: Vintage Books, 1985), p. 73.
7 Virgil, *The Aeneid*, p. 211. Gary Schmidgall compares Caliban to Allecto in *Shakespeare and the Courtly Aesthetic* (Berkeley: University of California Press, 1981), p. 75.
8 Donna B. Hamilton, *Virgil and The Tempest: The Politics of Imitation* (Columbus: Ohio State University Press, 1990), p. 92.

resembles Sinon's treachery against his own country. But Caliban is also a parody of Aeneas. His lust for Miranda evokes Aeneas' sojourn with Dido, but in a "diminished form." Caliban, Stephano, and Trinculo's dousing in the horse pond is analogous to Aeneas' encounter with the river Avernus, and their discovery of Prospero's "glistering apparel" parodies Aeneas' search for the golden bough. But however intriguing such comic parallels may be, they do not tell us how Shakespeare conceived of Caliban's personality and physiognomy. To find specific models for the "savage and deformed slave" we must turn elsewhere.

Shakespeare unquestionably read Ovid's *Metamorphoses*. Arthur Golding's translation of 1567 was probably the source for Prospero's "Ye elves" speech in Act IV, scene i.[9] Moreover, John Gillies argues, Caliban is "circumscribed by imagery which echoes the Ovidian iconography of the masque and (to a degree) he can be thought of as Shakespeare's version of the unreclaimed natural forces that resist the power of Ovid's Ceres."[10] Caliban's animal nature also hints at traditional Roman satyrs (familiar from Ovid and other Roman writers) – creatures half human, half goat, who signified sexual drives and the narrow boundary between humanity and bestiality. Like Polyphemus, satyrs signify (in Hayden White's words) "human regression to an animal state."[11] In their sensual, animal nature they can also be seen as prototypes of the early European wild man.

II

Before turning to the wild man, we mention in passing other possible – but scarcely probable – influences that originated in the medieval period. Raymond Urban suggests, for example, that Caliban, Stephano, and Trinculo burlesque organized religion in their worship of the man in the moon and reverence for celestial liquor as his bible. Similar burlesques were invented by vagabond clerics in medieval

9 Geoffrey Bullough, *Narrative and Dramatic Sources of Shakespeare*, 8 vols. (London: Routledge & Kegan Paul, 1957–75), Vol. VIII, pp. 314–15.
10 John Gillies, "Shakespeare's Virginian Masque," *ELH*, LIII (1986): 673–707, esp. p. 698.
11 White, "The Forms of Wildness," p. 22.

Europe and perpetuated by drinkers in Shakespeare's London who frequented taverns named "The Man in the Moon."[12]

Caliban does more, of course, than drink. His bestial nature, the opposite of Ariel's spirituality, may have been created in imitation of the psychomachia of medieval cycle and moral plays. Prudentius' poem "Psychomachia" (ca. 400 AD) depicted the battle of virtues and vices for the individual soul. English cycle plays later adopted a similar structure. In the Wakefield "Creation" (ca. 1400), for example, Malus Angelus opposed Bonus Angelus beneath God's throne. This opposition of good and evil angels persisted through the fifteenth-century morality plays and became an informing structure in many Renaissance dramas. Marlowe's *Dr. Faustus* depicts virtuous and evil angels fighting over Faustus' soul. This shaping pattern occasionally appears in Shakespeare's plays, though the forces of good and evil lose their one-dimensional simplicity. Othello is torn between the malevolent Iago and the virtuous Desdemona. Lady MacDuff opposes Lady Macbeth, and Cordelia drastically contrasts with her sisters. Such moral oppositions inform the relationship between Caliban and Ariel. As our introduction suggests, Shakespeare clearly intended Caliban to contrast with Ariel, although both characters are too complex to be dismissed merely as personifications of vice and virtue. Nevertheless, from Prospero's viewpoint (which is in some respects godlike), Ariel is the good and faithful servant, Caliban the devilish rebel.

Another source for Caliban may lie in early Celtic lore. Noel Cobb contends that Caliban "is actually a kind of demi-god of the forests." He resembles the archetypal Celtic wizard, Merlin, in his role as "Ward of the Wood." An early French text describes Merlin as a herdsman, with

a great club in his hand, clad in a great hide, the fur of which was longer than the breadth of the largest hand known, and it was neither black nor white but smoked and browned and seemed to be a wolf skin.[13]

---

12 Raymond A. Urban, "Why Caliban Worships the Man in the Moon," *Shakespeare Quarterly*, XXVII (1976): 203–05.

13 Noel Cobb, *Prospero's Island: The Secret Alchemy at the Heart of The Tempest* (London: Coventure, 1984), pp. 121–22.

Because an animal skin seems to have been Caliban's traditional costume throughout the eighteenth century (a convention that may have extended back to Shakespeare's original production),[14] the Celtic legend of Merlin may warrant more attention than it has customarily received.

III

Merlin is but one variation of the wild man of European tradition. His ancestry was classical: He had precursors in ancient Babylonia, Greece, and Rome. By the early Middle Ages, Christian thought had fused a variety of quasi-human man-beast figures – satyrs, centaurs, fauns, giants, and green men – into a widely recognized generic figure that had only minor differences within western Europe. The names varied a bit, or course: *wildeman* in Germany; *l'homme sauvage* in France; *selvaggi* in Italy; wild man, wodewose, or green man in England. By whatever name, he was a crucial figure in European folklore and pageantry.

Richard Bernheimer, the acknowledged authority on the species, defines the wild man as "a hairy man curiously compounded of human and animal traits, without, however, sinking to the level of an ape."[15] This man-beast is naked, covered with an animal skin or twisted vines. He lives in the forest and sleeps in a cave or under thick branches. His food is raw meat, berries, and other forest fare. According to Hayden White, "From biblical times to the present, the notion of the Wild Man was associated with the idea of the wilderness – the desert, forest, jungle, and mountains – those parts of the physical world that had not yet been domesticated or marked out for domestication in any significant way."[16] He is, in sum, a borderline figure in a borderline environment, the body of a man with the

---

14 See *The Tempest*, ed. Frank Kermode, "The Arden Shakespeare," 6th ed. (London: Methuen, 1958), p. 63.

15 Richard Bernheimer, *Wild Men in the Middle Ages* (Cambridge, Mass.: Harvard University Press, 1952), p. 1. See also Robert H. Goldsmith, "The Wild Man on the English Stage," *Modern Language Review*, LIII (1958): 481–91; see also the lavishly illustrated *The Wild Man: Medieval Myth and Symbolism* (New York: Metropolitan Museum of Art, 1980), by Timothy Husband.

16 White, "The Forms of Wildness," p. 7.

habits of an animal living in an animal's world: humankind at its most primitive.

The wild man has other, more serious shortcomings. Having degenerated into beastliness, he has no knowledge of God and consequently no right reason. Nor has he any true language; at best he can mutter a few intelligible sounds. But the wild man has some extraordinary powers that civilized humans do not have. With the removal of society's restraints, the degenerated man has superhuman strength, sexual prowess, and knowledge of nature's secrets. In some depictions he used these powers for good – but usually not. Sometimes he wielded a huge club or tree trunk against his foes or ravished women who came too near his wilderness retreat. Until the seventeenth century, he was as ferocious as he was uncivilized. White observes that "in whatever way he is envisaged, the Wild Man almost always represents the image of the man released from social control, the man in whom the libidinal impulses have gained full ascendency."[17] Yet the wild man was not doomed to eternal barbarity; proper tutelage could redeem him. When cleaned and dressed and exposed to civilization's finer thoughts and customs (and often to the right woman) the wild man quickly reformed. He was humanity gone astray, not humanity extinguished.

Over the centuries, the wild man served several psychological and intellectual needs. On an obvious level, he symbolized humanity's lustful, animalistic characteristics: His less admirable moods and visages were rough, lewd, cruel – "brutish" or "beastial" in the vocabulary of Shakespeare's day. The wild man's bestial attributes were only partly literal, however, for he remained human in body while behaving in many respects as an animal.[18] And his "wildness" implied more than it does in today's terminology. Above all, the wild man was opposed to "civilitie," those customs that enabled humans to live together in "civil amity." The wild man opposed and

17 White, "The Forms of Wildness," p. 21.
18 See Bernheimer, *Wild Men*, p. 7. Other discussions of Caliban as a wild or bestial man are John E. Hankins, "Caliban, the Bestial Man," *PMLA*, LXII (1947): 793–801; and G. M. Pinciss, "The Savage Man in Spenser, Shakespeare and Renaissance English Drama," in G. D. Hibbard, ed., *The Elizabethan Theatre VIII, Papers Given at the English International Conference on Elizabethan Theatre ... 1979* (Port Credit, Ontario: P. D. Meany, 1982), pp. 69–89.

2. A wild man, as depicted on an early seventeenth-century ballad, "The Mad, Merry Pranks of Robin Good-fellow," reproduced in Joseph Strutt, *Sports and Pastimes of the People of England* (1810).

rejected civilization – its values and beliefs, its virtues and order. In Freudian terms, the wild man was id, the instinctive impulses that often ran afoul of legal and social constraints. To play the part of the wild man, as Europeans often did in carnivals or skits, was to set aside for a time the constraints of an obsessively orderly and authoritarian age.[19] In the psychological as well as the social and

19 For discussion of the "carnivalesque" and its impact on the Elizabethan theatre, see Michael D. Bristol, *Carnival and Theatre: Plebeian Culture and the Structure of Authority in Renaissance England* (New York: Methuen, 1985). See also Jan Kott, *The Bottom Translation: Marlowe and Shakespeare and the Carnival Tradition*, trans. Daniela Miedzyrzecka (Evanston, Ill.: Northwestern University Press, 1987).

political spheres of life, the wild man signified humanity's struggle against the civilizing and, thereby, controlling forces of church, state, and community (Figure 2).

During the Middle Ages the wild man appeared throughout Europe in indigenous folk rituals. The English wodewose first emerged in medieval folk festivals as an ivy-clad figure who participated in mock battles between winter and summer. Gradually these green men or wild men were assigned to bear torches and clear the way before a procession. A green knight appeared in the 1309 tournament before Edward II at Stepney, and a heraldic wodewose is mentioned in accounts dating back to 1347. By the sixteenth century, the wild man was a regular feature of Lord Mayor's Day pageants and processions. He walked along the parade route at the beginning of the procession, lighting fireworks to clear a path through the crowd. The lord mayor's show of 1553 included two "grett wodyn with ij grett clubes all in grene, and with skwybes borning . . . with gret berds and syd here."[20] The inventory for the 1556 lord mayor's pageant lists a "woodewarde & other pastymes to be had wt men castyng of squybe of fyre afore the Baachelers."[21] In 1568, Hugh Watts and Christopher Beck agreed to "serve for woodhousis or Ivie men."[22] The Merchant Taylors' accounts indicate that green men were needed for lord mayor's pageants in 1602, 1605, and 1610.[23] Shakespeare's contemporaries knew well the conventional wild man of English pageantry.

During the establishment of Tudor rule, the traditional wodewose had been appropriated for ideological purposes in royal entertainments. Wild men shot fireworks on the Thames during Anne Boleyn's 1533 coronation procession[24] and frequently appeared in entertainments for Queen Elizabeth. In spectacles designed to celebrate the monarch's power, wisdom, and beauty, the wild man represented

20 Robert Withington, *English Pageantry: An Historical Outline*, Vol. II (Cambridge, Mass.: Harvard University Press, 1918), pp. 13–14.
21 R. T. D. Sayle, *Lord Mayors' Pageants of the Merchant Taylor's Company* (London: Privately printed, 1931), p. 22.
22 Sayle, *Lord Mayors' Pageants*, p. 48.
23 Sayle, *Lord Mayors' Pageants*, passim.
24 Joseph Strutt, *Sports and Pastimes of the People of England*, 2nd ed. (London: T. Bensley, 1810), p. 331.

the natural forces she controlled. Her civilizing presence could tame the savage beast, just as her armies could tame the wilderness and her seamen could tame Spain's fleets. When Robert Dudley, Lord Leicester, entertained Elizabeth at Kenilworth in 1575, she was met at the end of the hunt by an "Hombre Saluagio, with an Oken plant pluct vp by the roots in hiz hande, himself forgrone all in moss and Iuy."[25] Despite his unkempt appearance, this "salvage man" sported some social graces: He addressed the queen in an elaborate poem by George Gascoigne, in the form of a conventional dialogue between a speaker and his echo. Just as Caliban initially responds with wonder to Prospero's invasion of his island, the salvage man learns from the echo song of the wondrous creatures who invade his woods. In a moment akin to Caliban's determination to sue for grace, the salvage man falls on his knees and cries:

> O Queen! I must confess, it is not without cause:
> These civil people so rejoice, that you should give them laws.
> Since I, which live at large, a wild and savage man,
> And have run out a wilful race, since first my life began,
> Do here submit myself, beseeching you to serve:
> And that you take in worth my will, which can but well deserve.
> Had I the learned skill, which in your head is found:
> My tale had flow'd in eloquence, where now my words are drown'd.[26]

The salvage man celebrates Elizabeth's power by his willingness to abandon his wild ways and voluntarily submit to her rule of law. The poem was later widely distributed as an object lesson for her people.

Though the entertainment at Cowdray (1591) was staged on a smaller scale than Leicester's extravaganza, it was no less political and no less illustrative of the centrality of wild men in Elizabethan spectacle. In a pageant affirming the loyalty of Sussex in general and Lord Montague in particular, Elizabeth confronted a pilgrim in the Montague gardens. He took her to see an ancient oak on which

---

25 Robert Laneham, *Captain Cox, his Ballads and Books, or Robert Laneham's Letter*, ed. Frederick J. Furnival (London: Taylor & Co., 1871), p. 14.

26 George Gascoigne, *Gascoigne's Princely Pleasures* (London: Printed for J. H. Burn, 1821), pp. 12–21.

her arms were carved intertwined with the arms of all the noblemen of Sussex. Beneath the tree stood a wild man, dressed in ivy, affirming not only the loyalty of Catholic citizens but also Elizabeth's control over nature and over the wild hearts of her people.[27] In the same way, Caliban's final speech indicates Prospero's moral control.

Elizabeth was similarly addressed by a wild man in 1592 at Bisham. Again, the savage creature feels her civilizing presence and submits to her power:

my untamed thoughts waxe gentle, and I feele in myselfe civility, A thing hated, because not knowen, and unknown, because I knew not you. Thus Vertue tameth fiercenesse, Beauty, madnesse. Your Majesty on my knees will I followe, bearing this Club, not as a Salvage, but to beate downe those that are.[28]

The published reports of such royal pageants highlighted the queen's love for her people and the civilizing impact of her government; the green man who symbolized unruly nature was thereby implicitly associated with the wild lands – especially Ireland and America – that were to be tamed by Elizabethan laws and customs.

Such pageantry did not disappear in 1603. Much of it was distilled in the elaborate court masque – a genre that helped shape Shakespeare's *Tempest* – and civic pageantry still greeted members of the royal family. The pageant at Chester on St. George's Day, 1610, in honor of Prince Henry, identified the prince with St. George, England's patron saint and dragon-killer. The pageant's wild men accompanied the dragon:

Two disquised, called Greene-men, their habit Embroydred and Stitch'd on with Iuie-leaues with blacke-side, hauing hanging to their shoulders, a huge blacke shaggie Hayre, Sauage-like, with Iuie Garlands vpon their heads, bearing Herculian *clubbes in their hands, and artificiall Dragon, very liuely to behold, pursuing the Sauages entring their Denne, casting Fire from his mouth, which afterwards was slaine.*[29]

27 Jean Wilson, *Entertainments for Elizabeth I* (Totowa, N.J.: Rowman & Littlefield, 1980), p. 91.
28 Wilson, *Entertainments*, p. 44.
29 *Chester's Triumph, 1610* (Chetham: Printed for the Chetham Society, 1844), sig. A3v.

Shakespeare's Caliban

After the dragon's demise, a knight on horseback made an oration "in Honour of the King, his Crowne and Emperiall Monarchie." St. George's victory symbolizes the imperial power of James I.

Green men had been as ideological in the Elizabethan theatre as in sixteenth-century civic pageantry; they were often used to display courtesy's civilizing power and the monarchy's ability to tame the people's wildness. *Gorboduc* (1562), by Thomas Sackville and Thomas Norton, taught the perils of an unsure succession. The play begins with a dumb show:

First, the music of violins began to play, during which came in upon the stage six wild men clothed in leaves. Of whom the first bare on his neck a fagot of small sticks, which they all, both severally and together, assayed with all their strengths to break; but it could not be broken by them. At the length, one of them plucked out one of the sticks, and brake it; and the rest plucking out all the other sticks one after another, did easily break them, the same being severed; which being conjoined, they had before attempted in vain. After they had this done, they departed the stage, and the music ceased. Hereby was signified that a state knit in unity doth continue strong against all force.[30]

George Whetstone's *Promos and Cassandra* (1578) depicts wild men much as they appeared in London processions: They clear the street for a royal progress. The Merchant Taylors' master calls for "[t]wo men, apparrelled, lyke greene men at the Mayors feast, with clubbes of fyre worke."[31]

The Misfortunes of Arthur, performed for the queen in 1587 by the Gentlemen of Gray's Inn, associates the wild man with the equally unkempt Irish "salvage"; like the wild man, the Irish man needed the restraints of Elizabethan rule to become civilized. This dumb show presents "a man bareheaded, with blacke long shagged haire downe to his shoulders; apparailed with an Irish Iacket and shirt, hauing an Irish dagger by His side and a dart in his hand. Who first with a threatning countenance looking about; and then spying the

30 Thomas Sackville and Thomas Norton, *Gorboduc*, ed. Irby B. Cauthen, Jr. (Lincoln: University of Nebraska Press, 1970), p. 8.
31 George Whetstone, *Promos and Cassandra* (London: Imprinted by Richard Ihones, 1578), sig. H1r.

King, did furiously chase and drive him into *Mordred's* house. . . .
The Irish man signified Reuenge and Furie."[32]

Whereas theatrical wild men – unlike Caliban – usually were one-dimensional, an anonymous play first printed in 1598 develops a genuine character. *Mucedorus* was revived in the Jacobean period with new additions. Shakespeare must have known it well, because his company performed it at court around 1610.[33] Its wild man, Bremo, carries a club, lives in the woods, and savagely attacks all travelers. He even intends to gobble the dainty flesh of the heroine, fair Amadine: "Now glut thy greedie guts with lukewarme blood." Despite such cannibalistic impulses, Bremo is smitten by Amadine's beauty:

> My limmes do tremble and my sinewes shake.
> My unweakned armes have lost their former force. . . .
> Shall I spare her *Bremo*, spare her, do not kill,
> Sayth space her which never spared any. . . .
> I think her beawtie hath bewitched my force.[34]

Bremo forces Amadine to live in the woods with him until the valiant knight Mucedorus slays Bremo and rescues the lady. Bernheimer suggests that the conflict between the knight and the wild man was a natural outgrowth of the medieval concept of courtly love, a motif that also informs much early Renaissance English drama. In the medieval narrative "Sir Gawain and the Green Knight," for example, Gawain, who is renowned for his courtesy, is challenged by the green giant of irrepressible nature.[35] By slaying Bremo, Mucedorus imposes codes of civility on raw sexual instinct. Instead of being transformed into submission – like the wild man of Elizabethan entertainments – Bremo is destroyed.

---

32 *Certaine Devices and shewes presented to her majestie by the Gentlemen of Grayes Inne at her Highnesse Court in Greenewich* (London: Printed by Robert Robinson, 1587), p. 12.

33 See the title page of the 1610 edition: *A most pleasant comedie of Mucedorus . . . Amplified with new additions, as it was acted before the Kings Maiestie at White-hall on Shroue-sunday night. By his Highness Seruants vsually playing at the Globe* (London: Printed for William Jones, 1610).

34 Anon., *Mucedorus* (London: W. Jones, 1598), sigs. D2r–v.

35 See Bernheimer, *Wild Men*, pp. 122–28.

In sum, Shakespeare's fellow dramatists, and the poet Edmund Spenser (discussed later), freely drew on both sides of this ambiguous but readily understood convention. The wild man might appear as the ferocious cannibal of antiquity and the early Middle Ages, or he might be a rough-hewn woodsman or benign savage, but whatever his guise, he was a convenient social symbol. He appeared in a wide variety of media, including prose, poetry, drama, song, painting, sculpture, book illustrations, and tapestry.[36] Shakespeare and his audience experienced a lifetime of vicarious familiarity with this legendary creature. How plausible it would have been for the dramatist to incorporate some wild-man characteristics into a pastoral drama like *The Tempest*.

Caliban's affinity to the wild man is obvious. The earliest portrayals of Caliban apparently stressed his hairiness and animalistic appearance. (In 1821 Edmond Malone contended that Caliban's costume had always consisted of "a large bear-skin, or the skin of some other animal; and he is usually represented with long shaggy hair." This attire, said Malone, without sharing the source of his knowledge, "was originally prescribed by the poet himself and has been continued, I believe since his time."[37]) Caliban carries wood – the wild man's club or tree trunk – and lives in a subterranean cave. He tries to ravish Miranda and boasts of the sexual prowess he almost put to use. He is immoderately fond of intoxicants. (A German tradition, well known in England, made liquor the key to unlocking the wild man's secrets – reflected, perhaps, in Stephano and Trinculo's "celestial liquor."[38]) Caliban certainly had forest secrets: "all the qualities o' th' isle, / The fresh springs, brine pits, barren places and fertile" (I.ii.337–38). And until Prospero and Miranda taught him their language, Caliban gabbled incoherently, at least to their ears. Perhaps the most fundamental link between Caliban and the wild man is their similarity in parentage: During the Middle Ages, both satyrs and wild men were thought to be products of unnatural unions. The son of a witch and a devil nicely fits the bill.

36 See esp. Husband, *Wild Man*, p. 4.
37 Edmond Malone, ed., *The Plays and Poems of William Shakespeare* . . . (London: Printed for F. C. and J. Rivington et al., 1821), Vol. XV, p. 13. See also *The Tempest*, ed. Kermode, p. 63.
38 Bernheimer, *Wild Men*, p. 25.

In several important respects, however, Caliban and the wild man differ. Caliban lacks the wild man's superhuman strength, his powerlessness in the presence of a beautiful maiden, and his rapid progress toward civility under proper tutelage. (Caliban, it might be argued, had been absorbing civility until his assault on Miranda, and by the end of the play he is on his way toward social and spiritual redemption.) In any event, the wild-man tradition was, as we have noted, flexible enough to encompass many variations. Caliban conforms strikingly to the wild-man tradition, and Shakespeare's audiences may have recognized him accordingly. That does not, of course, rule out the possibility that Shakespeare added touches of his own – from the New World, where the wild man's savage ways often were attributed to native Americans, or from other literary traditions.

IV

The most "literary" appropriation of the wild-man myth appears in Edmund Spenser's *Faerie Queene*. Given the wild man's symbolic association with emblems of regal authority, it is not surprising that the poet included two "salvage men" in his allegorical epic, dedicated to Queen Elizabeth; both are potential literary antecedents for Caliban.[39] The first appears in Book IV, when Amoret meets him in the forest. He was a "wilde and salvage man,"

> Yet was no man, but onely like in shape,
> And eke in stature higher by a span,
> All ouergrowne with haire, that could awhape
> An hardy hart, and his wide mouth did gape
> With huge great teeth, like to a tusked Bore:
> For he liu'd all on rauin and on rape
> Of men and beasts; and fed on fleshly gore,
> The signe whereof yet stain'd his bloudy lips afore.
>
> (IV.vii.5)[40]

---

39 Bullough discusses Shakespeare's debt to Spenser in *Narrative and Dramatic Sources*, Vol. VIII, pp. 253–55.
40 Edmund Spenser, *The Faerie Queene*, ed. A. C. Hamilton (London: Longman, 1977), p. 473; cited henceforth by book, canto, and stanza number within the text.

Shakespeare's Caliban

This nightmare version of the wodewose embodies civilized society's
repressed appetites; he is cruel, violent, rapacious, cannibalistic.
He represents, as Edward Tayler contends, humanity in a state of
nature.[41] As the embodiment of lechery, this wild man can never
be wholly subdued. Whereas Spenser's knights adhere to a chivalric
code in which desire is sublimated, the "savage nation" wallows in
raw sexual appetite.

Spenser's other wild man is more admirable, perhaps because
his mysterious parentage includes noble blood. When he first sees
Serena and Calepine, his noble instincts surface:

> The saluage man, that neuer till this hour
> Did taste of pittie, neither gentlesse knew,
> Seeing his [Turpine's] sharpe assault and cruell stoure
> Was much emmoued at his perils vew,
> That even his ruder hart began to rew,
> And feele compassion for his euill plight,
> Against his foe that did him so pursew:
> From whom he meant to free him, if he might,
> And him auenge of that so villenous despight.

(VI.iv.3)

The salvage man proves an indefatigable fighter who ceases only
when commanded by Prince Arthur. The prince – emblem of royal
power – can control the violent forces the wild man represents. In
the context of Book VI of The Faerie Queene, this salvage man signifies
a lack of courtesy and civility, not brute force.[42]

Tayler argues persuasively that salvage men serve as moral exempla.
They are often a direct warning that "to this end man may come
if he forsake his rational nature"; moreover, they satirize civilized
society itself – "look how much more civilized the savage is than the
courtier with all his supposed advantages."[43] Caliban, too, has this
double edge. His attempt to rape Miranda proclaims his bestiality;
yet he is scarcely more depraved than Antonio and Sebastian, who,

41 See Edward William Tayler, Nature and Art in Renaissance Literature (New York:
Columbia University Press, 1964), pp. 109–12.
42 Arnold Williams suggests that the Salvage Man "is a benign creature, though
traces of demonic malignancy remain." Flower on a Lowly Stalk: The Sixth Book of
the Faerie Queene (East Lansing: Michigan State University Press, 1967), p. 73.
43 Tayler, Nature and Art, p. 108.

72

despite the supposed moral benefits of "civility," plan Alonso's murder.

It is hardly surprising that in their quest for Shakespeare's sources critics should frequently turn to Spenser's rich assortment of allegorical figures. In addition to the salvage men described earlier, several other Spenserian characters have been identified as Caliban's literary antecedents. James A. S. McPeek alluded in 1946 to the notion that the Hag's brutish son in Book III (designated by Spenser simply as the Chorle) is a source for Caliban. McPeek saw Caliban prefigured more fully, however, in the Freckled Beast of the same adventure. The Hag created this monster to track down the helpless maiden Florimell for her son. After a series of textual comparisons – the Hag to Sycorax, Florimell to Miranda, and the Freckled Beast to Caliban – McPeek concluded that "Caliban owes his main features to the fusion in Shakespeare's mind of the general picture of the laesy hag-seed Chorle and the specific characteristics of this Freckled Beast."[44]

Another possible Spenserian influence on Caliban may be the Blatant Beast, Calidore's antagonist in Book VI of *The Faerie Queene*.[45] Spenser describes the beast as "a Monster bred of hellishe race" (VI.i.7), begot from Cerberus and Chimaera (or, alternatively, Echidna and Typhon, in VI.x.10–11). He was raised in "*Stygian* fen" (VI.i.8) and sent into the world to plague humanity. The Blatant Beast seizes Serena and tries to rape her, but Calidore, Spenser's courteous hero, frightens him into "fearefull flight" (VI.iii.25). The beast appears again in the sixth canto, where he is described as a "hellish Dog,"

A wicked Monster, that his tongue doth whet
Gainst all, both good and bad, both most and least,

44 James A. S. McPeek, "The Genesis of Caliban," *Philological Quarterly*, XXV (1946): 378–81, quotation on pp. 379–80.
45 Schmidgall argues that the Blatant Beast, like Caliban, represents the aberration of normal courtly behavior and that both were drawn for similar symbolic purposes. See *Shakespeare and the Courtly Aesthetic*, pp. 202–08. Michael Srigley sees similarities between the Blatant Beast and Caliban in that both foment social strife. See Srigley, *Images of Regeneration: A Study of Shakespeare's The Tempest and its Cultural Background* (Uppsala: Studia Anglistica Upsaliensia, No. 58, 1985), p. 112.

Shakespeare's Caliban

And poures his poysnous gall forth to infest
The noblest wights with notable defame:

(VI.vi.12)

Calidore finally subdues this monster in the twelfth canto, but the
victory is only temporary. As Spenser ruefully concludes *The Faerie
Queene*, he describes the Blatant Beast breaking his iron chain to run
through the world once again (VI.xii.38), where he continues to
prey, especially on gentle poets.

Humphrey Tonkin associates this allegorical figure with Hydra,
the mythical many-headed monster "considered emblematic of envy
and evil-speaking."[46] Arnold Williams sees it as "the essential evil
of slander, indeed, of all discourtesy." In form, the Blatant Beast
is like a dog, but in many of its actions it resembles a wild boar,
crashing through the woods to interrupt polite conversations and
ceremonies.[47] The beast, contends Donald Cheney, "challenges . . .
the fragile texture of human community."[48]

The Blatant Beast's similarities to Caliban are perhaps more structural than physical. Both characters ostensibly are the products of
mysterious, infernal unions. Both are contentious. Both disrupt polite
society, particularly by destroying the ceremonies that symbolize
and thereby reify social harmony. Caliban is "puppy-headed," and
Spenser's beast is a "monstrous dog." But Caliban is also described
as human, a trait never ascribed to the allegorical beast. Spenser's
Blatant Beast functions solely as an object, an allegory of slander
that destroys others but cannot itself be destroyed. Caliban, in contrast, is a subject; he speaks for himself throughout *The Tempest*,
explaining his thoughts and feelings. His humanity and subjecthood
make him a far more sophisticated character than the Blatant Beast.

Caliban could have been influenced by either of Spenser's salvage
men, or by the Chorle, the Freckled Beast, or the Blatant Beast.
None of these allegorical forebears can explain his full complexity.
As a combination of the indigenous, untutored savage and (perhaps)

46 Humphrey Tonkin, *Spenser's Courteous Pastoral: Book Six of "The Faerie Queene"*
   (Oxford: Clarendon Press, 1972), p. 33 (n. 2).
47 Williams, *Flower on a Lowly Stalk*, p. 68.
48 Donald Cheney, *Spenser's Image of Nature: Wild Man and Shepherd in "The Faerie
   Queene"* (New Haven, Conn.: Yale University Press, 1966), p. 184.

the scion of a devil, Caliban has characteristics of several Spenserian figures. Spenser must remain, however, one among many possible literary influences that Shakespeare may have exploited in creating Caliban.

V

Among other traditions that could have influenced Shakespeare's conception of Caliban was Europe's fascination with monsters and other nonhuman creatures. The wild man, of course, had some monstrous elements, but he was essentially human. Not so the true monsters of Europe's imagination. Ancient and medieval literature abounded with reports of incredible creatures that usually inhabited faraway places – "at the round earth's imagined corners," in John Donne's apt phrase.[49] Since the dawn of storytelling, quasi-human monsters had paraded through poetry, histories, travel accounts, iconography, and illustrations.

Such material would have been readily available to Shakespeare through Philemon Holland's 1601 translation of Pliny, a standard catalogue of wonders from ancient Greece widely read in the Middle Ages and the Renaissance.[50] Moreover, travel accounts of the New World incorporated Old World stories like Pliny's into their lore. Throughout Europe, popular pamphlets advertised monstrosities – in Rudolf Wittkower's words – for "prognostications, satire, political and religious propaganda and, above all, business, which can always rely on the attraction of the horrible."[51]

Like its literary cousin the wild man, the monster might be gentle

---

49 John Donne, "Holy Sonnet," in *The Complete Poetry of John Donne*, ed. John T. Shawcross (New York University Press, 1968), p. 340.
50 Pliny, *Historie of the World*, trans. Philemon Holland (London: Printed for A. Islip, 1601).
51 Rudolf Wittkower, "Marvels of the East: A Study in the History of Monsters," *Journal of the Warburg and Courtauld Institutes*, V (1942): 159–97, esp. p. 193. John Block Friedman also traces the prevalence of monster lore in medieval literature in *The Monstrous Races in Medieval Art and Thought* (Cambridge, Mass.: Harvard University Press, 1981). For fascination with human monsters in Shakespeare's times, see Katherine Park and Lorraine J. Daston, "Unnatural Conceptions: The Study of Monsters in Sixteenth- and Seventeenth-Century France and England," *Past and Present*, XCII (1981): 20–54.

or vicious or merely curious. But strange indeed they were, with animal heads on human bodies, or headless men with faces on their chests (Othello's "anthropophagi"), or one-legged creatures whose single huge foot was also an umbrella. Even Edward Topsell's *Historie of Foure-Footed Beastes* (1607) and *Historie of Serpents* (1608) portrayed with utter seriousness nonexistent creatures, including satyrs (part man, part lusty devil), "mantichoras" (part man, part lion), and the seven-headed hydra of antiquity – of which Topsell was skeptical, but he illustrated it nonetheless.[52] Who could prove that such monsters did not exist? Fascination with grotesques had waned in the late medieval period, only to revive in the age of reconnaissance. Throughout the sixteenth century, cartouches on maps – to cite only one visual genre – featured sea monsters, giants, and the like, and as late as 1596 Walter Raleigh told of monsters in Guinea. Monster accounts diminished in the seventeenth century as geographic and zoological knowledge advanced, but belief in such creatures died hard. Surely Shakespeare's audience was ready to believe in bizarre fusions of man and beast (Figure 3).

While Renaissance explorers brought home strange accounts that were told as fact, writers of fiction also included monsters in their romances of wandering knights and forlorn damsels. Bullough suggests that the Spanish romance *The Mirrour of Knighthood*, translated into English during the 1580s by Robert Parry, provides a model of Caliban in Fauno, the offspring of the evil woman Artimaga and the devil.[53] Parry's translation describes Artimaga as "so abhominable and euill, that neuer the lyke was seene nor heard of amongst women. . . . [S]he neuer beleeued in God but in the diuell." Like Shakespeare's Sycorax, Artimaga couples with the devil; he appears to her in the shape of a monstrous beast found in the deserts of Africa. Part human, part animal, this monster combines the ugliest and most ferocious attributes of several creatures:

His bodie was as bigge as a great bull, in forme and shape lyke a Lion, with his feete full of rugged haire and the clawes of his feete as bigge as twice a

52 Edward Topsell, *The Historie of Foure-Footed Beastes* (London: Printed by William Iaggard, 1607), esp. pp. 13, 441–42; Topsell, *The Historie of Serpents* (London: Printed by William Iaggard, 1608), esp. p. 201.
53 Bullough, *Narrative and Dramatic Sources*, Vol. VIII, pp. 253, 304–10.

3. A curious combination of fish and rooster – believed by some modern
authors to be Caliban's likely prototype – in Conrad Gessner, *Icones
Animalium* (1560).

man's finger, and a span long, his breast as big as of a horse, and necked
like an Elephant, and from that part upward both head and face like a man,
with a long beard of hard and thick haire, but the head was verie bigge, and
out of the middest of his forehead came forth an horne as big as a mans
arme and as long.

From this union derives a creature "deformed, monstrous and
diuellish." Artimaga dies giving birth to "the most horriblest and
terriblest creature that euer nature formed." Named Fauno after his
father, this monster grows "to be as bigge as an Elephant[;] his
forme and figure was much more horrible than that of his father."[54]
Like Caliban, he is the only inhabitant of a deserted island. But
unlike Caliban, he tears to pieces all who come ashore.

Caliban's parentage and monstrous birth may indeed derive from
The Mirrour of Knighthood, but as Shakespeare presents him, he has
neither Fauno's strength nor his ferocity. Moreover, Caliban, unlike

54 *The Third Part of the First Booke of the Mirrovr of Knighthood*, trans. R.P. (London:
Thomas East, 1586?), pp. 59r–61v.

Fauno, is described as having a human shape. Perhaps Trinculo and Stephano describe him as a monster because they have heard so many travelers' tales of grotesques. When they are shipwrecked on a desert island, they find (they think) what Renaissance tales and romances have led them to expect.

Gary Schmidgall suggests another "probable source" for *The Tempest* in the Palmerin romance epic, translated into English by Anthony Munday. A figure much like Prospero – the Knight of the Enclosed Isle – serves as one of this saga's heroes. Schmidgall lists seventeen similarities between *Primaleon* and *The Tempest*, including a storm at sea, the marriage of the magician's daughter to the son of his enemy, the presentation of a wedding masque, and the return to civilization at the conclusion. None of these similarities concern Caliban, however. Schmidgall briefly relates Shakespeare's "monster" to Maiortes, a man transformed into a dog by Circean magic. Still, Schmidgall admits that there are no substantial hints for Caliban and Ariel in the *Primaleon*. As a combination of New World "savage" and Old World "deformation," Caliban remains, in Schmidgall's terms, "an elaborate allegory of human vice and ignorance."[55]

VI

Monsters and wild men were featured in medieval and Renaissance plays on the Continent, particularly in the *commedia dell'arte* of the Italian Renaissance. If Shakespeare relied upon a *commedia scenari* (plot outlines – there were no scripts) for *The Tempest*, Caliban may well have descended from one or more of these carnivalesque figures. K. M. Lea suggested in 1934 that a particular type of *scenari* captured Shakespeare's attention: On the coast of Arcadia, a magician "has a somewhat malicious interest in the love-affairs of a group of nymphs and shepherds among whom one may be his daughter and another

55 Gary Schmidgall, "*The Tempest* and *Primaleon*: A New Source," *Shakespeare Quarterly*, XXXVII (1986): 424–39, quotation from p. 438. Schmidgall relies on *The Famous and Renowned History of Primaleon of Greece*, trans. Anthony Munday (London: T. Snodham, 1619). For further intriguing comments on *Primaleon of Greece* and *The Tempest*, see Bruce Chatwin, "The Marvels of Patagonia," *Geo* (July 1982): 67–69; and Bruce Chatwin, *In Patagonia* (New York: Summit Books, 1977), pp. 95–97.

the lost son of the Magnifico or the Doctor," who have been ship-wrecked on this coast. "The magician's attendants are satyrs, de-mons, or rustics of the cruder sort." The magician works to thwart the plot of the Arcadians and/or the intruders against him. But at the end, he "discovers the relationship between himself, the lovers, and the strangers," renounces his magic, "and sometimes agrees to leave the island and return to civic life."[56]

Because no transcript of these *scenari* survives, it is difficult to say what Shakespeare may have borrowed from the *commedia* tradition. To Allardyce Nicoll the similarities are so striking that "it is virtually impossible not to believe that Shakespeare had witnessed the per-formance of an improvised pastoral of this kind." He cites further parallels with *The Tempest*, including "the food offered by spirits to the famished mariners and its sudden snatching away."[57] David Young also concludes that Shakespeare was "deliberately resorting to the organization and manner of the pastoral tragicomedies of *commedia dell'arte*" when he composed *The Tempest*. Caliban, he argues, is "the wild man who in this play replaces the more charac-teristic natural men of the pastoral mode, the shepherds, hermits, and savages."[58] The Trinculo-Stephano subplot – particularly the farcical gaberdine scene – seems the most likely candidate for *commedia* derivation; even conservative critic Geoffrey Bullough admitted that the parallel was so strong as to "make it seem likely that Shakespeare knew some *commedia dell'arte* situations and *lazzi* [comic tricks]."[59] If Shakespeare was as well versed in the tradition as these commen-tators suggest, he may have substituted Caliban for the *commedia's* satyrs or wild men.

Caliban might relate to another stock *commedia dell'arte* figure, the *harlequin*. Dennis Sparacino contends that "the grotesqueness ol Caliban's appearance suggests the fantastic black leather mask of the

56 K. M. Lea, *Italian Popular Comedy: A Study in the Commedia Dell'Arte, 1560–1620 With Special Reference to the English Stage* (Oxford: Clarendon Press, 1934), Vol. II, pp. 444–45.
57 Allardyce Nicoll, *The World of Harlequin: A Critical Study of the Commedia Dell'Arte* (Cambridge University Press, 1963), pp. 119–20.
58 David Young, *The Heart's Forest: A Study of Shakespeare's Pastoral Plays* (New Haven, Conn.: Yale University Press, 1972), quotations from pp. 152, 187.
59 Bullough, *Narrative and Dramatic Sources*, Vol. VIII, p. 261.

harlequin." Caliban may embody the lecherousness of the *zanni* and the clown's buffoonery. His primary function, Sparacino believes, is to make us laugh.[60] Still, Caliban does not sport the harlequin's brightly colored motley. Although Touchstone or Feste may be the harlequin's direct descendant, Caliban is at most a distant cousin.

VII

Caliban may also be an antimasque figure in Shakespeare's most masquelike play.[61] Stephen Orgel, an expert on the Stuart masque, explains that the formal court masque was generally separated into two sections. The first section, the antimasque, was performed by professional actors and represented a world of vice or disorder. Antimasque figures designed by Inigo Jones included wild men, satyrs, Indians, "phantasms," pygmies, tumblers and jugglers, and even the contents of a cooking pot.[62] The second part, or masque proper, was performed by members of the court and represented the triumph of their aristocratic community and their belief in hierarchy.[63] Often the set reflected this movement. The masque might begin with scenery depicting untamed nature, but it usually concluded with images of cosmic and earthly harmony.[64] This progression parallels the Elizabethan entertainments in which the royal presence tames and civilizes the natural forces represented by the wild man.

Caliban, Prospero's antimasque figure, inverts the masque's normal

---

60 Dennis N. Sparacino, "Caliban" (unpublished Ph.D. dissertation, New York University, 1973), pp. 59, 112.

61 For discussion of masque elements in *The Tempest*, see Stephen Orgel, *The Illusion of Power: Political Theatre in the Renaissance* (Berkeley: University of California Press, 1975); Schmidgall, *Shakespeare and the Courtly Aesthetic*; Ernest B. Gilman, "'All eyes': Prospero's Inverted Masque," *Renaissance Quarterly*, XXXIII (1980): 214–31; Glynne Wickham, "Masque and Anti-masque in 'The Tempest'," in *Essays and Studies 1975* (London: John Murray, 1975), pp. 1–14. See also *The Tempest*, ed. Kermode, pp. lxxi–lxxvi, and Bullough, *Narrative and Dramatic Sources*, Vol. VIII, pp. 261–65.

62 See Stephen Orgel and Roy Strong, *Inigo Jones, The Theatre of the Stuart Court* (Berkeley: University of California Press, 1973).

63 Orgel, *Illusion of Power*, p. 40.

64 Orgel and Strong, *Inigo Jones*, p. 39.

order. Instead of being tamed or simply disappearing, Caliban's plot provokes the disappearance of Prospero's own entertainment when Ceres, Iris, and Juno vanish. As Robert Egan suggests, "the product of Prospero's art, having failed to acknowledge or come to terms with things as they are, cannot endure in the presence of that reality."[65] The antimasque continues after the masque's disruption. Stinking from their visit to the horse pond, Caliban, Stephano, and Trinculo become subject to their own show, a spectacle engineered by Ariel (as was the masque of Ceres and Juno) that burlesques the product of Prospero's art. Dazzled by the sumptuous garments hanging before Prospero's cave, Trinculo and Stephano mistake the appearance for the thing – royal robes that make "King Stephano" a worthy peer. Only Caliban sees through the illusion and realizes the folly of doting on "such luggage." The antimasque concludes with the Folio's stage direction:

A noyse of Hunters heard. Enter divers Spirits in shape of Dogs and Hounds, hunting them about: Prospero and Ariel setting them on (TLN 1929–31).

Like the Neapolitan party, the conspirators are chased about the island, caught in a distraction beyond their control.

Thus, in Act IV, as in Act III, Shakespeare presents an exact reversal of the normal order of the Jacobean masque. Ernest B. Gilman argues that "the inverted masque first asserts, but then partially denies or shadows, the imperial power of the imagination conventionally celebrated in the Stuart masque." It also "exposes, retrospectively, the contrary forces *within* the masque" and prompts "the audience to replot what it has just seen."[66] If Prospero is in any way a surrogate for James I (who also displayed an interest in magic), the antimasque may represent the forces that could disrupt James's ideally ordered hierarchy. Prospero learns to acknowledge Caliban as his own; James, on the other hand, ignored, to the realm's subsequent peril, the unruly elements in his own kingdom.

65 Robert Egan, *Drama Within Drama: Shakespeare's Sense of His Art* (New York: Columbia University Press, 1975), p. 108.
66 Gilman, "'All eyes'," pp. 218, 222.

VIII

The literary antecedents discussed thus far are fairly specific – wild man, monster, harlequin, antimasque. Each has particular points of resemblance with Caliban; any or all may have influenced Shakespeare. Other suggestions are more difficult to classify, mainly because they stress allegorical readings of *The Tempest* as a whole. Caliban is assigned a particular meaning or thematic role, dependent upon the critic's overall scheme.[67]

Whereas the "new historicists" summarized in Chapter 2 often link *The Tempest* to the court of James I, other critics have found more specific topical references in Shakespeare's play. Frances Yates believes, for example, that Prospero is partly based on Dr. John Dee, a magician-cum-scientist who was consulted by Elizabeth I, but who had fallen from favor in James's court. As a good magus with a reforming interest, Prospero "would belong with Prince Henry and his interests." Caliban, in contrast, is associated with black magic. His mother Sycorax was, after all, a witch who practiced magic to torture Ariel. Caliban is made of "earth" and embodies the bestial, animal world.[68] Or, in Michael Srigley's terminology, Caliban is the "equivalent of the *prime materia* or crude raw material[,] . . . the *elementum primordiale* of the alchemist." Through the play he emerges as "earthy Primordial Man, the rabbinical Adam fashioned out of red clay, a creature of darkness formed by demonic powers, given to rebellion and discontent, and yet haunted by intimations of something higher."[69] If he were successful in his quest to steal Prospero's books, he would become the proverbial sorcerer's apprentice, taking the tools Prospero controls for good to produce chaotic evil.

Allegorical interpretations like those of Yates and Srigley place Caliban in convenient binary opposition to Ariel. Whereas Caliban is earthy, dark, bestial, evil, and driven by appetite, Ariel is airy,

---

67 For a more generalized and philosophical discussion of allegory in *The Tempest*, see A. D. Nuttall, *Two Concepts of Allegory: A Study of Shakespeare's The Tempest and the Logic of Allegorical Expression* (London: Routledge & Kegan Paul, 1967), esp. pp. 136–60.

68 Frances Yates, *Shakespeare's Last Plays: A New Approach* (London: Routledge & Kegan Paul, 1975), pp. 93–97, quotation from p. 96.

69 Srigley, *Images of Regeneration*, pp. 43, 113.

light, spiritual, moral, and guided by reason. And though at some basic level this opposition is built into *The Tempest*'s structure – as it was into the medieval morality plays mentioned earlier – it nevertheless oversimplifies both Caliban's and Ariel's complexity. Perhaps Shakespeare did incorporate contemporary political issues into his play, but to focus on any specific concern to the exclusion of all others is to pluck the heart out of Caliban's – not to say the entire play's – mystery.

IX

When he created Caliban, Shakespeare may have recalled the wild man of civic pageantry and the antimasque figures of his fellow dramatist Ben Jonson. He may also have remembered images of his own creations from several plays he had already staged. Caliban is roughly analogous to previous comic characters, described as "idiotes" by Northrop Frye,[70] who served as foci of the anticomic mood, the locus for the audience's cynical side that resists romantic comic endings. *As You Like It*'s Jaques is skeptical about love, *Twelfth Night*'s Malvolio wants revenge, *Much Ado*'s Don John runs away, and *The Merchant of Venice*'s Shylock grieves over his ducats and his daughter. All are banished from those plays' last moments lest they destroy the mood of joy and reconciliation. Yet their discordant voices linger, leavening the sweetness of the happy conclusion.

Caliban, of course, does appear in the final scene but is dismissed many lines before the play's conclusion. He does not seek revenge like Malvolio; instead, he promises to be wise hereafter and sue for grace – a speech that signifies some sort of new knowledge, even if less than full regeneration. Caliban cannot be banished by the Neapolitans, but he is left behind while they return to Naples and civilization. As the play concludes, he remains – like Shylock and Malvolio – a marginalized figure who can never be incorporated into the newly created social/family unit.[71]

70 Northrop Frye, *A Natural Perspective: The Development of Shakespearean Comedy and Romance* (New York: Columbia University Press, 1965), p. 93.
71 For a fascinating account of the dynamics of Prospero and Caliban's parent–child relationship and its similarity to relationships in other Shakespearean plays, see Meredith Anne Skura, "Discourse and the Individual: The Case of Colonialism in *The Tempest*," *Shakespeare Quarterly*, XL (1989): 42–69, esp. pp. 57–66.

Shakespeare's Caliban

Another parallel exists in Shakespeare's other "fairy-tale comedy,"
A Midsummer Night's Dream (ca. 1594). Ariel is, in many respects,
like Puck: He can put a girdle around the earth in forty seconds.
Caliban is like Bottom; he can hear the island's music, as Bottom
dimly remembers his dream. But the music escapes them both;
when they awake, they long to dream again. Caliban's earthy, misshapen body is akin to Bottom's ass's head, a symbol of the fleshly
instincts that weigh down the spirit.[72]

Most scholars position *The Tempest* as Shakespeare's last noncollaborative experiment with tragicomedy or romance.[73] In *Pericles*,
Cymbeline, *The Winter's Tale*, and *The Tempest*, Shakespeare explored
nature's relationship to art and culture. The natural innocence and
inexperience of Marina and Perdita are repeated, for example, in
Miranda. All three young women confront a corrupt world without
becoming corrupted themselves. And Caliban is not the only nature
on whom nurture will not stick. As Joan Hartwig observes, Caliban
may be related to *Cymbeline*'s morally repulsive Cloten, the king's
stepson who would rape Imogen if he could, or to *The Winter's
Tale*'s Autolycus, incorrigible pickpocket and "snapper-up of un-
considered trifles." All three, argues Hartwig, are antimasque figures
who parody their plays' respective heroes: Posthumus, Leontes,
and Prospero. "They exert dramatically an energy, sexual and physical, that the figures they parody do not generate in themselves."[74]
Caliban, in particular, parodies not only Prospero but also the Neapolitan men of sin: Alonso, Antonio, and Sebastian. Still, of these
three parodic figures, Caliban is surely the most sophisticated and

72 James Black associates Bottom with Elizabethan monster lore in "The Monster
in Shakespeare's Landscape," in Hibbard, ed., *The Elizabethan Theatre VIII*, pp.
51–68. He mentions Caliban as a monstrous figure, but the main focus of his
discussion is *King Lear* and *A Midsummer Night's Dream*.
73 Several critical books categorize *Pericles*, *Cymbeline*, *The Winter's Tale*, and *The
Tempest* within a distinct genre, romance or tragicomedy. Cf. E. M. W. Tillyard,
Shakespeare's Last Plays (London: Chatto & Windus, 1938); Barbara A. Mowat,
The Dramaturgy of Shakespeare's Romances (Athens: University of Georgia Press,
1976); Howard Felperin, *Shakespearean Romance* (Princeton, N.J.: Princeton University Press, 1972); and Joan Hartwig, *Shakespeare's Tragicomic Vision* (Baton
Rouge: Louisiana State University Press, 1972).
74 Joan Hartwig, "Cloten, Autolycus, and Caliban: Bearers of Parodic Burdens,"
in *Shakespeare's Romances Reconsidered*, ed. Carol McGinness Kay and Henry E.
Jacobs (Lincoln: University of Nebraska Press, 1978), pp. 90–103, esp. p. 103.

complex.[75] As Shakespeare's final embodiment of the parodic figure, Caliban may have been influenced by the playwright's earlier experiments with such marginalized characters.

X

Caliban's possible literary paradigms are many and varied. Shakespeare's creative genius may have been sparked by what he read in Homer, Virgil, Ovid, or Spenser, by what he heard about the *commedia dell'arte*, or by what he saw in a court masque. From any or all of these sources – from the wild man, monster, harlequin, or antimasque – the dramatist may have found, too, a common pattern that in turn shaped Caliban. All of these literary paradigms signify physical and social forces of disorder. On the personal level, they embody the id that must be repressed and sublimated if the individual is to survive; on the social level, they express "carnivalesque" forces that challenge dominant hierarchies. These figures, and Caliban too, are marginalized from the "civilized" world, but that very marginalization allows them license to embody and express repressed appetites and instincts. As a liminal figure imprisoned in the borders of everyday reality, Caliban has appealed to various ages and cultures in dramatically disparate ways.

75 Shakespeare's *Cymbeline* also includes two salvage men who, by virtue of their noble birth (they are the king's sons), display courtesy and civility, even though they have been kidnapped at birth and raised in the wilds. Though they, like Caliban, might be classified as literary "wild men," Guiderius and Arviragus are polar opposites to *The Tempest*'s "salvage and deformed slave." Caliban's parentage prevents him from being noble, whereas theirs prevents them from being anything else.

Part III
Receptions

Chapter 4
Literary criticism

The poor monster's my subject, and he shall not
suffer indignity.

The Tempest (III.ii.34–5)

Every man has a right to create his own savage for
his own purposes. Perhaps every man does.

Clifford Geertz (1973)

From the Restoration to the present, Shakespeare's *Tempest* has
inspired dramatists, poets, and critics. Legions of authors have
written prose commentaries, some have contrived dramatic sequels
to Shakespeare's play, and a few have created poems and new plays
with *The Tempest* as an explicit or implicit model. In order to draw
coherent conclusions from a literary avalanche, this chapter focuses
only on critical commentary, adaptations, early poems, and offshoots,
leaving stage history and Caliban's most recent interpretations,
appropriations, and adaptations for separate discussion.

No eyewitness accounts of *The Tempest*'s early productions survive, but the one contemporaneous reaction is intriguing. Whether
or not Ben Jonson saw Shakespeare's final play at court or at the
Globe, he seems to have disapproved of Caliban. In *Bartholomew
Fair* (1614), Jonson's scrivener observes that the fair will contain
no Calibans:

If there be never a Servant-monster i' the Fair, who can help it? he says; nor
a nest of antics? He is loth to make Nature afraid in his plays, like those that

89

beget *Tales, Tempests,* and such like drolleries, to mix his head with other men's heels.[1]

Alas, Jonson provides no commentary on Caliban's appearance or actions; by categorizing the monster with antics, drolleries, and dancers of jigs, Jonson apparently saw him as both fearful and comic.

No specific allusions to *The Tempest* document Jacobean and Caroline reactions to Caliban, but Michael Drayton's poem "The Moone-Calf," published in 1627, may have been inspired by Shakespeare's monster. By presenting the Moone-Calf as the offspring of "the World" and the devil, Drayton satirizes the social abuses of his day. When the Moone-Calf is born, its monstrosity is best embodied by its gender – partly male, partly female, both joined together. Such deformity is a physical emblem of the Moone-Calf's corrupt moral nature.[2] Caliban, according to Prospero, is morally corrupt despite his essentially human yet deformed body.

Nor is there any record of *The Tempest*'s performance after 1613.[3] Thanks to Heminges and Condell's Folio, however, the text could be read even if it was rarely performed as Shakespeare wrote it. And when *The Tempest* was performed and appreciated, Caliban was at best incidental. John Dryden wrote in his preface to a Restoration adaptation (1670) that Shakespeare's original

it self had formerly been acted with success in the Black-Fryers: *and our excellent* Fletcher *had so great a value for it, that he thought fit to make use of the same Design, not much varied, a second time. Those who have seen his* Sea-Voyage, *may easily discern that it was a Copy of* Shakespear's Tempest: *the Storm, the desart-Island, and the Woman who had never seen a Man, are all sufficient testimonies of it.*

1 Ben Jonson, *Bartholomew Fair,* ed. Edward B. Partridge (Lincoln: University of Nebraska Press, 1964), pp. 10–11.
2 Michael Drayton, *The Works of Michael Drayton,* Vol. III (Oxford: Basil Blackwell, 1931; repr. 1961), pp. 166–202.
3 We have combed *The Shakspere Allusion-Book: A Collection of Allusions of Shakspere from 1591 to 1700,* 2 vols. (reissued Oxford University Press, 1930), but find no references to any performances of *The Tempest* between 1613 and the Restoration. G. E. Bentley's *The Jacobean and Caroline Stage,* 7 vols. (Oxford: Clarendon Press, 1941–68), records no performances after 1613.

Dryden added that Sir John Suckling had also imitated the play in *The Goblins*, particularly in the character of Regmella, a Miranda figure.[4] There seems to be a consensus here: Jonson, Fletcher, and Suckling admired various features of *The Tempest*, but Caliban was not among them. When the play was copied, he was omitted or at least marginalized.

I

Critical attitudes toward Caliban in the Restoration and the eighteenth century were based on Dryden and William Davenant's extensive adaptation of Shakespeare's text. First performed in 1667 and published in quarto in 1670, *The Tempest: Or, The Enchanted Island* retained only one-third of Shakespeare's original and gave Caliban a monstrous twin sister, Sycorax. Dryden and Davenant also altered the main action, providing Miranda with a sister, Dorinda, and Prospero with a foster son, Hippolito, the rightful duke of Mantua. Improbable as it may sound, Hippolito had been kept hidden in a rock on the island for twelve years and had never seen a woman.

From its inception, Hippolito was a breeches role, portrayed by a woman dressed in masculine attire. The result was a titillating series of double entendres. In the words of theatre historian Jocelyn Powell, "The whole part is set up for it, as the woman on stage asks the mixed audience what women are like. By having a boy played by a girl, the audience is made continually aware of the ideas involved in the encounters of the 'characters', while any exploration of the emotional basis of these ideas is avoided."[5]

The addition of Hippolito inevitably affects interpretations of Caliban, for the former, an uncivilized but handsome young man, represented for Restoration audiences humanity in a state of nature. In this sense his role parallels Miranda's. As she represents natural innocence uncorrupted by the court, Hippolito embodies sexual

4 See the Preface to John Dryden and William Davenant's *The Tempest: Or, The Enchanted Island* (London: 1670), reprinted in George Robert Guffey, *After the Tempest* (Los Angeles: William Andrews Clark Memorial Library, Augustan Reprint Society, Special Series, No. 4, 1969), sig. A2r.
5 Jocelyn Powell, *Restoration Theatre Production* (London: Routledge & Kegan Paul, 1984), p. 72.

naiveté. Hippolito is unskilled in the courtly arts of loving and dueling; Dorinda teaches him to love, Ferdinand to fence. This noble savage – unlike Caliban – is educable. As the play concludes and he has finally channeled his passion toward one woman, he steals Miranda's line from the First Folio: "O brave new world that has such people in't." When the Neapolitan party prepares to leave the enchanted island, it is clear that he and Dorinda will learn together the graces of European civilized society.[6]

In *The Enchanted Isle*, Caliban's monstrosity and ignorance burlesque the hero's simplicity. The cast list, in fact, no longer characterizes Caliban as a "salvage and deformed slave." Instead, he and his sister Sycorax are "Two monsters of the Isle." The text also describes the pair as "half-fish." Caliban's major stage business is to follow Trinculo slavishly and to curry favor by arranging a sexual alliance between Sycorax and his new master. Despite Sycorax's ugliness and immorality, Trinculo resolves to marry her so he can be king of the island. In contrast to Shakespeare's Caliban, who appreciates the island's natural treasures and its wondrous music, Dryden and Davenant's monster is insensitive to everything. His speeches are drastically cut. He is primarily a lackey to Stephano and Trinculo, whose parts are greatly expanded. Caliban embodies little humanity except its worst vices; he is a pimp and a grotesque.

Dryden and Davenant's changes to Shakespeare's original influenced not only theatrical productions but also seventeenth- and eighteenth-century critical interpretations, for many editions of *The Tempest* printed the Dryden-Davenant version as if it were Shakespeare's text. Accordingly, critics who thought and wrote about *The Tempest* often had the Dryden-Davenant version in mind.

Their changes may be symptomatic of Restoration fears and uncertainties. One theatre historian characterizes the seamen's subplot as "anti-commonwealth satire,"[7] and another argues that Dryden

6 Gunnar Sorelius notes that Fletcher and Suckling's imitations of *The Tempest* and Dryden's adaptation are all concerned with the study of primitive man; hence their fascination with the woman who has never seen a man and the man who has never seen a woman. See *"The Giant Race Before the Flood": Pre-Restoration Drama on the Stage and in the Criticism of the Restoration* (Uppsala: Studia Anglistica Upsaliensia, No. 4, 1966), p. 156.

7 Robert D. Hume, *The Development of English Drama in the Late Seventeenth Century* (Oxford: Clarendon Press, 1976), pp. 256–57.

and Davenant's Prospero, unlike Shakespeare's, cannot move from repression toward acceptance and forgiveness. He is a besieged character, left "without the means to cope with or reconcile himself to the manifold threats he perceives in his world." This Prospero "can never acknowledge his relationship to Caliban; at the end . . . he merely orders the savage back into the cave."[8] Like the discontents in Charles II's England, Caliban is to be contained lest he subvert the well-ordered state. Thus, very early in his career, Caliban was appropriated for political purposes.

Thomas Shadwell's operatic version of *The Tempest* (1674), which a modern critic has described as probably the most popular play of the Restoration period,[9] is similarly structured. Hippolito is the natural innocent; Caliban and Sycorax are ugly, bestial, and crude. In response to Shadwell's success, the rival King's Company produced a burlesque a year later. Thomas Duffett's *Mock Tempest* of 1675 transforms the storm and its special effects into a brawl in a brothel. Caliban does not appear until the final scene, when he and sister Sycorax join a chorus of bawd and pimp to sing the concluding masque. Caliban's lines are reminiscent of Bottom's as Pyramus:

> *Sweet* Sycorax, *my Mopsa dear,*
> *My Dove, my Duck,*
> *My Honey suck-*
> le which hast neither prick nor peer,
> *I'le do't, take tail of Shirt,*
> *Cleanse Eye from Dirt. . . .*
> *Dear* Dowdy *be jocund, and sleek*
> *The dainty fine furrowes of thine Olive Cheek:*
> *I cannot deny*
> *My pretty Pigs nye,*
> *With a Nose like a Rose*
> *And a lip as green as a Leek.*[10]

Caliban then signals the final chorus by announcing the impending sunrise, when bawds and pimps retire to their beds.

---

8 Katharine Eisaman Maus, "Arcadia Lost: Politics and Revision in the Restoration *Tempest*," *Renaissance Drama*, XIII (1982): 189–209, quotation from p. 197.

9 Guffey, *After the Tempest*, p. ix.

10 Reprinted in Guffey, *After the Tempest*, p. 52.

The Mock Tempest and Shadwell's opera (the latter version held the boards until 1756) indicate what Caliban represented to the Restoration. Shadwell's monster and Duffett's pimp embody gross immorality and rebellion against divinely ordered authority. Caliban's finer characteristics – love of the island, appreciation of natural beauty, poetic language – are expunged, and the contentious forces he symbolizes must be carefully controlled.

When he was not writing his own versions of Shakespeare's plays, Dryden served as literary critic and sage. He derided Caliban as an extraordinary but repugnant creation:

[Shakespeare] seems there to have created a person which was not in nature, a boldness which at first sight would appear intolerable; for he makes him a species of himself, begotten by an incubus on a witch . . . ; as from the distinct apprehensions of a horse, and of a man, imagination has formed a centaur; so from those of an incubus and a sorceress, Shakespeare has produced his monster. Whether or no his generation can be defended, I leave to philosophy; but of this I am certain, that the poet has most judiciously furnished him with a person, a language, and a character, which will suit him, both by father's and mother's side; he has all the discontents and malice of a witch, and of a devil, besides a convenient proportion of the deadly sins; gluttony, sloth, and lust are manifest; the dejectedness of a slave is likewise given him, and the ignorance of one bred up in a desert island. His person is monstrous, as he is the product of unnatural lust; and his language is as hobgoblin as his person; in all things he is distinguished from other mortals.[11]

Dryden appears to have described his own Caliban more than Shakespeare's, a Caliban without imagination, without love of beauty, without any redeeming qualities – a "hobgoblin" who epitomizes humankind's worst traits. Or, as Ariel sanctimoniously concludes in the Dryden-Davenant plays:

> The monsters *Sycorax* and *Caliban*
> More monstrous grow by passions learn'd from man.[12]

11 John Dryden, *Of Dramatic Poesy and Other Critical Essays*, ed. George Watson, Vol. I (London: J. M. Dent & Sons, 1962), pp. 252–53.
12 Dryden and Davenant, *The Tempest: Or, The Enchanted Island*, p. 72.

Although Restoration critics referred to Caliban as the "monster," his bestiality was human nature at its lowest. In his discussion of Renaissance tragedy (1677), Thomas Rymer commented that "'tis not necessary for a man to have a nose on his face, not to have two legs: he may be a *true* man, though awkward and unsightly, as the *Monster* in *The Tempest*."[13] Caliban's humanity was vital to the era's moralists; only as part of humankind could he represent human vices and thereby serve as a moral metaphor.

II

Eighteenth-century commentaries on Caliban continued to treat him as a monster, but they also focused on two other issues. Critics especially marveled that Shakespeare could create such a character without clear literary antecedents and concluded that Caliban proved the power of the dramatist's imagination. Eighteenth-century commentary also puzzled over Caliban's language, which impressed some as strikingly original and monsterlike, others as not so special. In his account of Shakespeare's life (1709), Nicholas Rowe argued that the character of Caliban (presumably Shakespeare's, not Dryden and Davenant's)

shews a wonderful Invention in the Author, who could strike out such a particular wild Image, and is certainly one of the finest and most uncommon Grotesques that was ever seen.[14]

Rowe also reported a conversation from the mid-seventeenth century among London's educated royalists, including Lucius Cary (Viscount Falkland), Chief Justice Henry Vaughan, and the distinguished jurist John Selden.[15] They concluded, Rowe noted, *"That*

---

13 *Shakespeare: The Critical Heritage: 1623–1692*, ed. Brian Vickers, Vol. I (London: Routledge & Kegan Paul, 1974), p. 186.
14 Nicholas Rowe, *Some Account of the Life of Mr. William Shakespear* (Ann Arbor, Mich.: Augustan Reprint Society, 1948), pp. xxiv–xxv, esp. p. xxiv.
15 Charles Gildon reports that Falkland, joined by John Hales of Eton and other "Persons of Quality," met at Mr. Hales's chambers at Eton to dispute Shakespeare's merits. He concludes that "upon a thorough Disquisition of the point the Judges chosen by agreement out of this Learned and Ingenious Assembly unanimously gave the Preference to SHAKESPEARE." See Vickers, ed., *Shakespeare: The Critical*

Shakespear *had not only found out a new Character in his* Caliban, *but had also devis'd and adapted a new manner of Language for that Character.*"[16]

Charles Gildon stressed Caliban's bestiality in his *Shakespeare's Life and Works* (1710). "*Caliban*," he wrote, "as born of a Witch, shews his Original Malice, ill Nature, Sordidness, and Villany."[17] But others focused on Caliban's striking originality. Joseph Addison observed in *The Spectator*, No. 279 (1712), that "[i]t shews a greater genius in Shakespeare to have drawn his Caliban, than his Hotspur, or Julius Caesar: the one was to be supplied out of his own imagination, whereas the other might have been formed upon tradition, history, and observation."[18] Lewis Theobald's Preface to an adaptation of *Richard II* (1720) argued that Caliban demonstrates the depth of Shakespeare's imagination: "*The Strength, and Vigour, of his Fancy have been confess'd, and admir'd, in the extravagant and supernatural Characters of his own Creation, such as his* CALIBAN."[19] Later in the century (1747), William Guthrie remarked that "Nature never created a Caliban till Shakespear introduced the monster, and we now take him to be nature's composition."[20]

In the same year (1747), William Warburton published the *Works of William Shakespeare in Eight Volumes*. His note for I.ii.362 of *The Tempest* repeated Rowe's comments about Caliban's language. "*Shakespear*," Warburton suggested, "hath very artificially given the air of the antique to the language of *Caliban*, in order to heighten the grotesque of his character." That was not only Warburton's opinion. He recalled the conversation among Falkland, Vaughan, and Selden about Caliban's language. Warburton assumed that "what they meant by it, without doubt, was that *Shakespear* gave his language a certain grotesque air of the Savage and Antique; which it

Heritage, Vol. II, pp. 66–67. Perhaps Shakespeare's unique characterization of Caliban was part of Falkland's case.

16 Rowe, *Some Account*, p. xiv.
17 Vickers, ed., *Shakespeare: The Critical Heritage*, Vol. II, p. 229.
18 Joseph Addison, "*The Spectator*," in *The British Essayists*, Vol. I, ed. Lionel Thomas Berguer (London: T. & J. Allman, 1823), p. 112.
19 Lewis Theobald, Preface to *The Tragedy of King Richard II* (London: Printed for G. Strahan et al., 1720), sig. A2v.
20 William Guthrie, *An Essay Upon English Tragedy* (London: Printed for T. Waller, 1747), p. 11.

certainly has."[21] Two years later, John Holt's *Remarks on the Tempest* (1749) disagreed with Warburton:

Mr. *Warb.* would have done well, to explain what he meant . . . by *Antique* with Respect to the Language of *Caliban*; and also to have assign'd a Reason why he calls his Character *Grotesque*? Because there is nothing absolute in Phrase or Idiom in his Speech, though his Stile is peculiarly adapted to his Origin; nor is there any Thing absurd, capricious, or unnatural in his Character, taking the Doctrine of Witches and their engendering with Daemons (which was fully credited in *Shakespear's* Time) for granted.[22]

Holt took the standard Enlightenment view of Caliban's character. Caliban, he argued, "is work'd up to a Height answerable to the Greatness of the Imagination that form'd it." Holt added that Caliban's "Language is finely adapted, nay peculiarized to his Character, as his Character is to the Fable, his Sentiments to both, and his Manners to all; his Curiosity, Avidity, Brutality, Cowardice, Vindictiveness, and Cruelty, exactly agreeing with his Ignorance, and the Origin of his Person."[23] He then described Caliban's education: Not only was the monster ignorant of language before Prospero's arrival, he also lacked the knowledge even of what was healthful or hurtful for him. When he learned language, it "enabled him to sort and separate his Ideas, and know his own Purposes, or those Meanings he had received from *Prospero*."[24] In sum, Caliban is incurably ignoble. His vices control his actions. Language and culture could curb those vices, but cursed with innate depravity, the education can never fully "take."

Joseph Warton shared these perceptions of Caliban in essay No. 97 of *The Adventurer* (1753). Caliban, Warton asserted, "is represented as a prodigy of cruelty, malice, pride, ignorance, idleness, gluttony, and lust." Shakespeare paints "the brutal barbarity, and unfeeling savageness of this son of Sycorax, by making him enumerate, with a kind of horrible delight, the various ways in which it was possible

21 *The Works of Shakespear in Eight Volumes*, Vol. I, ed. Alexander Pope and William Warburton (London: Printed for J. & P. Knapton et al., 1747), p. 19.
22 John Holt, *Some Remarks on The Tempest* (London: Printed for the author, 1750), p. 28.
23 Holt, *Some Remarks*, pp. 16–17.
24 Holt, *Some Remarks*, p. 29.

for the drunken sailors to surprize and kill his master." Yet the monster is a nonpareil of Shakespearean creation, for in Caliban's formation "he could derive no assistance from observation or experience." In accord with his negative view of Caliban's vices, Warton regretted the monster's last speech, wishing that Shakespeare had instead "preserved this fierce and implacable spirit in Calyban, to the end of the play."[25]

This fiendish Caliban also inspired at least one eighteenth-century poetic imagination. John Gilbert Cooper's "The Tomb of Shakespeare; a Poetical Vision" (1755) described his conception of Caliban:

> Another form succeeded to my view,
> A two-legg'd brute which Nature made in spleen,
> Or from the loathing womb unfinish'd drew.
>
> Scarce could he syllable the curse he thought,
> Prone were his eyes to earth, his mind to evil,
> A carnal fiend to imperfection wrought,
> The mongrel offspring of a Witch and Devil.[26]

As a participant in a parade of Shakespearean characters around the artist's tomb, Caliban here epitomized bestiality, the darkest side of human nature.

The debate over Caliban's language continued. When Benjamin Heath published *A Revisal of Shakespeare's Text* in 1765, he included several long notes on the subject. Returning to the original comments of Falkland, Vaughan, and Selden, Heath concluded that "they must be understood to mean, that the poet had given him [Caliban] a language adapted to the brutality of his manners, and the coarseness of his sentiments; and accordingly we commonly find him expressing himself in terms which betray his diabolical origin, and the baseness of his slavish nature." Heath differed with Warburton over the antique and savage qualities of Caliban's diction, concluding that his speech "seems to be just of the same date

---

25 Joseph Warton, "*The Adventurer*, No. 97," in Berguer, ed., *The British Essayists*, Vol. XXV, pp. 29–34.
26 Vickers, ed., *Shakespeare: The Critical Heritage*, Vol. IV, p. 180.

with that of his master Prospero, of whom, indeed, he learned it. As to the epithet, savage, . . . I know of no savage terms or expressions in the part of Caliban."[27]

The notes to Samuel Johnson's 1765 edition of The Tempest, reprinted in later editions, say little about Caliban. Johnson did, however, contribute his views to the debate over the monster's language. He argued that Falkland, Vaughan, and Selden "mistook brutality of sentiment for uncouthness of words." Caliban, argued Johnson, could not have invented a "language of his own without more understanding than Shakespear has thought it proper to bestow upon him." Besides, his language indicates his temperament. "His diction is indeed somewhat clouded by the gloominess of his temper and the malignity of his purposes," but anyone who entertained the same thoughts would speak the same way.[28]

The debate did not end there. In his Essay on the Dramatic Character of Sir John Falstaff (1777), Maurice Morgann concluded that Shakespeare "has personified malice in his Caliban; a character kneaded up of three distinct natures, the diabolical, the human, and the brute." Morgann characterized Caliban as Ariel's opposite: "Caliban is the passion itself, or rather a compound of malice, servility, and lust, substantiated; and therefore best shewn in contrast with the lightness of Ariel and the innocence of Miranda."[29] Caliban, in short, was "the other" in a binary opposition between body and spirit, evil and good, guilt and innocence – a view that fit comfortably with eighteenth-century moral certainties.

A final illustration of the eighteenth century's propensity to see Caliban as a devil figure appears in the 1793 edition of Shakespeare's plays, which contained not only Dr. Johnson's commentary on the text but also notes by George Steevens. The latter glossed Caliban's gleeful "O ho! O ho!": "This savage exclamation was originally and constantly appropriated by the writers of our ancient Mysteries and

27 Benjamin Heath, A Revisal of Shakespear's Text (London: Printed for W. Johnston, 1765), pp. 9–10.
28 Samuel Johnson, Johnson on Shakespeare, ed. Walter Raleigh (Oxford University Press, 1908), p. 66.
29 Maurice Morgann, An Essay on the Dramatic Character of Sir John Falstaff (London: Printed for T. Davis, 1777), pp. 75–76n.

Moralities, to the Devil; and has, in this instance, been transferred to his descendant Caliban."[30]

Although many critics commented on Caliban's language, rarely did they mention his appearance. But some evidence remains. Engravings of Shakespearean characters assembled for David Garrick's 1769 jubilee depict a hairy Caliban, covered with furs and grizzle Captain Edward Thompson, who attended the jubilee, later described the monster as he appeared at Stratford:

> There was Caliban too, a most monstrous ape,
> No beast had before such a whimsical shape,
> Yet was nearly being hang'd for attempting a rape.

This seems to be more of a commentary on Caliban's general hairiness – perhaps inspired by Europe's fictional wild man – than a precursor of the Darwinian approach to Caliban that appeared a century later (Figure 4). And elsewhere in the same satiric poem Thompson refers to Caliban as "The scaly vile Monster" who made the participants "sick with his damn'd smell of fish."[31] Caliban apparently was perceived in the eighteenth century as covered with fur but scaly around the arms and legs.

Adaptations also indicate the era's view of Caliban. Toward the end of the eighteenth century, London was agog over young William Henry Ireland's scandalous forgeries of Shakespearean documents. Trying to impress a father preoccupied with antiquarian hobbies, William Henry purchased legitimate pieces of sixteenth-century paper, imitated Elizabethan handwriting, and forged evidence of Shakespeare's life and religious views.[32] Other writers capitalized on the ensuing furor. In 1797, Francis Godolphin Waldron asserted that his *The Virgin Queen* was in "imitation of our immortal SHAKESPEARE." This spurious adaptation probably was never performed in a theatre, but it does elucidate late-eighteenth-century

---

30 George Steevens and Samuel Johnson, eds., *The Plays of William Shakespeare*, Vol. III (London: Printed for T. Longman et al., 1793), p. 38n.
31 Edward Thompson, *Trinculo's Trip to the Jubilee* (London: Printed for C. Moran et al., 1769), pp. 33, 28.
32 For an entertaining account of the Ireland forgeries, see S[amuel] Schoenbaum, *Shakespeare's Lives* (Oxford University Press, 1970), pp. 201–33.

4. Caliban, mouthing "A plague upon ye Tyrant that I serve," at the Shakespeare Jubilee, Stratford-upon-Avon, as illustrated in *The Public Advertiser* (23 August 1769).

onceptions of Caliban. He begs, for example, to be taken with Prospero to Milan, whereupon Miranda argues with her father that

> the creature's much reform'd
> Since your forgiveness of his last offence;
> And, by commixture with so many men,
> He hourly humanizes: pity 'twere
> In lonesome wretchedness to leave him now,
> The speechless brutes his sole society,
> Perforce a savage to become again.[33]

Prospero relents. Caliban is duly clad in silk garments instead of his former "rugged hide," but his "humanization" is only on the surface. On shipboard he plots against Prospero once again and gets drunk with Stephano and Trinculo. In his euphoria he wor-

33 Francis Godolphin Waldron, *The Virgin Queen; A Sequel to Shakespeare's Tempest* (London: Printed for the author, 1797), p. 12.

ships the ship as a god because it miraculously moves through water. Sycorax appears in the night to promise revenge on Prospero if he can be gotten to land – she has no power over the sea – so Caliban, Stephano, and Trinculo throw the ship's stores overboard to force a landing. Prospero, having relinquished his magic wand, is now vulnerable; too late he realizes what Caliban has done and that Antonio and Sebastian are also conspiring against him. When the ship lands at Tunis, Caliban lasciviously seizes both Miranda and Ferdinand's sister Claribel. Sycorax, his loving mother, encourages him:

> Young Caliban! born to annoy
> All those who are not of his kind;
> With mother's form, and father's mind![34]

When Sycorax burns the ship and all seems lost, Ariel descends with Prospero's magic wand. Prospero regrets his original lenity and forever banishes Caliban, Sycorax, Antonio, and Sebastian. *The Virgin Queen*'s Caliban has inherited his devil-father's vices he cannot be reformed or his sins eradicated. He must be rigidly controlled or, better yet, excluded from civilized society.

III

Eighteenth-century interpretations of *The Tempest* reflect neoclassical emphasis on man as a rational animal who can and should control his baser passions. As Waldron's adaptation demonstrated, Prospero's wand is necessary to keep Caliban's evil instincts in check. Not surprisingly, this view began to change toward the end of the eighteenth century. The American and French revolutions' rhetoric about the rights of individual man, Rousseau's speculations on man's natural nobility in an uncivilized state, and the romantic poets' appreciation of poetic imagination attuned to the "spontaneous overflow of powerful feelings" subtly influenced attitudes toward Shakespeare's monster. If Caliban were even partly human, and if there was a brotherhood of men, he could no longer be despised as inherently unequal and inferior.

34 Waldron, *The Virgin Queen*, p. 65.

Literary criticism

Writers and poets in the late eighteenth and early nineteenth centuries began to reexamine *The Tempest*; instead of automatically assuming Prospero's point of view, they occasionally looked at the play's scenario at least partly from Caliban's perspective. They empathized with his desperate attempt to regain control of his island and his life. They increasingly argued that it was not all Caliban's fault, that Prospero, too, bore some responsibility for Caliban's anger and despair. This turnabout did not happen overnight, but with the emergence of the romantic poets, reactions to Caliban became less moralistic, more sympathetic.

The comments of the German romanticist Augustus William Schlegel provide a case in point: "Caliban has become a by-word as the strange creation of a poetical imagination. . . . Caliban is malicious, cowardly, false, and base; and yet he is essentially different from the vulgar knaves of a civilized world." Schlegel saw Caliban as "rude, but not vulgar; he never falls into the prosaic and low familiarity of his drunken associates, for he is, in his way, a poetical being."[35]

Samuel Taylor Coleridge's lecture on *The Tempest* (1811–12) also demonstrates more sympathy for Caliban:

The character of Caliban is wonderfully conceived: he is a sort of creature of the earth partaking of the qualities of the brute and distinguished from them in two ways, 1. by having mere understanding without moral reason, 2. by not having the instincts which belong to mere animals. – Still Caliban is a noble being: a man in the sense of the imagination, all the images he utters are drawn from nature, & are all highly poetical.[36]

Yet in his first lecture of 1818–19, Coleridge argued that Caliban "has the dawnings of understanding without reason or the moral sense, and in him, as in some brute animals, this advance to the intellectual faculties, without the moral sense, is marked by the

35 Augustus William Schlegel, *A Course of Lectures on Dramatic Literature*, trans. John Black (London: Henry G. Bohn, 1846), p. 395. Schlegel delivered his lectures in 1808; they were first translated into English in 1815.
36 Samuel Taylor Coleridge, *The Collected Works of Samuel Taylor Coleridge. Part V. Lectures, 1808–1819, on Literature*, Vol. I, ed. R. A. Foakes (Princeton, N.J.: Princeton University Press, 1969), p. 364.

appearance of vice."[37] Caliban's language displays poetical awareness of nature's beauties, but he lacks moral sensibilities and therefore cannot be fully human.

William Hazlitt also recognized Caliban's imaginative power. In
his discussion of Shakespeare's characters (1817) he suggested that
Caliban is "one of the wildest and most abstracted of all Shakespear's
characters, whose deformity whether of body or mind is redeemed
by the power and truth of the imagination displayed in it." Hazlitt,
like Schlegel, drew a key distinction. Caliban's deformity "is the
essence of grossness, but there is not a particle of vulgarity in it.
Shakespear has described the brutal mind of Caliban in contact
with the pure and original forms of nature; the character grows
out of the soil where it is rooted uncontrouled, uncouth and wild."
Stephano and Trinculo, by contrast, have no redeeming qualities.
"In conducting Stephano and Trinculo to Prospero's cell, Caliban
shews the superiority of natural capacity over greater knowledge
and greater folly."[38]

A year later, on 14 February 1818, Hazlitt published in *The Yellow
Dwarf* a response to Coleridge's lecture. This time Hazlitt took a
more political view of Caliban, arguing that he, not Prospero, was
the legitimate ruler of the island. The Neapolitans, he charged,
were usurpers. In his reassessment of Hazlitt's Shakespeare criticism, Jonathan Bate praises Hazlitt for being "the first to read *The
Tempest* in terms of imperialism" and to see Caliban as a dispossessed
native.[39] Caliban should receive the reader's and the audience's
sympathy by right as well as through poetic power.

In 1838 William Charles Macready broke from the Dryden-Davenant
tradition and produced *The Tempest* in Shakespeare's original text.
The performance inspired at least one critic to see a kinder, gentler
Caliban. Patrick MacDonnell praised George Bennett's interpretation of the monster's role because it delineated "the rude and un-
cultivated savage, in a style, which arouses our sympathies." This
audience response heralds the new Caliban, no longer despised for

37 Coleridge, *Lectures, 1808–1819*, Vol. II, p. 270.
38 William Hazlitt, *Characters of Shakespeare's Plays* (London: Printed by C. H. Reynell
for R. Hunter, 1817), pp. 118–20.
39 Jonathan Bate, *Shakespearean Constitutions: Politics, Theatre, Criticism, 1730–1830*
(Oxford: Clarendon Press, 1989), p. 144; see also pp. 178–79.

his vices, but instead the focus of pity and human understanding. For MacDonnell, Caliban is "a creature in his nature possessing all the rude elements of the savage, yet maintaining in his mind, a strong resistance to that tyranny, which held him in the thralldom of slavery: Caliban creates our pity more than our detestation." And with MacDonnell, a trend began that lasts to the present day: Sympathy for Caliban entails criticism of Prospero. MacDonnell took it to be Prospero's fault that Caliban tried to rape Miranda, for "this wild and untutored creature, was imprudently placed enough in the way, to enable him, to make the attempt complained of: the noble and generous character of Prospero, therefore suffers, by this severe conduct to Caliban."[40]

MacDonnell's sympathy for a creature held in the "thralldom of slavery" may also be characteristic of the mid-nineteenth century – at least in some parts of the Anglo-American world. To the eighteenth century, Caliban's enslavement was the logical result of his depravity, his rightful station in a natural hierarchy of reason over passion, virtue over vice, civility over savagery. Such complacency was bound to be disturbed in the early nineteenth century by the growing fervor of the abolitionist movement in England and the United States. To many English and American observers slavery became a grim reality; whether the commentator was for or against emancipation, Caliban was perceived in a new light.[41]

A case in point is the 1848 burlesque *The Enchanted Isle*, by Robert and William Brough, in which Caliban is described as "a smart, active lad, wanted (by Prospero) to make himself generally useful, but by no means inclined to do so, an hereditary bondsman, who in his determination to be free, takes the most fearful liberties." Instead of consorting with Stephano and Trinculo, Caliban joins Easa Di Baccastoppa and Smuttifacio, "foreign propagandists" from Naples who satirize the libertarian impulse in Italy during the revolutions of 1848.

The Broughs' burlesque elaborates on the slavery theme. When

40 P. MacDonnell, *An Essay on the Play of The Tempest* (London: John Fellowes, 1840), pp. 16–19.
41 We were directed to the materials on slavery discussed later by Trevor Griffiths, "'This Island's Mine': Caliban and Colonialism," *The Yearbook of English Studies*, XIII (1983): 159–80.

Shakespeare's Caliban

Miranda calls Caliban for his first appearance ("Come here, slave!"), he enters *"with a Wellington boot on one arm and a brush in his hand."* His first words mimic abolitionist slogans:

> Slave! Come, drop that sort of bother;
> Just let me ax, "Aint I a man and a brother?"

He promises the audience to "tell a round unvarnished tale" (*Othello*, I.iii.107), and to the tune of "Georgy Barnwell" he sings:

> Sons of freedom, hear my story,
> Pity and protect the slave;
> Of my wrongs the inventory
> I'll just tip you in a stave.
> Tiddle ol, &c.
> [*Brushes the boot to the chorus.*]
> From morn till night I work like winkin',
> Yet I'm kicked and cuffed about,
> With scarce half time for grub or drinkin',
> And they never let me have a Sunday out.
> Tiddle ol, &c.
> And if jaw to the gov'nor I gives vent to,
> He calls up his spirits in a trice,
> Who grip, squeeze, bite, sting, and torment – oh!
> Such friends at a *pinch* are by no means nice.
> Tiddle ol, &c . . .
> But I'll not stand it longer, that I'll not,
> I'll strike at once, now that my *mettle's* hot.

When Prospero chastises him for rebellion, Caliban cries:

> The love of liberty upon me seizes;
> My bosom's filled with freedom's pure emotions,
> And on the "Rights of Labour" I've strong notions.

The rebellion is short-lived, however. Prospero's fairies attack Caliban with their staves, chasing him off the stage.

The Brough brothers' satire depended on knowledge of Shakespeare's original. But the humor of their burletta is also topical,

106

melding Shakespeare's "salvage slave" with the plight of black "hereditary bondsmen" who longed for freedom.

When Caliban next enters, he is caricatured as a revolutionary. He appears *"marching to music, with a Cap of Liberty on his head, a red flag in one hand, a small bundle of firewood in the other."* Now he's ready to join forces with the incompetent Italian rebels, Easa Di Baccastoppa and Smuttifacio, who cry "Viva la Republique!" The three exit singing "There's a good time coming, boys." They enter three scenes later *"loaded with chains."* Caliban's submission to Prospero follows:

> Governor, we surrender at discretion,
> And to your government send in adhesion;
> We own that this a just and fair defeat is,
> So take these chains off, and let's sign some treaties.

The farce concludes with the engagement of Ferdinand and Miranda, but instead of Prospero's epilogue to the audience, Caliban incites the audience to "Get up a *devil* of a *demon*stration, / But not with *arms*, no, only with the *hand.*"[42]

Caliban is a comic butt in *The Enchanted Isle*, yet so is everyone else. He is not overtly described as black, but as a "hereditary bondsman" who echoes Othello, he is surely meant to be perceived as black. And despite the buffoonery, he is treated sympathetically.

Not so Caliban's association with black slaves in the 24 January 1863 issue of *Punch*. There a cartoon titled "Scene from the American 'Tempest'" depicts Caliban as a black "Sambo." Abraham Lincoln, dressed as a Union Officer, hands Caliban the Emancipation Proclamation; the Sambo figure points to a Confederate officer to the left and exclaims: *"You* beat him 'nough, massa! Berry little time, I'll *beat him too."* The cartoon labels this a "Nigger translation" of Caliban's line about Trinculo in Shakespeare's original, "Beat him enough. After a little time / I'll beat him too" (III.ii.82–83). Opposite this cartoon is a doggerel poem, "Old Abe in a Fix," that spoofs the political difficulties leading to Lincoln's proclamation. Both the

---

42 Lines from *The Enchanted Isle* are taken from Michael R. Booth, ed., *English Plays of the Nineteenth Century. Vol. V: Pantomimes, Extravaganzas and Burlesques* (Oxford: Clarendon Press, 1976), pp. 163–201.

PUNCH, OR THE LONDON CHARIVARI.—January 24, 1863.

SCENE FROM THE AMERICAN "TEMPEST."

Caliban (Sambo). "*YOU BEAT HIM 'NOUGH, MASSA! BERRY LITTLE TIME, I'LL BEAT HIM TOO.*"—Shakspeare. (*Nigger Translation.*)

5. *Punch,* reacting to Lincoln's Emancipation Proclamation, portrays Caliban as a newly liberated "Sambo" (24 January 1863).

cartoon and the poem, obviously, reflect British sympathy for the Confederate cause. With blatant racism, both use the term "nigger" and depict blacks according to white stereotypes. The association of Caliban with enslaved blacks (Figure 5) would resurface in the next century, though from a dramatically different political perspective.[43]

At the same time as he was being characterized as a "hereditary bondsman," Caliban was sometimes described in terms reminiscent of the Gothic "monster." Two years after the Broughs' travesty, Caliban appeared in an eerie light in Morris Barnett's pamphlet *The Tempest; A Lyrical Drama,* which proposes that Shakespeare's play be made into a full-fledged opera. The new plot would reveal the demonic Sycorax entrapped beneath a rock. The she-monster offers

43 See Chapter 6.

her devilish son three wishes and begs him first to wish that she be delivered from her bondage. When Caliban ignores her desperate cries, Sycorax hurls curses at her fiendish offspring. (Entrapped in her magic den, Sycorax is not exactly Charlotte Brontë's Bertha Mason, nor is Caliban Mr. Rochester, but there is a similarity!) Caliban uses the first of his three wishes to shut Ariel in a mighty tree. He then seizes Miranda, who, "despairing of help, is about to plunge a poignard into her heart, when the breathing of the second wish seals up her senses in a soft and balmy sleep." Later she miraculously awakens, seizes Calban's enchanted flowers, and makes the third wish: Caliban and his drunken cohorts become rooted to the spot and cannot move. As the operatic scenario closes, Caliban is doomed to remain alone on the island with his rock-bound mother. Though driven by demonic fury, the repulsive and grotesque Caliban cannot ravish the innocent maiden. He does, however, come close enough to titillate the audience.[44]

IV

As nineteenth-century social and political currents ebbed and flowed, Caliban's image shifted again. He had, after all, been an unlikely and short-lived romantic hero. When Darwinism spurred philosophical speculations about humanity's place in an evolving universe, critics quickly put Caliban to new sociobiological uses. The most famous instance is Robert Browning's "Caliban Upon Setebos," published in 1864. To Browning, Caliban is an amphibian – half man, half fish – who lives on the margins of humanity but reveals essential human traits such as selfishness and self-deception. Browning's poem, a satire on Victorian theologians, describes the conception of God that might occur to a less-than-human creature. Caliban judges his god Setebos by himself; if he is capricious with crabs on the beach – sometimes ignoring them, sometimes cruelly toying with them – so must Setebos be cruel and capricious, favoring Prospero for no reason. Caliban thinks Setebos can be appeased by ceremonial songs, such as

44 Morris Barnett, *The Tempest; A Lyrical Drama* (London: J. Mitchell, 1850), pp. 26–28.

Shakespeare's Caliban

What I hate, be consecrate
To celebrate Thee and Thy state, no mate,
For Thee, what see for envy in poor me?

Another passage summarizes Browning's conception of Shakespeare's fishlike monster:

> a sea-beast, lumpish, which he snared,
> Blinded the eyes of, and brought somewhat tame,
> And split its toe-webs, and now pens the drudge
> In a hole o' the rock and calls him Caliban.

Browning concludes his poem in resignation, observing that the best way to escape Setebos' ire "Is, not to seem too happy."[45] If Browning's Caliban reflects a strain of Victorian pessimism, he is nonetheless more human, thoughtful, and sympathetic than the monster of the eighteenth century.

Caliban as amphibian, somewhere between brute animal and human being, is made more explicit and timely in Daniel Wilson's *Caliban: The Missing Link* (1873). Wilson associated Caliban with a theoretical "intermediate being, between the true brute and man, which, if the new theory of descent from crudest animal organisms be true, was our predecessor and precursor in the inheritance of this world of humanity."[46] Wilson related Caliban's (assumed) fishlike appearance to Darwin's view that man evolved from some species of aquatic animal. At the same time, he contended that "though by some scaly or fin-like appendages, the idea of a fish or sea-monster, is suggested to all, the form of Caliban is, nevertheless, essentially human," with "huge canine teeth and prognathous jaws. . . . He is a novel anthropoid of a high type." Wilson attributed Shakespeare's pre-Darwinian foresight to explorers' descriptions of the New World's inhabitants. On his Mediterranean island, Prospero found "just such a monstrous being as travellers' tales had already made familiar to all men as natives of such regions."[47] Wilson thus foreshadowed the Indianization of Caliban while epitomizing Darwinian influences on *The Tempest*.

45 Robert Browning, *The Poetical Works* (Oxford University Press, 1964), pp. 492–95.
46 Daniel Wilson, *Caliban: The Missing Link* (London: Macmillan, 1873), pp. xi–xii.
47 Wilson, *Caliban*, pp. 75, 78, 72.

Wilson also continued the tendency to denigrate Prospero. Wilson argued that Prospero's word is not to be taken as fact, for he is a tyrant who needs Caliban's services and drives his slave in anger. In attempting to rape Miranda, Caliban "proved to be simply an animal, actuated by the ordinary unrestrained passions and desires which in the brute involve no moral evil, and but for the presence of Miranda would have attracted no special notice."[48] Caliban is not the son of a devil; he is an animal, part of the natural landscape. Caliban's speech is poetical; he wins our sympathies. "We feel for the poor monster, so helplessly in the power of the stern Prospero, as for some caged wild beast pining in cruel captivity, and rejoice to think of him at last free to range in harmless mastery over his island solitude."[49]

By the late nineteenth century, Caliban had become more firmly entrenched as a vehicle for philosophical speculation. Another fanciful portrait of Caliban appeared in France in 1878 in Ernest Renan's *Caliban: Suite de "La Tempête,"* a closet drama that begins where *The Tempest* ends. Instead of leaving Caliban behind to rule over his Mediterranean island, Renan's Prospero takes him back to Italy, installs him in the wine cellar, and extracts whatever service a perpetual state of drunkenness allows. But Caliban has begun to change. As Ariel describes him, "little by little, thanks to language and reason, thy deformed features have become harmonized, thy web-fingers have separated themselves one from the other, and from a poisonous fish thou hast become a man."[50] That Caliban, exposed to proper language and thought, could make such a transformation speaks to the nineteenth-century belief in humanity's continuing progress and ability to improve itself, but Caliban's evolution has its limits. While Prospero is once more absorbed in his art, the unruly mob (Renan's symbol of the Paris Commune of 1871) makes Caliban its leader and revolts. Caliban becomes duke, and with his new position he acquires new respect for Prospero; in Act V Caliban refuses to deliver Prospero to the Inquisition. But Caliban has also

48 Wilson, *Caliban*, p. 85.
49 Wilson, *Caliban*, p. 91.
50 Ernest Renan, *Caliban: A Philosophical Drama Continuing "The Tempest" of William Shakespeare*, trans. Eleanor Grant Vickery (New York: The Shakespeare Press, 1896), p. 18.

become something of an elitist himself, reflecting Renan's suspic
ion of democracy's positivist proclivities. The play concludes with
Ariel's disappearance; shorn of his magic and its agent, Prospero
must die. Renan's Caliban is irresistible but uninspiring democracy
Prospero, according to critic Ruby Cohn, "tends to speak for the
idealistic, cultured, aristocratic aspect of man – a man much like
Renan himself."[51]

Christopher Pearse Cranch disclaimed any influence from Renan,
rather, his twenty-page verse dialogue, "Ariel and Caliban" (1887),
shows Caliban evolving morally as well as intellectually and physically. Bored with his freedom and Prospero's absence, Ariel under-
takes Caliban's moral education. Caliban explains: "I was never
taught to curb / My passions and I lived a lonely life." Ariel teaches
Caliban to "Learn to be a lord / In nobler style, and with a human
love / of all things good." As the poem concludes, the fairy-sprite
lifts the fleshy monster aloft, and both leave the island to seek a
better land where they will find "Contact with men of a superior
mould / In bonds of law and human brotherhood."[52]

Not every late-nineteenth-century commentator saw Caliban as
educable. Oscar Wilde, notorious libertine though he may have
been, took a more eighteenth-century view of Shakespeare's monster.
To Wilde, Caliban was a deformed, bestial slave who represented
human depravity. In the Preface to *The Picture of Dorian Gray*, Wilde
wrote:

There is no such thing as an immoral book. Books are well written, or badly
written. That is all. The nineteenth century dislike of Realism is the rage of
Caliban seeing his own face in a glass. The nineteenth century dislike of
Romanticism is the rage of Caliban not seeing his own face in a glass.

When Dorian Gray looks at his portrait, he sees the Caliban in his
own nature. Wilde's view not only looks back to the eighteenth
century but also foreshadows W. H. Auden's post-Freudian con-

---

51 Ruby Cohn, *Modern Shakespeare Offshoots* (Princeton, N.J.: Princeton University
   Press, 1976), pp. 272–75, quotation on p. 273. See also Roger Toumson, *Trois
   Calibans* (Habana: Casa de las Américas, 1981), pp. 489–638. For further dis-
   cussion of Renan, see Chapter 6 below.
52 Christopher Pearse Cranch, *Ariel and Caliban with Other Poems* (Boston: Houghton
   Mifflin, 1887), pp. 1–20, esp. pp. 11, 12, 16.

ception of Caliban as the darkness inside us we seldom face but cannot avoid.[53]

Wilde was an eccentric in the midst of late-Victorian optimism. Caliban as the Darwinian missing link with an evolving moral sensibility dominated western imaginations until the 1920s. To many commentators and adapters, he seemed to embody not only humanity's fallen conditon but also its efforts to rise from a mire of ignorance and corruption. Alfred A. Wheeler described the Caliban who was to be left behind in his 1907 poem "Caliban": "As the frighted soul / Took wing, the empty carcass but remains." The speaker concludes:

> Earth, with thy cleansing chemistries, absorb
> This man; melt his gross shape; let flesh and bone
> In thy dread crucible sink out of sight
> And bubble up in primal elements,
> Which, if thy will must give them back to light,
> Send through the channels of some waking tree,
> When first the spring stirs hunger in its roots,
> And as the life of branch and bud and flower,
> Transfigured, let their pure perfection shine,
> Unconscious they were once a fallen man.[54]

The age believed with Renan, Cranch, and Wheeler that Caliban – symbol of fallen humanity – could be left behind. Or, at the very least, he could be transcended. This optimistic view of the human condition is perhaps most fully revealed in Percy MacKaye's mammoth community masque, performed at Lewisohn Stadium in New York (1916).[55] In this production, Caliban is aspiring humanity; his education consists of pageants depicting stages of civilization from ancient Egypt to the present. MacKaye's self-proclaimed goal was

53 Oscar Wilde, *The Annotated Oscar Wilde*, ed. H. Montgomery Hyde (New York: Crown Publishers, 1982), p. 138.
54 Alfred A. Wheeler, "Caliban," *The Century*, 1907 (from clippings of Horace Howard Furness at the Furness Library, University of Pennsylvania, Philadelphia).
55 Percy MacKaye, *Caliban by the Yellow Sands* (Garden City, N.Y.: Doubleday, Page, & Co., 1916). Lawrence W. Levine shows how MacKaye's masque demonstrates the elevation of Shakespeare to "highbrow" culture in *Highbrow/Lowbrow: The Emergence of Cultural Hierarchy in America* (Cambridge, Mass.: Harvard University Press, 1988), p. 80.

"to present Prospero's art as the art of the theater culminating in Shakespeare and to lead Caliban step by step from his aboriginal path of brute force and ignorance to the realm of love, reason and self-discipline."[56] Thus his Caliban illustrates MacKaye's conviction that the human race had progressed during 4,000 years.

MacKaye's community masque expressed Edwardian complacency. Like his predecessors, MacKaye could comfortably view Caliban from the perspective of Anglo-Saxon superiority. Caliban represented what the English had been in a far-distant, pre-evolutionary past. He also symbolized colonized nations before they received the blessings of western culture and civilization. Separated from modern civilizations by his lack of government, culture, and manners, Caliban was the untutored "other". He was to be mastered, educated, and acculturated, but never acknowledged. Such smugness could not survive the fury of world war and depression.

V

As later generations reaped the whirlwind of two world wars and an attempted genocide, writers once more turned to Shakespeare's *Tempest*. Influenced by Freudian analysis of the darker side of human nature – the sexual and violent impulses lurking beneath the surface – they saw Caliban as a symbol of the inexorable, ineradicable evil within the human psyche. The most eloquent statement, composed in the midst of World War II, reflects profound disillusionment with the idealism of the late-Victorian period. W. H. Auden's *The Sea and the Mirror* begins poignantly with Prospero's farewell to Ariel. The magus's words betray his own disenchantment and world-weariness:

> Now, Ariel, I am that I am, your late and lonely master,
>   Who knows now what magic is: – the power to enchant
> That comes from disillusion. What the books can teach one
>   Is that most desires end up in stinking ponds.

---

56 Jane P. Franck, "*Caliban* at Lewisohn Stadium, 1916," *Shakespeare Encomium*, ed. Anne Paolucci (New York: The City College, 1964), pp. 154–68, quotation from p. 159.

So much for Prospero's dream of regeneration and harmony. More to our purposes, Prospero accepts responsibility for Caliban, recognizing the symbiotic nature of their relationship:

> But Caliban remains my impervious disgrace.
> We did it, Ariel, between us; you found on me a wish
> For absolute devotion; result – his wreck
> That sprawls in the weeds and will not be repaired:
> My dignity discouraged by a pupil's curse,
> I shall go knowing and incompetent into my grave.

Once he learns Prospero's language, Caliban's curse is inevitable.

In Auden's Part II, each of the characters who sails home to Naples reflects on the past and hopes for the future. Antonio's resolute determination not to reform is expressed in an allusion to Shakespeare's most melodramatic villain, Richard, duke of Gloucester:

> *Your all is partial, Prosper;*
> *My will is all my own:*
> *Your need to love shall never know*
> *Me: I am I, Antonio,*
> *By choice myself alone.*

The poem's final section is a dense, stream-of-consciousness prose monologue by Caliban to the audience. It begins by rejecting Shakespeare's original Epilogue. Speaking on behalf of the spectators to the dramatist, Caliban concludes: "Imprisoned, by you, in the mood doubtful, loaded, by you, with distressing embarrassments, we are, we submit, in no position to set *anyone* free." After a digression on Ariel, the speaker returns to the role of Caliban to address Prospero (who has been transformed into a Prufrockian middle-class English citizen): One day, says Caliban, Prospero will look in the mirror and find, instead of the Ariel he had expected,

a gibbering fist-clenched creature with which you are all too unfamiliar, for this is the first time indeed that you have met the only subject that you have, who is not a dream amenable to magic but the all too solid flesh you must acknowledge as your own; at last you have come face to face with me, and are appalled to learn how far I am from being, in any sense, your dish.

115

This discovery makes Prospero realize that he can never escape the Caliban within himself:

Can you wonder then, when, as was bound to happen sooner or later, your charms, because they no longer amuse you, have cracked and your spirits, because you are tired of giving orders, have ceased to obey, and you are left alone with me, the dark thing you could never abide to be with. . . . I must own that, after all, I am not just the person I would have chosen for a life companion myself; so the only chance, which in any case is slim enough, of my getting a tolerably new master and you a tolerably new man, lies in our both learning, if possible and as soon as possible, to forgive and forget the past, and to keep our respective hopes for the future, within moderate, very moderate, limits.

The result is almost Sartrian. At the poem's close, Caliban observes that "There is nothing to say. There never has been – and our wills chuck in their hands – There is no way out. There never was."[57] *The Tempest*, like life itself, has lost its metaphysical certainty.

Caliban could be a symbol of inner evil without engendering such profound pessimism, however. Critic G. Wilson Knight also wrote about Caliban during World War II, but his interpretation built on turn-of-the-century evolutionary concepts. For Knight, *The Tempest* was the ultimate statement of Shakespeare's worldview, its characters the culmination of years of experimentation. Caliban, argued Knight, derives from "all Shakespeare's imagery of nausea and evil expressed through reptiles, or . . . creatures of black magic, as in *Macbeth*." Caliban is himself "a water-beast, growing from the ooze and slime of those stagnant pools elsewhere associated with vice. . . . But he has a beast's innocence and pathos too."[58] Integral to the symbolic pattern Knight saw in *The Tempest*, Caliban – like Ariel, Prospero, and Miranda – could be perceived as an aspect of Shakespeare's psyche. Caliban opposed Ariel's fire and air, contributing "the world of creation, smelling of earth and water, with the salt tang of the physical, of sexual energy, and with, too, all

---

57 W. H. Auden, *Collected Poems*, ed. Edward Mendelson (New York: Random House, 1976), pp. 307–41.
58 G. Wilson Knight, *The Crown of Life* (Oxford University Press, 1947; repr. New York: Barnes & Noble, 1966), p. 211.

those revulsions and curses to which it gives birth." Thus, Caliban's deformity symbolizes "the anomalous, and therefore provisional, ascent of evil within the creative order."[59] As a primitive monster, Caliban "is a *sub specie aeternitatis* study of creation's very inertia and retrogression in laborous advance, growing from slime and slush, slug and furry beast, to man in his misery and slavery, though shot through with glory; and learning, in his own despite, the meaning of lordship and grace."[60] In short, *The Tempest* seemed to Knight a myth of Britain's soul. Prospero was a sort of Nietzschean superman who embodied "the compulsion of man to super-humanity, drawing man in his own despite to god-in-man." The play, in turn, foretold the genius of British colonization,

(i) her in-ruling severe, yet inclusive and tolerant, religious and political instincts, of which her first colonial adventures and the Puritan revolution were active examples; (ii) her inventive and poetic genius variously concerned with the tapping and use of natural energy; and (iii) her colonizing, especially her will to raise savage peoples from superstition and blood-sacrifice, taboos and witchcraft and the attendant fears and slaveries, to a more enlightened existence.[61]

Although he could not know it when he wrote in 1947, Knight here outlined the directions that postwar criticism would take.

59 Knight, *The Crown of Life*, pp. 223, 240.
60 Knight, *The Crown of Life*, p. 240.
61 Knight, *The Crown of Life*, p. 255.

Chapter 5
The American school

O brave new world.

The Tempest (V.i.183)

In Caliban, he [Shakespeare] propounded an answer
to the greatest of American enigmas.

Sidney Lee (1907)

Not until the late eighteenth century did commentators begin to
associate *The Tempest*'s plot, language, and characters with Europe's
exploration and colonization of America. The earliest New World
connections to draw attention (discussed in Chapter 2) concerned
incidentals – Setebos, Bermuda, and Caliban's possible etymological
roots in "cannibal." But even as critics became aware of Shakespeare's
extensive familiarity with the travel literature of his day, they insisted that he meant nothing consequential; the American allusions,
they assumed, were random, incidental, almost accidental. In 1797,
Richard Sill could have been speaking for a generation of *Tempest*
interpretation when he contended that "Shakespeare has undoubtedly derived the greatest share of his ideas, as to incident,
from the narratives of discovery of the New World. He throws
them into his budget, from whence they are indiscriminately drawn
whenever he finds occasion."[1] Caliban was seldom considered one

---

1 Charles Dirrill [Richard Sill], *Remarks on Shakespeare's Tempest* (Cambridge, England:
Benjamin Flowers, 1797), p. 65.

of the American "ideas." He was, as documented in the preceding chapter, portrayed from the Restoration to the end of the eighteenth century as a quasi-human monster, even if at times the image was more benign (or, as in the Dryden-Davenant version, comical) than ferocious.

Presumptions of a bestial Caliban began to erode in the early nineteenth century, partly because assumptions about *The Tempest's* indebtedness to American colonization grew slowly more explicit and significant. In 1808, Edmond Malone argued for the crucial influence of the Bermuda pamphlets, especially Jourdain's *Discovery of the Barmudas;* these works, Malone insisted, triggered Shakespeare's imagination and provided much of *The Tempest's* narrative framework.[2] Malone said nothing about Caliban, largely because the pamphlets he championed had no obvious prototypes, but by emphasizing a New World inspiration for *The Tempest* he launched a trend that led inexorably to a reconsideration of Prospero's slave. And in 1821 his posthumous variorum edition of *The Tempest* hailed the recent suggestion of "my very learned friend Dr. Vincent, Dean of Westminster" that Antonio Pigafetta's Patagonian giant (described in Chapter 2) was "the remote progenator of the servant-monster in The Tempest." Despite the giant's obvious dissimilarity to *The Tempest's* evidence about Caliban, Malone quoted extensively from Richard Eden's second version (1577) of Pigafetta's description and concluded that "there can, I think, be little doubt that in the formation of that [Caliban] character" Shakespeare had this passage "in his thoughts." But Malone saw other sources for Caliban too – creatures in Pliny's *Natural History* and Spenser's *Faerie Queene*, with hints of the devil and Shakespeare's own Robin Goodfellow.[3]

Many nineteenth-century Shakespeareans followed Malone's lead in suggesting that Caliban might have some American roots; none made it central to his interpretation. An 1837 summary of the presumed influence on Shakespeare of American exploration literature

2 Edmond Malone, *An Account of the Incidents, from Which the Title and Part of the Story of Shakespeare's Tempest Were Derived; and Its True Date Ascertained* (London: C. & R. Baldwin, 1808), bound with an Appendix dated 21 January 1809. An expanded version of Malone's argument appears in *The Plays and Poems of William Shakspeare*, 21 vols., Vol. XV, ed. Edmond Malone (London: Rivington's, 1821), pp. 379–434.
3 Malone, ed., *Plays and Poems of Shakspeare*, Vol. XV, pp. 11–14, esp. p. 12.

endorsed Pigafetta's narrative as one of many possible sources, but
included also, with evident approval, the German scholar Schlegel's
description of Caliban as "a mixture of gnome and savage, half
daemon, half brute."[4] In 1875, A. W. Ward conjectured that
Shakespeare used Caliban partly as a satire on Montaigne's noble
savage, and a year later J. S. Phillpotts saw in Prospero's appropriation of Caliban's island a prototype of England's dispossession
of American aborigines.[5] But by and large, nineteenth-century
commentators explained Caliban in more traditional terms – "in
both soul and body, a sort of intermediate nature between man and
brute, with an infusion of something that belongs to neither[;] . . .
part man, part demon, part brute." Horace Howard Furness's
authoritative 1892 variorum *Tempest* gave appreciable attention to
Caliban, but scarcely mentioned the possibility that he had Indian
origins.[6]

I

Not until the end of the nineteenth century did a Shakespearean
contend unequivocally that Caliban was Shakespeare's portrayal
of an American native. In 1898, Sidney Lee,.a prominent English
scholar who would later be knighted for his voluminous writings
on Shakespeare and his editorship of the *Dictionary of National
Biography*, went far beyond nineteenth-century contentions that the
dramatist incorporated information from several travel books and
pamphlets. Bermuda, Lee declared in his biography of Shakespeare,
is Prospero's island, and "Caliban is an imaginary portrait, conceived with matchless vigour and vividness, of the aboriginal savage

4 *The Dramatic Works of William Shakspeare*, 10 vols., Vol. I, ed. Samuel Weller
Singer et al. (Boston: Hilliard, Gray, 1837), pp. 1–5. The quotation from Schlegel
is most readily found in Augustus William Schlegel, *A Course of Lectures on Dramatic Art and Literature*, trans. John Black, rev. A. J. Morrison (London: Henry
G. Bohn, 1846), p. 395.
5 Adolphus William Ward, *History of English Dramatic Literature to the Death of Queen
Anne*, 2 vols., Vol. I (London: Macmillan, 1875), p. 442; *The Tempest*, ed. J. Surtees
Phillpotts, "The Rugby Edition" (London: Rivington's, 1876), p. xvii.
6 *The Works of Shakespeare*, 11 vols., Vol. I, ed. H. N. Hudson (Boston: James Monroe,
1851–56), p. 9; *A New Variorum Edition of Shakespeare. Vol. IX: The Tempest*, ed.
Horace Howard Furness (Philadelphia: Lippincott, 1892), pp. v–viii, 5, 65 (n. 364),
67 (n. 379), 379–88.

of the New World."[7] During the next quarter-century, Lee became increasingly specific about Caliban's American roots. In a long article (1907) he argued that *The Tempest* was "a veritable document of early Anglo-American history" in which Shakespeare "squarely faced" the mysterious nature of the American native. "At the end of his working life, when his mental power had reached its highest stage of development," Lee wrote, "Shakespeare . . . offered the world his final conception of the place the aboriginal American filled in human economy. In Caliban he propounded an answer to the greatest of American enigmas."[8]

Lee doubted that Shakespeare had *noble* savages in mind or that any single tribe was Caliban's prototype. Instead, Lee – apparently influenced by Herbert Spencer's glosses on Darwinian theory, and reflecting an insensitivity to Native Americans that characterizes much nineteenth- and twentieth-century writing about Caliban – propounded that

Caliban is no precise presentation of any identifiable native American. He is an imaginary composite portrait, an attempt to reduce the aboriginal types of whom the dramatist and his contemporaries knew anything to one common denominator. . . . Traits of the normal tractable type of Indian to which the Virginian and Caribbean belonged freely mingled in the crucible of his [Shakespeare's] mind with those of the irredeemable savages of Patagonia. . . . Shakespeare's American is not the Arcadian innocent with whom Montaigne identifies him. He is a human being, endowed with live senses and appetites, with aptitudes for mechanical labour, with some knowledge and some control of the resources of inanimate nature and of the animal world. But his life is passed in that stage of evolutionary development which precedes the birth of moral sentiment, of intellectual perception, and social culture. He is a creature stumbling over the first stepping-stones which lead from savagery to civilization.[9]

7 Sidney Lee, *A Life of William Shakespeare* (London: Smith, Elder, 1898), p. 257. For an extensive biographical sketch of Lee, see the entry in the *Dictionary of National Biography, Supplement 1922–1930*.
8 Sidney Lee, "The Call of the West: America and Elizabethan England." Part 3: "The American Indian in Elizabethan England," *Scribner's Magazine*, 42 (1907): 313–30, esp. p. 326. Part 3 also appeared in Sidney Lee, *Elizabethan and Other Essays*, ed. Frederick S. Boas (Oxford: Clarendon Press, 1929), pp. 263–301, esp. pp. 292–93.
9 Lee, *Elizabethan and Other Essays*, pp. 295–96.

During the next two decades, Lee altered only slightly his initial interpretation of Caliban. In 1913, Lee hypothesized that Shakespeare learned about Indians not only from travel accounts but also from Indians displayed in England; the latter allowed Shakespeare to observe "at first hand the aboriginal temperament." The result was "a full-length portrait of the aboriginal inhabitant of the New World," who was fully human "but lacking moral sense, moral control, and ratiocination."[10] In the revised and enlarged edition of his *Life of William Shakespeare* (1923), Lee backed off a bit from his earlier extreme assessment of the play's American origin by acknowledging that Shakespeare probably borrowed the theme of an exiled magician from a story popular in many European nations; however, "the episode of the storm and the conception of Caliban were more obvious fruit of reported incident in recent voyages across the Atlantic Ocean. . . . Caliban was Shakespeare's ultimate conception of the true quality of aboriginal character."[11]

Joining Sidney Lee in the emerging "American school" of *Tempest* interpretation were several American and English scholars. In 1898 – the same year Lee first argued for an Indian Caliban – Reverend Frank M. Bristol of Washington, D.C. (later Episcopal bishop of Chicago) declared that *The Tempest* "has an entirely American basis and character," and Caliban "is an American." Elsewhere in his brief *Shakespeare and America*, Bristol was ambivalent, almost contradictory. After asserting that "There can be no doubt that Shakespeare had in his mind the American Indian when he conceived the character of Caliban," Bristol conceded that "the Indian element is so mixed up with elements of monstrosity as to be lost."[12] The English critic Walter Alexander Raleigh (like Lee, knighted in 1911 for distinguished scholarship) was less equivocal. "*The Tempest* is a fantasy of the New World," he insisted in 1905; "Shakespeare, almost alone, saw the problem of American settlement in a detached light." As

10 Sidney Lee, "Caliban's Visits to England," *Cornhill Magazine*, n.s., XXXIV (1913): 333–45, esp. pp. 333, 341, 343.
11 Sidney Lee, *A Life of William Shakespeare*, rev. ed. (New York: Macmillan, 1923), pp. 426, 429. A similar view, often verbatim, appears in subsequent editions of the biography and in Lee's "Caliban's Visits to England," pp. 333–45.
12 Frank M. Bristol, *Shakespeare and America* (Chicago: W. C. Hollister, 1898), pp. 82, 50–51.

illustrations, Raleigh offered the similarity of Stephano to Virginia's disreputable early settlers and the likelihood that Miranda was modeled after Roanoko Island's Virginia Dare, the first English child born in America. Caliban, Raleigh asserted, came straight from the colonization literature of Shakespeare's day:

Caliban, with his affectionate loyalty to the drunkard, his adoration of valour, his love of natural beauty and feeling for music and poetry, his hatred and superstitious fear of his task-master, and the simple cunning and savagery of his attempts at revenge and escape – all this is a composite wrought from fragments of travellers' tales, and shows a wonderfully accurate and sympathetic understanding of uncivilized man.[13]

Rudyard Kipling imagined a saltier and more specific scenario. He had recently visited Bermuda and was convinced that it was *The Tempest*'s island. Shakespeare, Kipling mused, may have gotten much of *The Tempest*'s tone from overhearing a drunken sailor's slurred story of maritime adventures, real and imagined; among the sailor's blurry recollections was, Kipling suggested, a castaway, "hiding under the ribs of a dead whale which smelt abominable." Kipling thus contributed to the Americanization of *The Tempest* and, obliquely, of Caliban.[14]

Although English writers dominated the turn-of-the-century reinterpretation of *The Tempest*, they did not monopolize it. In 1902, Edward Everett Hale, Boston clergyman and author, ignored Caliban but as staunchly defended *The Tempest*'s American affinities as anyone before or since. In a paroxysm of regional pride, Hale's paper to the American Antiquarian Society rejected Bermuda as the play's setting in favor of Cuttyhunk Island, off the coast of Cape Cod. He compared Cuttyhunk's topography, as described in several accounts of Bartholomew Gosnold's brief outpost in 1602, with that of Prospero's island; both, for example, had oaks, pines, and cedars,

13 Walter A. Raleigh, "The English Voyages of the Sixteenth Century," introduction to Richard Hakluyt, *The Principal Navigations Voyages Traffiques & Discoveries of the English Nation*, 12 vols. (Glasgow: James MacLehose & Sons, 1905–07), Vol. XII, pp. 112–13.
14 Rudyard Kipling, *How Shakespeare Came to Write the "Tempest"* (New York: Dramatic Museum of Columbia University, 1916), pp. 25–32, esp. p. 30; first published in *Spectator*, 2 July 1898.

but none of the palm and citrus trees so prevalent on southern islands. From such evidence, and on the false assumption that *The Tempest* was first performed in 1603, when Gosnold's expedition was major news, Hale asserted that "there can be no doubt that the local coloring of the 'Tempest' is in part derived from the narrative of Gosnold's adventures." Hale concluded – tongue perhaps partly in cheek – that "we have a right to claim Miranda as a Massachusetts girl." That, implicitly, made Caliban a Wampanoag Indian.[15]

II

The trend toward an American-focused interpretation of *The Tempest* by scholars on both sides of the Atlantic drew much of its inspiration from a concurrent cultural and political rapprochement between England and the United States. Throughout most of the nineteenth century, Anglo-American relations – diplomatic, social, and intellectual – had been strained, sometimes hostile. Early in the century, England still begrudged the independence of her former colonies, whereas the new republic resented Britain's domineering attitude and the continuing presence of British forts on the American frontier. Those grievances and a host of others had pitted the United States against England in the War of 1812; three years of bloodshed and destruction, followed by scattered hostilities along the Canadian border, kept tensions high until midcentury. England's failure to support wholeheartedly the American Union during the Civil War sparked new resentment, and several lesser crises after the war fueled the animosity. In 1891, Kipling observed with only slight exaggeration that America "makes a sandbag of the

15 Edward Everett Hale, "Gosnold at Cuttyhunk," *American Antiquarian Society, Proceedings*, n.s., XV (1902–03)[1904]: 98–102, reprinted with an introduction by Henry Cabot Lodge in *Prospero's Island* (New York: Dramatic Museum of Columbia University, 1919), p. 37. The key document was John Brereton, *A Brief and True Relation of the Discovery of the North Part of Virginia* (London: George Bishop, 1602). Brereton's relation and two other accounts of the Gosnold expedition are reprinted in *Massachusetts Historical Society, Collections*, 3rd ser., VIII (1843), and, with extensive annotations, in David B. Quinn and Alison M. Quinn, eds., *The English New England Voyages, 1602–1608*, Hakluyt Society Publications, 2nd ser., No. CLXI (1983). Most commentators on *The Tempest*'s sources ignore the Gosnold tracts.

mother country, and hangs her when occasion requires."[16] But eventually the mood changed. On the eve of the twentieth century, the two English-speaking democracies discovered reasons for co-operation and mutual respect.

The rapprochement is best illustrated by America's – especially Woodrow Wilson's – partiality toward Britain during the prologue to World War I, but the tendency toward Anglo-American cooperation and appreciation had been building for at least two decades before 1917.[17] On the American side, the rapprochement stemmed largely from a growing confidence in the nation's military strength, its population growth, and its industrial production. Pride in American achievements and prospects encouraged a more benevolent view of the nation's roots, especially among Americans of English descent who deplored the recent influx of immigrants from southeastern Europe. On the English side, the rapprochement reflected a recognition that in an increasingly contentious and interdependent world the United States was Britain's most plausible ally. In 1907, British ambassador James Bryce articulated the new attitude in a public tribute to Virginia's tricentennial. "In this season of fair weather," he proclaimed,

it is natural that your eyes should look back across the sea to an ancient motherland, from whom you were for a time divided by clouds of misunderstanding that have now melted away into the blue. Between you and her there is now an affection and a sympathy such as perhaps there never was before. . . . Today she rejoices with you in your prosperity and your unity. She is proud of you, and among her many achievements there is none of which she is more proud than this, that she laid the foundations of your vast and splendid Republic.[18]

16 Rudyard Kipling, *American Notes* (Boston: Brown & Co., 1899), p. 53.
17 Bradford Perkins, *The Great Rapprochement: England and the United States, 1895–1914* (New York: Atheneum, 1968), pp. 3–11, 64–88; Stuart Anderson, *Race and Rapprochement: Anglo-Saxonism and Anglo-American Relations, 1895–1904* (Rutherford, N.J.: Fairleigh Dickinson University Press, 1981), esp. pp. 11–25, 174–78. On the nineteenth-century background of Anglo-Saxon racism in America, see Reginald Horsman, *Race and Manifest Destiny: The Origins of American Racial Anglo-Saxonism* (Cambridge, Mass.: Harvard University Press, 1981).
18 James Bryce, *University and Historical Addresses: Delivered during a Residence in the United States as Ambassador of Great Britain* (New York: Macmillan, 1913), p. 12.

By the time of Bryce's panegyric, a virulent Anglo-Saxon racism had convinced the English-speaking peoples that they shared a unique superiority to all other "races" (by which they meant nationalities or ethnic groups) that mandated a common destiny of world leadership. As Bryce himself had observed in 1898, "sympathy of race . . . is a force of tremendous potency; for it affects not so much governments as the people themselves, who, both in America and in England, are the depositaries of power." This self-congratulatory ideology, according to its leading historian, "provided the primary abstract rationale" for the Anglo-American rapprochement.[19]

Among the rapprochement's many manifestations were a sharp increase in diplomatic cooperation, an economic coordination aimed at reciprocal benefits, and the formation of institutional liaisons between American and British churches. On a less significant but more conspicuous level were numerous marriages between titled Englishmen and American mercantile heiresses.[20] In the literary realm, English and American scholars suddenly remembered – or at least suddenly praised – their common intellectual roots. English readers began to appreciate American writers, and British publishers fed that new interest with editions of Nathaniel Hawthorne, Oliver Wendell Holmes, Mark Twain, Washington Irving, and others. Several young American writers gained recognition in Britain before they did at home; Gertrude Atherton and Robert Frost are illustrative. Across the Atlantic, Americans avidly read George Otto Trevelyan's histories, Mrs. Humphrey Ward's novels, and Kipling's stories.[21]

Shakespeareans on both sides of the ocean joined the celebration. Lee, Bristol, Raleigh, and Hale were soon followed by others, most notably Charles Mills Gayley, whose *Shakespeare and the Founders of Liberty in America* (1917) fused Anglo-American concerns over the World War with boundless praise for Shakespeare's influence on

19 Anderson, *Race and Rapprochement*, pp. 11–12.
20 Perkins, *Great Rapprochement*, pp. 163–87, 122–30, 151–53; Hesketh Pearson, *The Marrying Americans* (New York: Coward McCann, 1961), esp. p. 166, which reports that by 1909 more than five hundred American women had married titled foreigners. Pearson offers no separate figure for Anglo-American marriages, but relates many examples.
21 Perkins, *Great Rapprochement*, pp. 130–41.

both nations. "In this period of conflict, the sternest that the world has known," Gayley intoned,

when we have joined heart and hand with Great Britain, it may profit Americans to recall how essentially at one with Englishmen we have always been in everything that counts. That the speech, the poetry, of the race are ours and theirs in common, we know – they are Shakespeare. But that the institutions, the law and liberty, the democracy administered by the fittest, are not only theirs and ours in common, but are derived from Shakespeare's England, and are Shakespeare, too, we do not generally know.[22]

So strong was the nationalistic tug on the intellectual community that, in one case at least, it temporarily de-Americanized Caliban by identifying him with the Kaiser's Germany. In 1918, Sir Walter Raleigh, then professor of English at Oxford, delivered the annual Shakespeare Lecture to the British Academy. Revamping his earlier assessment of Caliban as "a wonderfully accurate and sympathetic understanding of uncivilized man," Raleigh, in an imaginative modernization of the first Trinculo-Stephano-Caliban scene, called the latter "an ugly low-born creature, of . . . violent criminal tendencies, a liar, and ready at any time for theft, rape, and murder." In Raleigh's wartime scenario, British soldiers nicknamed this creature "the monster, and the mooncalf, as who should say Fritz, or the Boche."[23]

Raleigh's metaphorical defection did not deter the Americanization of Caliban. Two years after Gayley, in America, had championed Anglo-American political and literary fellowship, Sir A. W. Ward gave it an implicit endorsement in his lecture to the British Academy on "Shakespeare and the Makers of Virginia." Ward praised Gayley's book, hailed the establishment of a fund for promoting cooperation in British and American historical research, and lauded the special relationship between the two English-speaking nations "not only in

22 Charles Mills Gayley, *Shakespeare and the Founders of Liberty in America* (New York: Macmillan, 1917), Preface. On Gayley, see Michael D. Bristol, *Shakespeare's America, America's Shakespeare* (London: Routledge, 1990), pp. 137–43.
23 Terence Hawkes, "Swisser-Swatter: Making a Man of English Letters," in John Drakakis, ed., *Alternative Shakespeares* (London: Methuen, 1985), pp. 35–41, esp. p. 39; Walter Alexander Raleigh, *Shakespeare and England* (British Academy annual Shakespeare Lecture) (Oxford University Press, 1918), p. 7.

127

blood but in some of the most enduring traditions of our national life." Ward listed recent publications that reflected Anglo-American cooperation, including Alexander Brown's *Genesis of the United States* and A. P. Newton's *Colonising Activities of the English Puritans*.[24] Ward might have cited as further evidence of the intellectual rapprochement the enthusiasm with which Shakespearean scholars were making *The Tempest* into an Anglo-American play, though probably neither he nor his audience was aware that they were part of a political-intellectual trend that had been under way for two decades and would continue for several more.

In 1926, Robert Ralston Cawley put a temporary capstone on the Americanization of *The Tempest*. His lengthy essay quoted, in adjacent passages, almost every imaginable parallel between *The Tempest* and the exploration narratives.[25] In addition to the familiar references to the wreck of *Sea Venture* and to the Patagonian god Setebos, Cawley documented Shakespeare's possible – often probable – sources for the island's flora and fauna, the shipwrecked party's conspiracies against Prospero, and other links between the play and its contemporaneous travel literature. "Nobody in his right mind," Cawley huffed, could doubt that Shakespeare "was aware to a considerable extent of the very language of the [exploration] narratives." Cawley also discussed at some length "the White Man and the Indian." Like the Indians, he pointed out, Caliban initially views the newcomers as gods and befriends them but is repaid with scorn and abuse; he originally owns the land but is soon dispossessed; he is taught a foreign tongue because the colonists find his own unintelligible; he acquires the European's vices rather than their virtues; he is a curio to be kidnapped and displayed in Europe for a few pence a look. Cawley, in sum, provided the specifics to support many of his predecessors' generalizations. Cawley disagreed with Lee only about the basis of Caliban's good/ evil duality. Rather than a fusion of various types of Indians, Cawley contended, the duality reflected Shakespeare's awareness of the colonists' changing attitudes: "The poet probably intended to sat-

24 A. W. Ward, *Shakespeare and the Makers of Virginia* (British Academy annual Shakespeare Lecture) (Oxford University Press, 1919), pp. 3–6, 14, esp. p. 5.
25 Robert Ralston Cawley, "Shakspere's Use of the Voyagers in *The Tempest*," *PMLA*, XLI (1926): 688–726.

irize the two extremist conceptions [initially benign, then bestial] of the people as he had those of their land."[26]

The Americanization of *The Tempest* did not go unchallenged. In the same year that Cawley codified its case, E. E. Stoll's acerbic address to the Modern Language Association accused scholars who emphasized Shakespeare's indebtedness to American events of pandering to the times. Stoll was especially contemptuous of Gayley's book:

It appeared during the war; it was no doubt prompted by the spirit of propaganda; and as often with propaganda, the end justifies the means. . . . He takes great pains to endeavor to prove acquaintance on Shakespeare's part with the promoters of colonizing in Virginia, and sympathy with their motives and aspirations – only, Shakespeare himself says not a word to that effect. Spenser, Daniel, Drayton, and the rest sing of the New World and Virginia, but not Shakespeare. So the argument recoils, and proves, if anything, the contrary.

Stoll did acknowledge a handful of verbal parallels between *The Tempest* and Elizabethan travel literature, but he considered them meaningless. Rather, Stoll insisted, "There is not a word in the *Tempest* about America or Virginia, colonies or colonizing, Indians or tomahawks, maize, mockingbirds, or tobacco. Nothing but the Bermudas, once barely mentioned as a faraway place, like Tokio or Mandalay."[27] Stoll, in the eyes of some scholars, then and later, was too literal and not entirely accurate; they find American allusions in *The Tempest* more significant than "the still vex't Bermoothes."[28] In any event, by denying *The Tempest*'s American influences, Stoll

---

26 Cawley, "Shakspere's Use of the Voyagers," pp. 714–21, esp. pp. 714, 719 (n. 20).
27 Elmer Edgar Stoll, "Certain Fallacies and Irrelevancies in the Literary Scholarship of the Day," *Studies in Philology*, XXIV (1927): 486–87. Stoll first presented this critique at the Modern Language Association convention in Cambridge, Mass., in December 1926; it was subsequently republished, with minor variations, in Stoll's collection of essays, *Poets and Playwrights: Shakespeare, Milton, Spenser, Jonson* (Minneapolis: University of Minnesota Press, 1930), pp. 210–40, esp. pp. 212–13.
28 For criticism of Stoll, see, for example, Charles Frey, "*The Tempest* and the New World," *Shakespeare Quarterly* XXX (1979): 32; and, implicitly, Peter Hulme, *Colonial Encounters: Europe and the Native Caribbean, 1492–1797* (London: Methuen, 1986), pp. 106–09.

and his followers tried to return Caliban to the earlier emphasis on Old World origins. Their efforts were largely unsuccessful. A close identification of *The Tempest* with American colonization and of Caliban with American natives was becoming axiomatic among Shakespearean scholars, largely through the efforts of Lee, Raleigh, Cawley, and the other Americanists.

Especially Lee. By stating his case so strongly (unlike most of his contemporaries he rarely equivocated and seldom acknowledged non-American prototypes) and so frequently (his biography of Shakespeare enjoyed twenty editions between 1898 and his death in 1926), Lee may have convinced a generation of Shakespeare scholars and buffs of something that their predecessors had scarcely imagined. Such influence is, of course, impossible to prove; Lee's adamant and abundant insistence on Shakespeare's indebtedness to Indian prototypes may have fallen on deaf ears. Yet he was surely read widely and cited frequently. It seems reasonable to assume that Lee's advocacy went a long way toward popularizing a new interpretation and making it acceptable among Shakespearean specialists and the general public.

It seems reasonable too – though equally unprovable – that if Lee was the proximate cause of *The Tempest*'s Americanization and Caliban's Indianization, the twentieth century's political-intellectual climate was their essential precondition, influencing Lee and his contemporaries simultaneously. The times were propitious for seeing *The Tempest* as "a veritable document of early Anglo-American history" (Lee's phrase), just as the times had not been conducive during the preceding century. The intellectual climate, in short, owed much (*how* much we can never know) to the political climate. Like all such climates, the Anglo-American rapprochement did not affect everyone: Some ignored it, some partially accepted it, and a few resistant minds rejected it altogether. But its overall influence appears to have been pervasive and persistent.

Even D. H. Lawrence, no admirer of American culture, connected Caliban to the New World. Ever the maverick, however, Lawrence's few lines about Caliban in the introductory chapter to *Studies in Classic American Literature* (1923) identified Shakespeare's monster with America's transplanted Europeans, not with its aborigines. To Lawrence, the bulk of the colonists seemed masterless: "Somewhere deep in every American heart lies a rebellion against the old parenthood of Europe." Twice Lawrence illustrated the Americans' restless search for independence with lines from Caliban's "freedom song": "Ca ca Caliban / Get a new master, be a new man." But Lawrence took minor liberties with Shakespeare's text. The Folio's *"Has a new Master, get a new Man"* (TLN 1230) did not fit the theme of restlessness quite so well as Lawrence's "Get a new master, be a new man."[29] Lawrence may have drawn unconsciously and ironically on Hector St. John de Crèvecoeur's glorification of "the American, this new man."[30] Lawrence also anticipated a trend that would emerge emphatically in the second half of the twentieth century: a more figurative use of *The Tempest* that focused on affinities between the play and New World colonization without claiming, as had Lee and others, that Shakespeare had consciously portrayed European imperialists and American Indians or that the American affinities excluded all others.

III

The new trend was eloquently inaugurated in 1960 by Leo Marx. In an article on "Shakespeare's American Fable" and, a few years later, in *The Machine in the Garden*, Marx depicted *The Tempest* as "a prologue to American literature." He found special affinities between the play and American colonization, but they were not the "external facts" – the shipwreck, the reference to Bermuda, and similar connections that had so impressed Lee, Cawley, and others. For Marx, such historical links "indicate only that Shakespeare was aware of what his countrymen were doing in the Western hemisphere." Rather, Marx stressed *The Tempest*'s action: its primitive setting, its European protagonist and his "struggle with raw nature on the one hand and the corruption within his own civilization on the other,"

29 D. H. Lawrence, *Studies in Classic American Literature* (1923; repr. New York: Viking Press, 1964), pp. 4–5. Lawrence's pejorative identification of Caliban with Caucasian Americans may have been inspired by an earlier trend among Latin American writers, especially Rubén Darío and José Enrique Rodó, though the Latin American application of the metaphor had quite different implications. For an extensive discussion of Darío and Rodó, see Chapter 6 herein.

30 J. Hector St. John de Crèvecoeur, *Letters from an American Farmer* (1782; repr. New York: Dutton, 1957), p. 39.

and the play's eventual reconciliation of nature and civilization. Marx did not argue that this sequence of events was "a uniquely American situation" but rather that America "affords a singularly vivid instance" of it.[31]

To show that early descriptions of America fit Prospero's island, Marx quoted not only from William Strachey, whose writings may well have influenced Shakespeare, but also from William Bradford, who wrote several decades after Shakespeare's death. Such an apparent anachronism was compatible with a "prophetic" rather than a literal reading of *The Tempest*:

The play, in its overall design, prefigures the design of the classic American fables. . . . Prospero's island community prefigures Jefferson's vision of an ideal Virginia, an imaginary land free both of European oppression and frontier savagery. The topography of *The Tempest* anticipates the moral geography of the American imagination.

In sum, if *The Tempest* was not written about America, America at least enacted much of what *The Tempest* prefigures. And although Marx does not explicitly identify Caliban with the Indians, the implication must have occurred to many readers. When Prospero is the emblem of European civilization and his island is a "New World Arcadia," Caliban's Indianness is correlative.[32]

If Leo Marx's Caliban is implicitly Indian, Leslie Fiedler's is explicitly (but not exclusively) Indian. Like Marx, Fiedler apparently cares less about Shakespeare's analogical intentions in the play than about the appropriateness of its emblems for subsequent American history. Writing amid the sociopolitical upheavals of the late 1960s and early 1970s, Fiedler recognizes in *The Tempest* "themes of colonialism and race."[33] The new sensitivity to the plight of minorities, espec-

---

31 Leo Marx, "Shakespeare's American Fable," *The Massachusetts Review*, II (1960): 40–71; reprinted with minor revisions in Leo Marx, *The Machine in the Garden: Technology and the Pastoral Ideal in America* (Oxford University Press, 1964), ch. 2; the quoted phrases are taken from the latter, pp. 35, 72.

32 Marx, *Machine in the Garden*, pp. 40–41, 61, 68–69, 72; Frey, "*The Tempest* and the New World," pp. 31–32. As Frey points out (p. 31), the "visionary" approach of Marx and others is more concerned with the play's posthistory than its prehistory.

33 Leslie A. Fiedler, *The Stranger in Shakespeare* (New York: Stein & Day, 1972), p. 230.

ially African Americans and Indian Americans, and a corollary suspicion of government and big business had created a congenial atmosphere for reading *The Tempest* as a paradigm of exploitation. This interpretation was not entirely new. Morton Luce's edition of *The Tempest* (1901) had already expounded the essential elements of the exploitation theme, seeing in Caliban "a dispossessed Indian, a more or less 'noble' savage." But Luce also perceived in Caliban a supernatural sea monster and an African slave. In Shakespeare's mind, Luce insisted, Caliban was first and foremost a monster; Caliban as exploited native was a subsidiary theme.[34] Half a century later, the French scholar Octave Mannoni would emphatically use Caliban as a symbol of the world's oppressed peoples, as would, slightly later, "negritude" writers of the early 1960s (more on these matters in the next chapter).[35] But Luce apparently had little impact on Fiedler and his followers, and even Mannoni and the negritude school may have been peripheral to America's revolution of the 1960s and 1970s. The political, social, and intellectual currents indigenous to those years probably provided stimulus enough.

Within that sociopolitical context, Fiedler interpreted Prospero's books as the "symbols of a literate technology with which the ruling classes of Europe controlled the subliterates of two worlds," and Prospero's suppression of the Caliban-Stephano-Trinculo plot emblemized

the whole history of imperialist America ... prophetically revealed to us in brief parable: from the initial act of expropriation through the Indian wars to the setting up of reservations, and from the beginnings of black slavery to the first revolts and evasions. With even more astonishing prescience, *The Tempest* foreshadows as well the emergence of that democracy of fugitive white slaves, deprived and cultureless refugees from a Europe they never owned. ... And it prophesies, finally, like some inspired piece of

34 *The Tempest*, ed. Morton Luce (London, Methuen, 1901), pp. xxxii–xxxix.
35 [Dominique] O. Mannoni, *Prospero and Caliban: The Psychology of Colonization*, 2nd ed., trans. Pamela Powesland (New York: Praeger, 1964); Roberto Fernández Retamar, "Caliban: Notes toward a Discussion of Culture in Our America," *The Massachusetts Review*, XV (1974): 11–16. On "negritude" writers, see Janheinz Jahn, *Neo-African Literature: A History of Black Writing*, trans. Oliver Coburn and Ursala Lehrburger (Düsseldorf-Köln, Germany, 1966; repr. New York: Grove Press, 1968), pp. 239–76. See also Chapter 6 herein.

science fiction before its time, the revolt against the printed page, the anti-Gutenberg rebellion for which Marshall McLuhan is currently a chief spokesman.[36]

Fiedler saw in Caliban not only an American Indian but also reflections of the African slave and the European wild man. A chapter on "The New World Savage as Stranger" portrays Caliban as a lusty native:

> . . . to say that Caliban was for Shakespeare an Indian means that he was a problem since the age had not been able to decide what in fact Indians were. And, in a certain sense, *The Tempest* must be understood as an attempt to answer that troubling question on the basis of both ancient preconceptions and new information about the inhabitants of the Americas. . . . [T]he point is to identify him with a kind of subhuman freak imagined in Europe even before the discovery of red men in America: the *homme sauvage* or "savage man," who, in the nightmares of Mediterranean humanists, had been endowed with sexual powers vastly in excess of their own. Such monstrous virility Shakespeare attributes to Caliban, associating him not with cannibalism, after all, but with unbridled lust.[37]

Although Fiedler identifies Caliban partly with the *homme sauvage* of medieval Europe and the Minotaur of ancient Crete ("bestial product of woman's lust to be possessed, without due rite or ceremony"), Fiedler principally sees him as a blend of several American Indian types, much as Sidney Lee had proposed three-quarters of a century earlier. Fiedler suggests that

> Caliban seems to have been created, on his historical side, by a fusion in Shakespeare's imagination of Columbus's first New World savages with Montaigne's Brazilians, Somers's native Bermudans, and those Patagonian "giants" encountered by Pigafetta.

Given this American lineage, Caliban's attempt on Miranda's virtue makes him "the first nonwhite rapist in white man's literature"; his freedom song is "the first American poem"; and when he guzzles

---

36 Fiedler, *Stranger in Shakespeare*, pp. 238–39.
37 Fiedler, *Stranger in Shakespeare*, pp. 233–34.

too much of Stephano's wine, Caliban is "the first drunken Indian in Western literature."[38]

Few modern critics are as expansive on *The Tempest*'s American connections as are Fiedler and Marx, but most take Caliban to be something of an Indian – either because it was Shakespeare's intention or because he is an appropriate signifier of New World natives. Bullough is a case in point: His Caliban is multigeneric – devil, wild man, and preternatural man – but also "a savage, enslaved Indian."[39] Charles Frey's perceptive discussion of the exploration narratives does not quite call Caliban an Indian, but in a footnote Frey refers to the "Patagonian Caliban."[40] G. M. Pinciss finds Caliban's roots in classical and medieval notions of primitive man yet concludes that "Shakespeare has made his savage a native inhabitant of the New World."[41]

Frank Kermode, the most widely acknowledged *Tempest* expert, is similarly eclectic: His Introduction to the Arden edition describes non-Indian aspects of Caliban's heritage – the natural man, the wild man – but argues too that "Caliban is a salvage man, and the West Indians were salvage men of a topical kind; hence the Indian element in this natural man." Kermode also observes that "as Lee showed, Caliban in some lights seems to be a representative Indian." And in a footnote to Act II, scene ii, Kermode explains Caliban's offer to show "every fertile inch" of the island to Stephano and Trinculo: "The colonists [in America] were frequently received with this kindess, though treachery might follow."[42]

---

38 Fiedler, *Stranger in Shakespeare*, pp. 233–34, 236–37. Fielder strays from the facts in suggesting "Somers's native Bermudans" as a prototype; there were no Indians on Bermuda in Somers's time, nor had there been earlier. The possible (but unlikely) exceptions are two Virginia Indians who may have been in the Somers expedition, en route back to America after earlier being kidnapped and taken to England. See Chapter 2, footnote 49.

39 Geoffrey Bullough, *Narrative and Dramatic Sources of Shakespeare*, 8 vols. (London: Routledge & Kegan Paul, 1957–75), Vol. VIII, p. 253.

40 Frey, "*The Tempest* and the New World," p. 37 (n. 20).

41 G. M. Pinciss, "The Savage Man in Spenser, Shakespeare and Renaissance English Drama," in G. R. Hibbard, ed., *The Elizabethan Theatre VIII, Papers Given at the English International Conference on Elizabethan Theatre . . . 1979* (Port Credit, Ontario: P. D. Meany, 1982), pp. 69–89, esp. p. 75.

42 *The Tempest*, ed. Frank Kermode, "The Arden Edition of the Works of William Shakespeare," 6th ed. (London: Methuen, 1958; repr. 1977), emphasizes Caliban

Some modern critics emphasize *The Tempest*'s American roots to the virtual exclusion of all others. David G. Nuzum argues that Shakespeare wrote *The Tempest* "in support of the Virginia Company in general and of the Bermuda [colonization] project in particular," thus giving English overseas ventures a favorable slant (in contrast to the view of his fellow playwrights) – a reading that makes Caliban, implicitly, personify the Indians.[43] Philip Brockbank declares *The Tempest* to be "a play . . . about colonization" and Caliban "[n]ot only . . . a theatrical epitome of the animal, anarchic qualities of the colonizers [but] . . . also the epitome of the primitive and uncivilized condition of the native American."[44] Jan Kott sets *The Tempest* "between Bermuda and Virginia," where Caliban, "an Indian," lives on "this American plantation."[45] To Gordon Zeeveld, Caliban is "Shakespeare's sole representation of the human population of the New World."[46] And A. L. Rowse, echoing Sidney Lee, proposes that "Caliban is . . . based on the various accounts of the American Indians coming home from the New World."[47] Of all modern advocates of Caliban-as-Indian, surely the most graphic is G. Wilson

as Indian on pages xxxiii, xxxvii–xxxix, and 67 (n. 148); for European sources, see especially pages lxii–lxiii, xxiv–xxv, and xxxiv–xlii. For other discussions (among many) of Caliban that view him, at least implicitly, as to some extent an intentional Indian, see D. G. James, *The Dream of Prospero* (Oxford: Clarendon Press, 1967), pp. 106–21; Corona Sharp, "Caliban: The Primitive Man's Evolution," *Shakespeare Studies*, XIV (1981): 268; and Paul N. Seigel, "Historical Ironies in 'The Tempest'," *Shakespeare Jahrbuch*, CXIX (1983): 107.

43 David G. Nuzum, "The London Company and *The Tempest*," *West Virginia Philological Papers*, XII (1959): 12–23.
44 Philip Brockbank, "'The Tempest': Conventions of Art and Empire," in John Russell Brown and Bernard Harris, eds., *Later Shakespeare*, Stratford-upon-Avon Studies, No. 8 (London: Edward Arnold, 1966), pp. 183–201, esp. pp. 184, 192.
45 Jan Kott, "*The Tempest*, or Repetition," *Mosaic*, X (1977): 9–36, esp. pp. 14, 19, 35. In an earlier publication, Kott seemed to deny American connections. In *Shakespeare our Contemporary*, trans. Boleslaw Taborski (Warsaw: 1962; repr. Garden City, N.Y.: Doubleday, 1964), Kott proposed that Prospero's island "was always the whole world. It is useless, therefore, to look for [its] longitude and latitude" (p. 176). Nonetheless, Kott described Caliban as "a symbol of Montaigne's good cannibals, but he is not a noble savage" (p. 197).
46 W. Gordon Zeeveld, *The Temper of Shakespeare's Thought* (New Haven, Conn.: Yale University Press, 1974), p. 250.
47 *The Annotated Shakespeare*, 3 vols. *Vol. 3: The Tragedies and Romances*, ed. A. L. Rowse (London: Clarkson N. Potter, 1978), pp. 860–64. See also A. L. Rowse, *The Elizabethans and America* (London: Macmillan, 1959), pp. 196–200.

Knight. In an essay on "Caliban as a Red Man," Knight reports that he has "concluded recent performances of my dramatic recital with a short delineation of Caliban in Red Indian guise."[48]

IV

Until recently, the Americanization of Caliban has been primarily a literary trend, fostered initially by Shakespearean specialists and subsequently by analysts of American literature.[49] In the past decade, however, just when literary critics were abandoning a literal for a figurative reading of Caliban's New World connections, English and American historians jumped on the American-school bandwagon. Histories of early English contact with America and its native inhabitants now almost invariably cite *The Tempest* as a play partly or wholly about colonization and Caliban as partly or wholly a Jacobean representation of the Indian. If the author cites an authority for this notion, it is usually Sidney Lee or Leslie Fiedler.

Two examples illustrate the current cross-disciplinary borrowing. Bernard Sheehan's *Savagism and Civility: Indians and Englishmen in Colonial Virginia* (1980) explores contrasting visions of paradise and savagery – "the ambiguities of the paradisaic vision" – through which the Old World saw the New.[50] Caliban, Sheehan suggests, epitomizes the Elizabethan-Jacobean notion of savagery – a blend of the human and the bestial, of goodness and evil. Shakespeare may have based Caliban's character on the wild-man tradition, but Prospero's slave also reflects the New World's denizens. "To Trinculo and Stephano," Sheehan maintains, "the monster Caliban is an Indian, the same sort of creature they and Shakespeare had seen exhibited more than once in London." Sheehan ends several pages

---

48 G. Wilson Knight, "Caliban as a Red Man," in Philip Edwards, Inga-Stina Ewbank, and G. K. Hunter, eds., *Shakespeare's Styles: Essays in Honor of Kenneth Muir* (Cambridge University Press, 1980), p. 219; reprinted in G. Wilson Knight, *Shakespearean Dimensions* (Sussex, U.K.: Harvester Press, 1984).

49 For a hint of Caliban as an Indian in an early historical work, see J. A. Williams, "England and the Opening of the Atlantic," in *The Cambridge History of the British Empire*, ed. J. Holland Rose et al. (Cambridge University Press, 1929; repr. 1960), p. 97.

50 Bernard Sheehan, *Savagism and Civility: Indians and Englishmen in Colonial Virginia* (Cambridge University Press, 1980), pp. 84–86.

on *The Tempest* with the assertion that Caliban "is an American savage, clearly humanoid though not fully human," who "attests to how easily the American Indians could fall victim to the European tendency to measure the New World and its people through the concept of savagism and to how readily savagism slipped into bestiality."[51]

The second example of Caliban in historians' hands is British art historian Hugh Honour's *New Golden Land* (1975). Honour holds that

Caliban, who owes his god Setebos to Pigafetta's account of Patagonia and other characteristics to Thomas Hariot's *Briefe and True Report of Virginia*, is an irredeemable "savage" no better than the degenerate, villainous nobleman, Antonio. . . . [T]he savage people of the New World prompted [Shakespeare], like Montaigne and other thinkers of the time, to reconsider what was then called "civility."

While denying that *The Tempest* is an allegory of colonialism, Honour nonetheless contends that "the lascivious Caliban . . . surely reflects the English settlers' view" of the Indians and that from Hariot's writings and John White's paintings (at least through de Bry's engraving) "Shakespeare probably drew some touches for Caliban's more amiable characteristics."[52]

Not all modern Shakespearean scholars or historians of early America subscribe to the American school. Among the former, Gareth

51 Sheehan, *Savagism and Civility*, pp. 86–88. Sheehan seems to misread Trinculo's and Stephano's identification of Caliban and the passage in which Prospero asserts that Caliban *has* a human shape.
52 Hugh Honour, *The New Golden Land: European Images of America from the Discoveries to the Present Time* (New York: Random House, 1975), pp. 66–71. For other discussions of *The Tempest* in connection with English colonization in America, see the Preface, "1611: The Tempest," in H. C. Porter, *The Inconstant Savage: England and the North American Indian, 1500–1660* (London: Gerald Duckworth, 1979); Robert F. Berkhofer, Jr., *The White Man's Indian: Images of the American Indian from Columbus to the Present* (New York: Knopf, 1978), p. 24; Gary B. Nash, *Red, White and Black: The Peoples of Early America*, 2nd ed. (Englewood Cliffs, N.J.: Prentice-Hall, 1982), p. 34; Neal Salisbury, "Prospero in New England: The Puritan Missionary as Colonist," in William Cowan, ed., *Papers of the Sixth Algonquian Conference, 1974*, National Museum of Man, Mercury Series (Ottawa: Canadian Ethnology Service, 1975), pp. 253–68. There is a hint of an American connection to *The Tempest* in Howard Mumford Jones, *O Strange New World: American Culture – The Formative Years* (New York: Viking Press, 1964), p. 107.

The American school

Lloyd Evans's Introduction to *The Tempest* does not mention America or Bermuda or Indians, and Paul A. Jorgensen harbors "a disturbing suspicion that the freedom-proclaiming, rebellious Caliban, who turns promptly from one god to another, is patterned upon the mobs in *Julius Caesar* (and of course England) and not freshly upon the latest knowledge of the American Indian."[53] Among historians who have resisted the American school's attractions, Olive Dickason (to cite a single example) is convinced by her investigation of early French accounts of the New World that Caliban is no Indian but instead "a depiction of the Wild Man in which the demonic aspects prevailed."[54] But with few exceptions, the American school has permeated *Tempest* interpretations from Sidney Lee's day through the 1980s.[55]

53 Gareth Lloyd Evans, *Shakespeare, V: 1606–1616* (Edinburgh: Oliver & Boyd, 1973); Paul A. Jorgensen, "Shakespeare's Brave New World," in Fredi Chiappelli et al., eds., *First Images of America: The Impact of the New World on the Old*, 2 vols., Vol. I (Berkeley: University of California Press, 1976), pp. 83–90, esp. p. 85. Cf. several other essays in the Chiappelli volumes that do reflect the American school, especially Stephen J. Greenblatt, "Learning to Curse: Aspects of Linguistic Colonialism in the Sixteenth Century" (Vol. II, pp. 561–80), and Arthur J. Slavin, "The American Principle from More to Locke" (Vol. I, pp. 139–64), who writes that *The Tempest* "plumbs the depths of the meaning of America, by bringing Caliban face to face with the meaning of civilization" (Vol. I, p. 147). Even Jorgensen (p. 87) adds an American touch.

54 Olive Patricia Dickason, *The Myth of the Savage: And the Beginnings of French Colonialism in the Americas* (Edmonton: University of Alberta Press, 1984), pp. 77, 299. Among other tacit dissenters to the American school are Richard Slotkin, whose brief paragraph in *Regeneration through Violence: The Mythology of the American Frontier, 1660–1860* (Middletown, Conn.: Wesleyan University Press, 1973), p. 35, suggests parallels between *The Tempest* and European colonization but associates Caliban with a Faustian lust in the conquerors rather than with Indians. See also the variety of metaphoric applications of Caliban in Richard Drinnon, *Facing West: The Metaphysics of Indian-Hating and Empire-Building* (Minneapolis: University of Minnesota Press, 1980), pp. 16, 95, 253, 267, 321. Only Drinnon's second reference conforms to the American school, and even it does not contend that Shakespeare had Indians in mind. And, not surprisingly, *The Wild Man Within: An Image in Western Thought from the Renaissance to Romanticism*, ed. Edward Dudley and Maximillian E. Novak (University of Pittsburgh Press, 1972), often mentions Caliban but never explicitly as an Indian; see pp. 29, 95–97, 101–04, 109, 310, 313.

55 For a historian's recent variation on the standard paradigm, perhaps under the influence of Leo Marx's and Leslie Fiedler's "prophetic" readings of *The Tempest*, see Ronald T. Takaki, *Iron Cages: Race and Culture in Nineteenth-Century America* (New York: Knopf, 1979), pp. 11–13. "In an uncanny way," Takaki writes, "America became a larger theatre for *The Tempest*. As it turned out, the play was

V

Whereas Lee and his disciples claimed an intentional connection between Caliban and the American Indian, and Leo Marx and others forged a metaphoric link, "new historicists" posit yet a different tie. In marked contrast to the old (and sometimes not-so-old) intentionalist readings and the newer allegorical or "visionary" approach, several commentators now focus almost exclusively on *congruities* between Shakespeare's play and its contemporaneous historical and imaginative literature.[56] Openly skeptical of claims that Shakespeare borrowed from specific texts, and implicitly indifferent to *The Tempest*'s various metaphoric applications, such critics as Peter Hulme contend that "the moment of production of *The Tempest* needs conceiving within an historical context which is not weighed down by random accumulations of supposed 'sources' or hamstrung by specious speculations concerning 'Shakespeare's mind'." Rather, Hulme seeks the text's political-literary climate – the "congeners" (James Smith's term) or the "linguistic and narrative force-field" (Charles Frey's) – that allows *The Tempest* to be seen from new and sharper angles.[57]

The breadth of perspectives opened by this approach is suggested

the thing: English fantasies of the stage were acted out in reality in the New World. As Englishmen made their 'errand into the wilderness' of America, they took lands from red Calibans and made black Calibans work for them." On the other hand, Takaki suggests (p. 11) that Caliban "could be African, American Indian, or even Asian."

56 The principal "new historicist" works treated here are Bruce Erlich, "Shakespeare's Colonial Metaphor: On the Social Function of Theatre in *The Tempest,*" *Science and Society*, XLI (1977): 43–65; Francis Barker and Peter Hulme, "Nymphs and Reapers Heavily Vanish: The Discursive Contexts of *The Tempest,*" in Drakakis, ed., *Alternative Shakespeares*, pp. 191–205; Peter Hulme, "Hurricanes in the Caribees: The Constitution of the Discourse of English Colonialism," in Francis Barker et al., eds., *1642: Literature and Power in the Seventeenth Century* (Proceedings of the Essex Conference on the Sociology of Literature, July 1980) (University of Essex, 1981), pp. 55–83; Paul Brown, "'This Thing of Darkness I Acknowledge Mine': *The Tempest* and the Discourse of Colonialism," in Jonathan Dollimore and Alan Sinfield, eds., *Political Shakespeare: New Essays in Cultural Materialism* (Ithaca, N.Y.: Cornell University Press, 1985), pp. 48–71; and Hulme, *Colonial Encounters*, ch. 3 ("Prospero and Caliban"). Greenblatt's "Learning to Curse" and Frey's "*The Tempest* and the New World" share the new interest in historical contexts and thus foreshadowed that trend.

57 Hulme, *Colonial Encounters*, p. 93.

in several recent essays. Francis Barker and Peter Hulme focus on English colonization as *"The Tempest*'s dominant discursive con-texts . . . [and] on the figure of usurpation as the nodal point of the play's imbrication into this discourse of colonialism." From this perspective, Caliban, rather than Prospero, is *The Tempest*'s dramatic center. Barker and Hulme complain that Shakespeareans have overlooked the play's complexity; instead, they say, critics heretofore have

tended to listen exclusively to Prospero's voice: after all, he speaks their language. It has been left to those who have suffered colonial usurpation to discover and map the traces of that complexity by reading in full measure Caliban's refractory place in both Prospero's play and *The Tempest*.[58]

Elsewhere, Hulme portrays *The Tempest* as the product of diverse literary and historical trends, especially "the Mediterranean and the nascent Caribee discourses." Caliban is

a Mediterranean wild man or classical monster – certainly a Polyphemus, possibly even a Minotour – with an African mother, whose pedigree leads back to Book X of the *Odyssey*. And yet at the same time he's a cannibal . . . ugly, hostile, ignorant, devilish – by birth but also having, through Sycorax, a particular connection with the moon . . . whose sign the Caribs could read, and which makes especially appropriate Caliban's particular form of monstrosity as "moon-calf."

The play's cast of characters makes the point succinctly: "Caliban, savage, deformed, slave – a multiple burden of Atlantic and Mediterranean descriptions."[59]

Paul Brown adds still another dimension to the geography of colonial discourse. Like Barker and Hulme, he proposes that familiarity with early English colonialism – its facts and literature – "will help us to establish a network of relations or discursive matrix *within and against which* an analysis of *The Tempest* becomes possible." But, Brown points out, the matrix includes Ireland as well as America;

58 Barker and Hulme, "Nymphs and Reapers," pp. 198, 204.
59 Hulme, "Hurricanes in the Caribees," p. 70; Hulme, *Colonial Encounters*, p. 108.

England's efforts to expand "the Pale" in the sixteenth and seventeenth centuries produced a lively literature about civility and incivility, mastery and masterlessness, order and disorder, that "provides the richest and most fraught discussion of colonialism at the moment of the play's inception." Brown does not advocate a rush to find *Tempest* sources in Elizabethan-Jacobean writings on Ireland, but "we should note a general analogy between text and context; specifically between Ireland and Prospero's island." The analogy has important implications for Caliban, of course: As Brown rightly observes, "the discourses regarding the Irish and the Amerindians were mutually reinforcing." Caliban, in that context, is neither Irishman nor Indian but a "savage incarnate" – a generalized reflection of "the other" in the English imperialists' drive for hegemony at home, on the nation's periphery, and overseas.[60]

In the hands of the new historicists, then, Caliban is the product of a literary and political milieu that includes but exceeds the American scene; he is an Indian and much else besides. They have simultaneously perpetuated Caliban's Americanization and expanded his genealogy. Yet in the mid-1980s, Jean Howard questioned whether the new readings of Shakespearean texts constituted a major trend in historical criticism or a new form of nostalgia.[61] More recently, a flood of *Tempest* studies prompted Meredith Skura to caution that although new historicism "has been one of the most salutary [trends] in recent years in correcting New Critical 'blindness' to history and ideology," it nonetheless "is now in danger of fostering blindness of its own."

The recent criticism not only flattens the text into the mold of colonialist discourse and eliminates what is characteristically "Shakespearean" in order to foreground what is "colonialist," but it is also – paradoxically – in danger

60 Brown, "*The Tempest* and the Discourse of Colonialism," pp. 51, 58, 57, 70 (n. 22), 62. For a critique of Brown, see Deborah Willis, "Shakespeare's *Tempest* and the Discourse of Colonialism," *Studies in English Literature, 1500–1900*, XXIX (1989): 277–89, esp. pp. 277–81, 288 (n. 11).

61 Jean E. Howard, "The New Historicism in Renaissance Studies," *English Literary Renaissance*, XVI (1986): 13–43, esp. p. 19. See also Edward Pechter, "The New Historicism and Its Discontents: Politicizing Renaissance Drama," *PMLA*, CII (1987): 292–303; Howard Felperin, "Making It 'Neo': The New Historicism and Renaissance Literature," *Textual Practice*, I (1987): 262–77.

of taking the play further from the particular historical situation in England in 1611.[62]

Before 1611, Skura argues, colonialist literary discourse was scanty and not yet self-justifying; if *The Tempest* is " 'colonialist,' it must be seen as 'prophetic' rather than descriptive." If Skura's critique is valid, it considerably diminishes the new historicists' interpretive originality.[63] In contrast to the intentionalists' acceptance of similarities in language and plot as evidence that historical texts shaped *The Tempest*, and the allegorists' perception of *The Tempest* as a prefiguration of later situations and events, the new historicists' positing of meaningful ties between the play and its contemporary colonial texts had seemed to inaugurate a third stage in the Americanization of Caliban. Skura implies that there is less distance between the allegorists and the new historicists than the latter proclaimed.

In any event, Caliban's Americanization seems likely to persist, even as a reaction sets in to the new historicists' particular reformulations of *The Tempest* and its politicoliterary context. So much of *The Tempest*'s contemporaneous literature involves New World colonization that any tally of "the common coinage" that Hulme and others identify must continue to include the early literature of American colonization, especially travel and promotional tracts, even if their precise connections to the play, and especially to Caliban, remain problematic. The new historicists have also, inadvertently, broadened the American school's ideological range. It now embraces the whole spectrum from Marxist materialists to cultural conservatives, from traditionalists to the avant-garde. In Caliban-as-Indian, diverse ideologies find a small but congenial common ground.

62 Meredith Anne Skura, "Discourse and the Individual: The Case of Colonialism in *The Tempest*," *Shakespeare Quarterly*, XL (1989): 42–69, esp. pp. 46, 47.
63 Skura, "Colonialism in *The Tempest*," p. 58.

Chapter 6
Colonial metaphors

I am subject to a tyrant . . . that by his cunning hath
cheated me of the island.

The Tempest (III.ii.40–41)

What is our history, what is our culture, if not the
history and culture of Caliban?

Roberto Fernández Retamar (1971)

A sociointellectual trend contemporaneous to the American school,
yet profoundly different in its assumptions and perspectives, has
flourished in the twentieth century outside the English-speaking
nations. Since the 1890s in Central and South America, and especially since 1950 in the Caribbean and Africa, writers from Third
World nations have contended that *The Tempest* embodies heretofore
neglected meanings for their societies and that Caliban conveys a
very different message than traditional scholarship has allowed.[1]

1 By "Third World" we mean, very loosely, "the developing countries of Asia,
Africa, and Latin America not politically aligned with Communist or Western
nations" (*American Oxford Dictionary*). We are aware of growing dissatisfaction
with the term and use it here reluctantly (in the absence of a better alternative)
because Caliban has been a frequent metaphor in Latin American and African
writings, as this chapter demonstrates, and occasionally in Asian texts; writers
from other geopolitical areas, moreover, have often applied *Tempest* metaphors
to what they identify as Third World contexts. A suggestive comment on use of
the label comes from Bapsi Sidhwa, "Third World, Our World," *The Massachusetts
Review*, XXIX (1988–89): 703–06.

Such authors – few are Shakespearean scholars, but many are distinguished in other fields – argue that Caliban is no mere fish or monster or even a North American Indian. His true significance lies instead in an emblematic identification with modern men and women, especially Latin Americans and Africans, no matter how anachronistic those identifications may seem to traditional Shakespeareans.

Authors who invoke *The Tempest* in Latin American or African contexts have differed drastically over whom or what Caliban symbolizes. Diametrical opposites are proposed: Caliban as exemplar of imperialist oppressors (the prevalent view in the late nineteenth and early twentieth centuries) or Caliban as emblem of oppressed natives (prevalent in recent decades). Advocates of the first approach found Shakespeare's monster a handy image for everything gross and vicious in a domineering nation or social class – Yankee imperialism, for example, or European racism. The second and now more widespread view stresses Caliban's implicit virtues – his innate sensitivity, rough dignity, articulateness, and intelligence – rather than his cruder characteristics. Thus recast, Caliban stands for countless victims of European imperialism and colonization. Like Caliban (so the argument goes), colonized peoples were disinherited, exploited, and subjugated. Like him, they learned a conqueror's language and perhaps that conqueror's values. Like him, they endured enslavement and contempt by European usurpers and eventually rebelled. Like him, they are torn between their indigenous culture and the culture superimposed on it by their conquerors. In sum, the Third World's image of Caliban before midcentury emphasized his foreignness, his "otherness"; since then he has been "ourselves."

The shift in Caliban's image from symbol of the oppressor to symbol of the oppressed occurred, not surprisingly, when mass movements in both Latin America and Africa brought to prominence a generation of cultural and political spokesmen who stressed indigenous heritages and national independence. Earlier Latin American intellectuals were tied emotionally and often ethnically to the Iberian Peninsula. They wrote in Spanish (or, in the case of Brazilians, in Portuguese) and looked to Europeans, especially French and Iberian intellectuals, for their ethnic identity and cultural heroes. As an Argentine scholar wrote in 1911, "Despite the [racial

145

Shakespeare's Caliban

and ethnic] mixtures, ... [o]ur spirit and our culture are Latin. But within our Latinism we belong, and will eternally belong, to the Spanish caste."[2]

For Central and South Americans as a whole, that statement was too broad; for the writer's own era of Latin American intellectuals it was essentially true. Trained in a European cultural context, and often educated in European schools, they found their symbols in European history and literature. But in recent decades, changing social forces have drastically modified the structure of Latin American intellectual life. A new generation of scholars and writers, many from non-European racial or ethnic stocks and cultural heritages, has insisted on new symbols or, at the very least, new interpretations of old symbols. Caliban is a prime example. A somewhat similar shift has occurred among African intellectuals: An earlier dependence on European education and European literature has been replaced by reemergent indigenous cultures. Along the way, Caliban has undergone a drastic interpretive change.

Either approach – Caliban as oppressor or Caliban as oppressed – differs fundamentally from traditional interpretive modes. Whereas traditional scholarship is at least partly concerned with the probable prototypes for Shakespeare's characters, most Third World authors who borrow emblems from *The Tempest* ignore, as irrelevant, Shakespeare's sources and intentions. The Third World interpretation of Caliban is symbolic, not historic; it adopts Caliban for what he represents to the observer, not for what Shakespeare may have had in mind. Few Third World exponents of *Tempest* images contend that Shakespeare expected his audience to see Caliban as a black African, brown mestizo, or white American.[3] Instead, they want

2 Manuel Gálvez, quoted in Harold Eugene Davis, *Latin American Social Thought: The History of Its Development since Independence, with Selected Readings* (University Press of Washington, D.C., 1963), p. 424. For the Spanish version, see Gálvez, *El solar de la raza* (Buenos Aires: Editorial Tor, 1936), p. 39.
3 A possible exception is Roberto Fernández Retamar, "Caliban: Notes towards a Discussion of Culture in Our America," *The Massachusetts Review*, XV (1973–74): 11–16. "There is no doubt," Fernández Retamar contends, "that *The Tempest* alludes to America, that its island is the mystification of one of our islands" (p. 15) and that "Caliban is our Carib" (p. 16). Fernández Retamar thus implies that Shakespeare intended Caliban to be a Caribbean and hence an ancestor of Latin American mestizos.

146

modern readers to accept Shakespeare's dramatic symbols because, retrospectively, they fit. New situations give the play's characters new meanings. As one exponent of Caliban metaphors explains, "The Tempest . . . presents figures that are suggestive, evocative and allusive; and it often relies on mythopoetic references for full effect. If we accept this, . . . [it has] applications appropriate for a present cultural dilemma."[4] The principal dilemma that faced users of Tempest (and especially Caliban) metaphors in the third quarter of the twentieth century was postcolonial self-fashioning.

I

Caliban's sociopolitical career has been longer and more diverse in Latin America than in Africa. He first appeared in late-nineteenth-century Spanish-American literature as a symbol of the region's political and cultural resentment of the United States. Rubén Darío, a young Nicaraguan nationalist, journalist, and poet (later also a diplomat and Nicaragua's leading intellectual), probably was the first writer to apply images from The Tempest to the Western Hemisphere's international rivalries. In 1893 he visited New York City; its crudeness, materialism, and vice convinced him that he was in "the gory, the cyclopean, the monstrous capital of the banknote," where "Caliban soaks up whiskey as he soaked up wine in Shakespeare's play."[5] Five years later, Darío's article "The Triumph of Caliban" denounced North Americans as "buffaloes with silver teeth"; "red-faced, heavy and gross . . . like animals in their hunt for the dollar."[6] That same year (1898), Paul Groussac, an Argentine writer, dubbed the early United States "Calibanesque."[7]

This casting of Caliban as a greedy, overbearing *yanqui* received major encouragement a few years later from the Uruguayan philosopher/politician José Enrique Rodó, who had recently published a

---

4 Max Dorsinville, *Caliban without Prospero: Essay on Quebec and Black Literature* (Erin, Ontario: Press Porcépic, 1974), p. 12.
5 Quoted in John T. Reid, *Spanish American Images of the United States, 1790–1960* (Gainesville: University Presses of Florida, 1977), p. 195.
6 Reid, *Spanish American Images*, p. 195. The original Spanish version, "El Triunfo de Caliban," is reprinted in *Escritos inéditos de Rubén Darío*, ed. E. K. Mapes (New York: Instituto de las Españas en los Estados Unidos, 1938), pp. 160–62.
7 Quoted in Fernández Retamar, "Caliban," p. 18.

biographical sketch of Darío. In a long essay entitled *Ariel* (1900), Rodó combined praise for Spanish-American characteristics with sharp but sophisticated criticism of the United States. Rodó structured his book as an impromptu lecture by a master teacher – affectionately called Prospero "after the wise sage of Shakespeare's 'Tempest'" – to his departing scholars, who have assembled around a bronze statue of Ariel.[8] Prospero urges his disciples to seek art, beauty, virtue, truth, and sensitivity; he warns them against materialism and utilitarianism. Sometimes implicitly, often explicitly, Prospero identifies those virtues with Spanish America or the Spanish "race," the vices with North America or the Anglo-Saxon "race."[9] Nearly a third of *Ariel* is aimed at *yanqui* shortcomings, tempered here and there by grudging praise for American achievements (mostly in the early years of the republic) and softened a bit by Rodó's affinity for generalizations and abstractions.

If *Ariel*'s target was ostensibly the United States, its intellectual inspiration was unquestionably France. Writing amid Latin America's modernist movement, Rodó and his contemporaries championed a new literary voice and a more nationalistic political stance. Yet the modernists could not wholly shed their own cultural training. While largely rejecting the Castilian tradition that had long dominated Spanish-American culture, they turned not to truly indigenous sources but to France's creative vitality. Their heroes were Victor Hugo, Baudelaire, Verlaine, and other French authors who flourished in what Latin American intellectuals believed to be the world's most free and stimulating cultural environment.[10]

Rodó's *Ariel* is a case in point. It was partly a response to Ernest Renan's dramatic epilogues to *The Tempest*. As we recounted in Chapter 4, Renan's first play, *Caliban, suite de La Tempête* (1878), ends with Caliban in command of Milan; Prospero is dead, and Ariel, rejecting human machinations, has vanished in the air to be

8 All quotations from *Ariel* in this book are from the English translation by F. J. Stimson (Boston: Houghton Mifflin, 1922). The quotation concerning Prospero is on page 3.
9 Rodó, *Ariel*, esp. pp. 89–123.
10 The modernist movement is discussed in Jean Franco, *The Modern Culture of Latin America: Society and the Artist*, rev. ed. (Harmondsworth, U.K.: Penguin Books, 1970), pp. 25–51; and Arturo Torres-Ríoseco, *The Epic of Latin American Literature* (Oxford University Press, 1942), pp. 86–132.

a universal spirit. The workaday world is left to the triumphant mob and an increasingly conservative and manipulative Caliban. The French intellectual community was not wholly sympathetic to Renan's formulation; some critics found it too cynical, too anti-democratic. Alfred Fouillée, especially, expressed philosophical dis-satisfaction. His *L'idée moderne du droit en Allemagne, en Angleterre et en France* (1878) argued that Ariel should return to the playwright's world as the necessary other dimension of Caliban; anything else, Fouillée contended, would be unjust and illogical. Renan responded with another play, *L'eau de jouvence: suite de Caliban* (1881), but it failed to fulfill Fouillée's suggestion, for in this, Renan's second epilogue to *The Tempest*, Ariel plays no significant role. Again the theme is cynical and elitist.[11]

Nearly two decades later, Rodó's *Ariel* implicity extended Fouillée's objection to Renan's pejorative dichotomy between refined aristoc-racy and utilitarian democracy. Like Fouillée, Rodó sought com-promise in the idealistic notion that social evolution would improve the human species through natural selection: Caliban's qualities would eventually merge with Ariel's as successive refinements made rough-and-tumble leaders more sensitive and intelligent. Thus, Ariel and Caliban, in Rodó's eyes, were complementary; they were con-current influences in a cultural dialectic that some day would produce an ideal civilization. Rodó hoped, in short, that Spaniards and Anglo-Saxons in America would reach "a higher concord in the future, that will be due not to a one-sided imitation of one race by the other, but to a reciprocity of influences and a skilful harmonizing of those attributes which make the peculiar glory of either race." The gentle Ariel was Rodó's symbol of Spanish-American civilization at its best, and though he refrained from blatant labeling, Rodó implied unmistakably that Caliban represented North American civilization at its worst. Ariel is "the spirituality of civilization, and the vivacity and grace of the intelligence; – the ideal end

11 Ernest Renan, *Caliban: A Philosophical Drama Continuing "The Tempest" of William Shakespeare*, trans. Eleanor Grant Vickery (New York: The Shakespeare Press, 1896), passim. For the influence on Rodó of Renan and Fouillée, see especially Gordon Brotherston's Introduction to *Ariel* (Cambridge University Press, 1967), pp. 3–7. *Ariel* mentions Renan more often than any other author, including Shakespeare.

to which human selection aspires; that superman in whom has disappeared . . . the last stubborn trace of the *Caliban,* symbol of sensuality and stupidity." Rodó feared that *yanqui* culture might overwhelm Spanish America before an amalgamation could occur. The history of the United States, Rodó presciently complained a year before Theodore Roosevelt acceded to the presidency, "is above all a very paroxysm of virile activity."[12]

Uncle Sam had, to be sure, cast greedy eyes at neighboring territories for almost a century, to the growing unease of Latin American spokesmen. Examples of Yankee expansionism abound: the annexation of Texas in 1845; the war against Mexico in 1846–48 and, at its conclusion, the confiscation of nearly one-third of Mexico's territory; frequent demands in the 1850s for the annexation of Cuba; armed encroachments in the 1880s and '90s in Central and South America and the Caribbean.[13] Thus, long before the Spanish-American War of 1898, Latin Americans feared Uncle Sam's imperialist intentions. How could they trust a nation whose secretary of state, Richard Olney, announced in 1895 that the United States was "practically sovereign on this continent, and its fiat is law upon the subjects to which it confines its interposition." Olney was ready to extend the fiat to the southern continent as well. Senator Henry Cabot Lodge, in his own mind at least, already had. In June 1895 Lodge asserted in the *North American Review* that the United States had "rightful supremacy in the Western Hemisphere."[14]

By its expansionist policy and aggressive rhetoric, the United States unwittingly encouraged the pan-Hispanic movement that began in the late nineteenth century. Earlier in the century, Latin Americans had resented Iberian colonial policies even more than North American encroachment. The resulting wars of liberation

12 Rodó, *Ariel,* passim, esp. pp. 90, 95, 63, 145, 4, 102. For a general discussion of "Arielism," see Franco, *Modern Culture,* pp. 61–70.

13 The major events in the United States' relations with Latin America can be found conveniently in Dexter Perkins, *Hands Off: A History of the Monroe Doctrine* (Boston: Little, Brown, 1941); and Samuel Flagg Bemis, *The Latin American Policy of the United States* (New York: Harcourt, Brace & World, 1943).

14 Ruhl J. Bartlett, ed., *The Record of American Diplomacy: Documents and Readings in American Foreign Relations* (New York; Knopf, 1948), p. 344; Henry Cabot Lodge, "England, Venezuela, and the Monroe Doctrine," *North American Review,* CLX (1895): 658.

Colonial metaphors

from Spanish and Portuguese control had drawn some of their inspiration from the United States' struggle for independence from Great Britain; Washington and Jefferson were hailed throughout the hemisphere.[15] But gradually "the Colossus of the North" became too powerful, too expansionist, too dictatorial. Secretary Olney's "doctrine" and Senator Lodge's bombast were prime evidence.

The clash between Spain and the United States in 1898 marked a critical juncture in the evolution of Latin America's attitude toward itself and toward its northern neighbor. Many Latin American commentators cheered the liberation of Cuba, but most resented Anglo-American intrusion in a Spanish-American affair. Their resentment grew more vociferous when the United States occupied Cuba, annexed Puerto Rico, and embarked on a prolonged war against Philippine insurrectionists. "The disaster of 1898," an American historian argues, "by which the Anglo-Saxon racial foe added several more notches to the stock of his imperialistic gun, aroused sympathy for the ancestral race and praise of its shining virtues."[16] Later the Chilean poetess and pan-Hispanic champion, Gabriela Mistral, would advocate "one Spanish-America united by two stupendous factors – the language which God gave us and the misery which the United States gives us."[17] It had been a continuing misery, exacerbated by Theodore Roosevelt's pseudolegal acquisition of the Panama Canal Zone in 1903 and his "corollary" to the Monroe Doctrine in 1904. The latter went a giant step further than Secretary Olney's earlier statement by asserting that the United States could intervene anywhere in the Western Hemisphere in cases of "[c]hronic wrongdoing, or an impotence which results in a general loosening of the ties of civilized society."[18] T.R., of course,

15 José de Onís, *The United States as Seen by Spanish American Writers, 1776–1890* (New York: Hispanic Institute in the United States, 1952), pp. 193–95.
16 Reid, *Spanish American Images*, pp. 123 (quotation), 130–31. On the pan-Hispanic movement, see also J. Fred Rippy, *Latin America in World Politics: An Outline Survey* (New York: Knopf, 1928), ch. 12.
17 Quoted in Donald Marquand Dozer, *Are We Good Neighbors? Three Decades of Inter-American Relations, 1930–1960* (Gainesville: University of Florida Press, 1959), p. 318.
18 Bartlett, ed., *Record of American Diplomacy*, p. 539. The quotation is from Roosevelt's annual message to Congress in 1904; a slightly different version appears in Roosevelt's letter to Elihu Root, quoted in Perkins, *Hands Off*, p. 238.

would be the judge of who was wrong or impotent or uncivilized. In 1904, Rubén Darío's poem "To Roosevelt" vividly expressed Latin American fears: "The United States is grand and powerful / Whenever it trembles, a profound shudder / Runs down the enormous backbone of the Andes."[19]

Against this backdrop, *Ariel*'s verbal assault on the United States and its ready acceptance by Rodó's contemporaries are not surprising. Rodó denied that his essay was an indictment of the United States, but it quickly acquired that reputation. And Rodó himself grew more critical of the United States in his later years, as continuing Yankee imperialism made Latin Americans increasingly wary of Anglo-America's intentions. Between *Ariel*'s appearance in 1900 and Rodó's death in 1917, the United States intervened often and forcefully in Mexico, Central and South America, and the Caribbean. Each event added fuel to the rhetorical fire that Rodó had ignited, and many disciples carried still further his condemnation of North American materialism and aggression; Rodó's subtle distinctions were lost in rampant Yankeephobia.[20] To South Americans, a Venezuelan writer reported in 1918, their non-Iberian northern neighbors were "rough and obtuse Calibans, swollen by brutal appetites, the enemies of all idealisms, furiously enamored of the dollar, insatiable gulpers of whiskey and sausages – swift, overwhelming, fierce, clownish."[21]

Rodó's death did nothing to dim *Ariel*'s popularity or influence. The return of the author's body to Uruguay in 1920 (he died in Italy) occasioned memorials throughout Latin America, and Rodó remains to the present a cultural hero in Spanish-speaking nations of the Western Hemisphere; in the 1940s his magnum opus was hailed as "the ethical gospel of the Spanish-speaking New World."[22] Through

19 *Selected Poems of Rubén Darío*, trans. Lysander Kemp (Austin: University of Texas Press, 1965), p. 69.
20 Brotherston, Introduction to *Ariel*, pp. 9–13; Reid, *Spanish American Images*, pp. 131, 192; Rippy, *Latin America in World Politics*, ch. 15.
21 Jesús Semprúm, quoted in Dozer, *Are We Good Neighbors?*, p. 4, from "El Norte y el Sur," *Cultura Venezolana*, I (1918): 132.
22 Torres-Ríoseco, *Epic of Latin American Literature*, p. 116. For recent reminders of Rodó's continuing influence, see James W. Symington, "Learn Latin American Culture," *New York Times*, 22 September 1984; and Jean Franco, "Coping with Caliban," *New York Times Book Review*, 22 May 1988.

more than fifty editions and countless printings, *Ariel* continues to wield enormous influence on Latin America's self-image and, especially, on its image of the United States.[23] "*Ariel*," a prominent Peruvian scholar born in 1900 attested, "we knew by heart."[24] And to know *Ariel* was almost always to subscribe to its thesis. To be sure, a few Latin American authors disagreed with Rodó's position from the outset, and a few more dissenters emerged later in the century when United States involvement in the world wars encouraged a kinder view of its idealism and industrial strength. But even then the Caliban/Ariel dichotomy remained central to Latin American imagery, and Caliban continued to symbolize the United States. During World War II, for example, another Peruvian writer couched a more benign view of Uncle Sam in the old metaphor:

Many [Latin Americans] thought they saw a spiritual antithesis between the United States, representing the vile part of Caliban, and Indo-America, playing the subtle role of Ariel. We now see that this is an exaggeration. There are many Ariels in the lands of the North and among us some Calibans who would shock Shakespeare himself.[25]

Thus the basic identities of Caliban and Ariel persisted, even if their respective characters became less distinct.

II

Despite Rodó's reputation and his book's popularity, Latin American writers in the past thirty-five years have repudiated his symbolic

23 Rodó, *Ariel*, p. v; Brotherston, Introduction to *Ariel*, p. 1. The major studies of Rodó include Victor Pérez Petit, *Rodó, su vida – su obra* (Montevideo: C. Garcia, 1937); Lauxar [Osvaldo Crispo Acosta], *Rubén Darío y José Enrique Rodó* (Montevideo: Agencia General de Libreria y Publicaciones, 1924); and Mario Benedetti, *Genio y figura de José Enrique Rodó* (Buenos Aires: Editorial Universitaria de Buenos Aires, 1966). An extensive annotated bibliography accompanies the most recent translation of Rodó's masterwork. See Margaret Sayers Peden, trans. and ed., *Ariel* (Austin: University of Texas Press, 1988), pp. 115–49; Peden lists the numerous editions of *Ariel* on pp. 115–23.
24 Luis Alberto Sánchez, quoted (with no citation) in Reid, *Spanish American Images*, p. 193.
25 Reid, *Spanish American Images*, pp. 192–98 (quotation on p. 197); translated from Manuel Seoane, *El gran vecino: América en la encrucijada*, 2nd ed. (Santiago, Chile: Editorial Orbe, 1944), p. 4.

strategy, while clinging to *Tempest* metaphors. Partly in response to Latin America's turn-of-the-century emphasis on cultural unity, partly as a reaction against a sudden influx of non-Iberian immigrants, and largely, perhaps, in belated recognition that most of the continent's population was not of European background, truly indigenous cultures reemerged throughout Latin America in the 1920s and '30s.[26] In a dramatic and perhaps inevitable transformation, Caliban at the same time became the emblem of exploited Latin Americans, and Prospero took on the menacing visage of Uncle Sam. Ariel again silently disappeared.

The reasons for the eventual rejection of Rodó's imagery are partly explained by *Ariel* itself. Despite the book's staunch advocacy of Latin American independence and spiritual superiority, it is palpably Eurocentric, with scarcely a nod toward the Western Hemisphere's cultural achievements.[27] The great heritage to which Rodó appeals throughout the essay is European and classical. His cultural pantheon includes Plato, Aristotle, and Cicero among the ancients; Taine, Bourget, and Comte among the moderns. At bottom, Rodó's vision of the clash between Latin America and the United States pits the Latin branch of the western tradition against the Anglo-Saxon branch – hardly a compelling vision for those who traced their heritage to American Indian or African roots. Consequently, the image of Caliban that Darío and Rodó used with such success in the late nineteenth and early twentieth centuries collapsed when the old intellectual elite lost its monopoly on Latin American cultural and political leadership. New leaders lauded a different heritage. In the words of a modern Cuban writer, "[O]ur culture – taking this term in its broad historical and anthropological sense – [is] . . . the culture created by the *mestizo* populace, those descendents of Indians and Blacks and Europeans . . . the culture of the exploited classes."[28] But if the reversal of Rodó's Ariel/Caliban metaphor was emphatic, it was also respectful. An authority on Rodó epitomized the twentieth-century shift in Latin American perspective when he observed that

---

26 Franco, *Modern Culture of Latin America*, pp. 82–140. In the visual arts, the emergent culture is perhaps best typified by Diego Rivera's murals.

27 Rodó's affinity for European culture is partly explained by his own family's recent migration to Uruguay; his father was a Catalan emigré.

28 Fernández Retamar, "Caliban," pp. 58–59.

Colonial metaphors

"Perhaps Rodó erred in naming the danger [to Latin America], but he did not err in his perception of where it lay."[29]

Caliban's metamorphosis had begun, arguably, in 1928, when Jean Guéhenno's *Calibán Parle* (1928) portrayed him more sympathetically than had earlier works. But the influence of Guéhenno, a French writer, on his Latin American contemporaries seems to have been slight on this matter, perhaps because he, like Rodó, was largely concerned with refuting Renan's extension of *The Tempest*.[30] Similarly, Argentinian Aníbal Ponce's *Humanismo burgués y humanismo proletario* (1938) favorably identified Caliban with the exploited masses in partial refutation of Renan; Ponce, too, had little overt influence on the Caliban metaphor.[31] But in 1950, Caliban's image shifted radically. The impetus was another French contribution: the publication in Paris of Octave Mannoni's *La psychologie de la colonisation*, translated into English in 1956 as *Prospero and Caliban: The Psychology of Colonization*.[32] Because Mannoni wrote about the African island of Madagascar, rather than the Americas, consideration of his argument and impact belongs elsewhere in this chapter.[33] Suffice it to say here that Mannoni forcefully and explicitly identified Caliban with colonized and exploited people in general, thereby making Prospero's slave an inappropriate symbol for the European-American population of the United States but eminently appropriate for many Latin Americans.

In the 1960s and '70s, West Indian writers, especially, and some Latin Americans avidly adopted Mannoni's imagery. In 1969, for

---

29 Benedetti, *Genio y figura de Rodó*, p. 95.
30 Jean Guéhenno, *Calibán Parle* (Paris: Bernard Grasset, 1928), passim. Guéhenno returned to this theme in *Caliban et Prospero: suivi d'autres essais* (Paris: Gallimard, 1969). For a claim that Rodó himself foreshadowed the reversal of Caliban images, see Emir Rodríguez Monegal, "The Metamorphoses of Caliban," *Diacritics*, VII (Fall 1977): 78–83, esp. p. 81.
31 Aníbal Ponce, *Humanismo burgués y humanismo proletario* (México: Editorial América, 1938). See also Rodrigo Garcia Treviño, *Aníbal Ponce el intelectual y el revolutionario* (México: Editorial América, 1938).
32 [Dominique] O. Mannoni, *Prospero and Caliban: The Psychology of Colonization*, 2nd ed., trans. Pamela Powesland (New York: Praeger, 1964). The importance of Mannoni and the emergence of *Tempest* metaphors in anticolonial literature are thoughtfully explored by Rob Nixon, "Caribbean and African Appropriations of *The Tempest*," *Critical Inquiry*, XIII (1986–87): 557–78, esp. pp. 562–66.
33 See Section III in this chapter.

155

example, three Caribbean authors – each perhaps unaware of the others' work in progress and each writing in a different language – drew on *The Tempest* metaphor. Aimé Césaire of Martinique published in French an adaptation of *The Tempest* for "un théâtre nègre"; his Caliban and Ariel are both slaves – the former black, the latter mulatto.[34] Simultaneously, the Barbadian poet Edward Kamau Brathwaite wrote in English a collection of poetry entitled *Islands*; one of the poems is "Caliban."[35] And in Cuba, Roberto Fernández Retamar, writing in Spanish, identified Caliban with the Cuban people in an essay on Fidel Castro.[36] Two years later (1971), Fernández Retamar's book *Caliban* explicitly and emphatically rejected José Rodó's formulation:

> Our symbol . . . is not Ariel, as Rodó thought, but Caliban. This is something that we, the *mestizo* inhabitants of these same isles where Caliban lived, see with particular clarity: Prospero invaded the islands, killed our ancestors, enslaved Caliban, and taught him his language to make himself understood. What else can Caliban do but use that same language – today he has no other – to curse him, to wish that the "red plague" would fall on him? I know no other metaphor more expressive of our cultural situation, of our reality. . . . [W]hat is our history, what is our culture, if not the history and culture of Caliban?[37]

Fernández Retamar's declaration, originally in Spanish, reappeared in English in 1974 in a special issue of *The Massachusetts*

---

34 Aimé Césaire, *Une tempête; d'apres "La tempête" de Shakespeare. Adaptation pour un théâtre nègre* (Paris: Editions du Seuil, 1969).

35 Edward Kamau Brathwaite, *Islands* (Oxford University Press, 1969).

36 Roberto Fernández Retamar, "Cuba hasta Fidel," *Bohemia*, 19 September 1969.

37 Fernández Retamar first published this statement in an article, "Caliban," in *Casa de Las Américas*, LXVIII (September-October 1971), and soon after in *Caliban: apuntes sobre la cultura en nuestra America* (México: Editorial Diogenes, 1971). It reappeared in an English translation – with minor variations – in *The Massachusetts Review*, XV (1973–74): 24; we quote from this version. For commentary, see Marta E. Sánchez, "Caliban: The New Latin-American Protagonist of *The Tempest*," *Diacritics*, VI (1976): 54–61; Rodríguez Monegal, "Metamorphoses of Caliban," pp. 79–81; "Roberto Fernández-Retamar: Caliban y La Literatura de Nuestura America," *ECOS: A Latino Journal of People's Culture & Literature*, Series in Cultural and Literary Theory, No. 1 (University of Illinois at Chicago, 1985); and Fernández Retamar, "Caliban Revisited," in his *Caliban and Other Essays*, trans. Edward Baker (Minneapolis: University of Minnesota Press, 1989), pp. 46–55.

Colonial metaphors

Review. The entire issue is entitled *Caliban* and is devoted to Latin American cultural expression. Guest editor Robert Márquez described the issue's purpose:

The stories, poems, play, essays and art work collected in this issue are . . . a contemporary echo of the rebellious Antillean slave in Shakespeare's final play. . . . [Caliban is a symbol of] a struggle for liberation and cultural authenticity whose roots must be traced back, from Salvador Allende, Che Guevara, and Toussaint L'Ouverture, to the original revolts of indigenous Indians and Black slaves. . . . Against the hegemonic, europocentric, vision of the universe, the identity of Caliban is a direct function of his refusal to accept – on any level – that hegemony. . . . This, then, . . . a fragment of the world-view of the victim, is the world of Caliban.[38]

In the years since that pathmark issue of *The Massachusetts Review*, the identification of Shakespeare's monster/slave with the dark-skinned peoples of Latin America has remained firmly entrenched in the region's cultural and political rhetoric. Recently, Brathwaite has added new dimensions to *The Tempest* metaphor in a history of the 1831–32 Jamaica slave revolt: Not only is Prospero the slave owner, Ariel the partially assimilated mulatto, and Caliban the rebel slave, but Alonso now symbolizes the British Parliament and Gonzalo the humanitarian but misguided missionaries.[39]

III

Robert Márquez's 1974 tracing of Caliban's ancestry to Indians and black slaves appeared to limit Caliban's physical sphere to the New World and Caliban's symbolic identity to its exploited inhabitants, whether aboriginal or imported from Africa. But other writers, especially Caribbeans of primarily African descent and native African writers of various nationalities, prescribe no geographic limits to the Prospero/Caliban metaphor. As Fernández Retamar acknowledged

---

38 Robert Márquez, "Foreword," *The Massachusetts Review*, XV (1973–74): 6.
39 Edward Kamau Brathwaite, "Caliban, Ariel, and Unprospero in the Conflict of Creolization: A Study of the Slave Revolt in Jamaica in 1831–32," in Vera Rubin and Arthur Tuden, eds., *Comparative Perspectives on Slavery in New World Plantation Societies* (New York Academy of Sciences, 1977), pp. 41–62, esp. p. 46.

nearly two decades ago, "The new reading of *The Tempest* has now become a common one throughout the colonial world."[40] Accordingly, Caliban is as much at home on the African continent as anywhere.

Caliban-as-African, much like Caliban-as-Latin American, endured an early identification with the oppressors rather than the oppressed and then experienced a parallel metamorphosis. In 1930 a South African journalist of English background, Leonard Barnes, published *Caliban in Africa: An Impression of Colour-Madness.*[41] Barnes's title page carried as epigram Trinculo's thoughts on first seeing Caliban:

What have we here? a man or a fish? dead or alive? A fish: he smells like a fish; a very ancient and fish-like smell; a kind of not the newest Poor-John. A strange fish!

Those lines appear at first glance to be a slur on black Africans; the racist attitudes prevalent throughout England and America in the 1920s and '30s encouraged such a reading. Barnes, however, had no such intent. He attacked, virtually slandered, certain Africans, to be sure, but not the blacks. The targets of his wrath were instead the Dutch Afrikaners – the creators and enforcers of apartheid. That system of racial segregation and the white-supremacist doctrine on which it is based are, Barnes contended, "worthy of the freckled whelp of Sycorax." In his only other specific reference to Shakespeare's monster, Barnes excoriated "several features in the characteristic Dutch outlook which no civilised person, whatever his nationality, can look upon with anything but contempt – for instance, the attitude to animals and persons of colour, and a certain deep intellectual insincerity," which, "like other Calibanesque traits . . . are things which good natures cannot abide to be with."[42]

Barnes drew few other *Tempest* parallels. He apparently assumed that his readers would readily recognize Caliban as a symbol of cruelty, stupidity, and sloth – the qualities he attributed to a major

40 Fernández Retamar, "Caliban," p. 24 (n. 29).
41 Leonard Barnes, *Caliban in Africa: An Impression of Colour-Madness* (London: Victor Gollancz, 1930).
42 Barnes, *Caliban in Africa*, pp. 118, 54.

segment of South Africa's white minority.[43] Thus, by 1930, Caliban's image had reached its nadir: Most metaphorical applications of *The Tempest* identified Caliban with the world's oppressors. Darío's and Rodó's *yanqui* Caliban and Barnes's Afrikaner Caliban held sway.

Twenty years later, Mannoni first identified Caliban with *black* Africans. His controversial *Prospero and Caliban* sought no connections between Shakespeare's intentions and Africans; rather, he borrowed symbols from *The Tempest* (and, less extensively, from *Robinson Crusoe*) to illustrate what he believed were Madagascan – indeed universal – personality types. Mannoni, a French psychoanalyst and social scientist who for several years in the 1940s headed France's General Information Department in Madagascar, was struck by European imperialism's profound and insidious impact yet perplexed by the Madagascan uprising of 1947–48. He expounded his analysis in a multipart "Ebauche d'une psychologie coloniale" in the French periodical *Psyché* in the late 1940s,[44] but not until he gathered and expanded the essays in 1950 did Mannoni apply *Tempest* signifiers, and not until the English-language editions of 1956 and 1964 were those signifiers highlighted in the book's title.

Mannoni's analysis of the Madagascan crisis proposed that colonial situations produce two basic personality types, which Prospero and Caliban conveniently represent: Colonials (Prosperos) tend to be competitive, to crave power, to lack patience – else they would have remained at home – and to seek an outlet overseas for their energies, their ambitions, and their deep insecurities. They become colonials partly because they are psychologically immature. "[I]f my analysis is correct," Mannoni hypothesized, "no one becomes a real colonial who is not impelled by infantile complexes which were not properly resolved in adolescence." Once in the colonial situation, Prosperos treat the people they rule as objects, as inferiors they

---

43 Barnes's book is discussed briefly in Charlotte H. Bruner, "The Meaning of Caliban in Black Literature Today," *Comparative Literature Studies*, XIII (1976): 240–53. This generally accurate and useful article somewhat misinterprets Barnes's use of the Caliban metaphor; he does not identify Caliban with black Africans.

44 See especially O. Mannoni, "Ebauche d'une psychologie coloniale," *Psyché*, II (1947): 1229–42, 1453–79; III (1948): 93–96. Mannoni's invocations of Daniel Defoe and Shakespeare appear most prominently in the central chapter, "Crusoe and Prospero," in Mannoni, *Prospero and Caliban*.

can control through the magic of technology, written language, and political authority. Calibans, of course, are the natives, who resent colonial rule but have little choice; they become dependent on Prosperos, even grateful to them sometimes, for bringing material and educational "progress."[45] Initially, Prospero may befriend the native – recall Caliban's plaintive "When thou cam'st first, / Thou strok'st me and made much of me . . . / and then I loved thee . . ." (I.ii.332–36). Soon the mood changes; Prospero becomes an exploiter, rather than a benefactor, and eventually almost ignores the native. Prospero's rejection of Caliban makes the native dependent, insecure, and in his own eyes inferior. The dependency created during the early years of colonization also leaves Caliban hopelessly enmeshed in a system not of his own making but essential to his survival.[46] Mannoni's characterization of the Malagasies is, admittedly, far more complex than this brief summary suggests, but two points about his paradigm should be apparent: First, Caliban is an African native – or indeed the native of any nation or continent subjugated by European Prosperos – and, second, he is a rather passive, obedient chap. The former conclusion has been widely accepted by Mannoni's admirers and detractors alike; the latter has generally been rejected, or at least modified, especially by black authors in the 1960s and '70s.[47]

If Mannoni's book was a major force in the transformation of Caliban as the oppressor to Caliban as the oppressed, some of the credit must go to Philip Mason, a longtime British civil servant in India and Africa and later director of the United Kingdom's Institute

45 Mannoni, *Prospero and Caliban*, pp. 97–98, 104–09, quotation on p. 104. Some of the themes developed by Mannoni appear also in Albert Memmi, *The Colonizer and the Colonized*, trans. Howard Greenfeld (Corrêa: 1957; repr. Boston: Beacon Press, 1967), without *Tempest* metaphors.

46 Mannoni, *Prospero and Caliban*, pp. 106–09, 128–31.

47 For sharp criticism of Mannoni's interpretation by a Third World author, see Aimé Césaire, *Discourse on Colonialism*, trans. Joan Pinkham (New York: Monthly Review Press, 1972), pp. 39–43. Mannoni explained the genesis of his thesis and briefly responded to some of its critics in prefaces to the 1956 and 1964 editions of *Prospero and Caliban* and in "The Decolonization of Myself," *Race*, VII (1966): 327–35. For trenchant criticism of Mannoni's understanding of racial dynamics in Madagascar, see the Foreword by Maurice Bloch to O. Mannoni, *Prospero and Caliban: The Psychology of Colonization* (Ann Arbor: University of Michigan Press, 1990).

of Race Relations. Mason wrote a Foreword to the American edition of *Prospero and Caliban* and later, in his own *Prospero's Magic: Some Thoughts on Race and Color* (1962), devoted considerable attention and praise to Mannoni's metaphor.[48] In some respects, Mason applies *Tempest* symbolism more globally and explicitly than did Mannoni – to India and Asia as well as Africa and America – and gives Shakespeare's characters modern roles. "Ariel is . . . the good native, the moderate nationalist, the gradualist, usually content to wait until it pleases Prospero to give him his freedom; . . . one quite expects Prospero to offer him a knighthood." Caliban, on the other hand, "is the bad native, the nationalist, the extremist – the man who will be Prime Minister after independence. He has to be shut up, . . . not for making seditious speeches but for wanting to violate Miranda." Mason halts his metaphorical flight at that point. "Here I think I must draw the line," he demurs, "and resist any further temptation to make a parlour game of analogies with colonialism; Shakespeare was not gifted with second sight and did not foresee the colonial situation."[49]

Probably not, but the power of Mannoni's adaptation of *The Tempest* has not diminished. Critics continue to address it, although few, including Mason, accept all its implications. Mason, for example, points out that Madagascar is unrepresentative in many ways of colonial situations, particularly in the character of French colonialism and in the nature of Malagasy culture. Still, Mason believes the archetypes in *Prospero and Caliban* are generally valid.[50] So does Frantz Fanon, of Martinique, whose *Black Skins, White Masks* (1952) devotes a chapter to "The So-Called Dependency Complex of Colonized Peoples." But Fanon objects emphatically to Mannoni's minimization of racism's impact on the Malagasies and his denial of the economic motives in colonization; Fanon sees the Malagasy dependency complex as a product of white colonization, not of any innate or culture-inspired condition. In short, Fanon accepts the Caliban characterization but attributes it to Prospero's tyranny rather

48 Mason, "Foreword" to Mannoni, *Prospero and Caliban*, pp. 9–15; Philip Mason, *Prospero's Magic: Some Thoughts on Class and Race* (Oxford University Press, 1962), pp. 78–79.
49 Mason, *Prospero's Magic*, pp. 88–89.
50 Mason, *Prospero's Magic*, pp. 78–81.

than Caliban's nature. Prospero is even more villainous for Fanon than he was for Mannoni.[51]

The shift in the personification of evil from Caliban to Prospero (and, almost unconsciously, the virtual exclusion of Ariel from contemporary symbolism) is, of course, essential to the reversal in Caliban's role from oppressor to oppressed. If Caliban is hero, Prospero must be villain. As Mason pointed out in 1962, "in my country until a generation ago we liked Prospero"; now, however, "some of us are beginning not to like him. . . . [W]e are perhaps moving towards some new conception of authority, in the family, in the state, and in international affairs."[52] That movement was inaugurated, or at least appreciably stimulated, by Aimé Césaire's *Une Tempête*. "To me," Césaire declared, "Prospero is the complete totalitarian. I am always surprised when others consider him the wise man who 'forgives.' . . . Prospero is the man of cold reason, the man of methodical conquest – in other words, a portrait of the 'enlightened' European." For Césaire, as for most Third World writers who now employ *Tempest* metaphors, the corollary of a totalitarian Prospero is an antiauthoritarian Caliban: "a rebel – the positive hero, in a Hegelian sense. The slave is always more important than his master – for it is the slave who makes history."[53]

IV

The Third World's adoption of Caliban is ironic. Although he readily symbolizes its oppressed and exploited peoples, he originally was a European construct – the product of an English imagination. Why, then, does Shakespeare's savage appeal so widely and profoundly

51 Frantz Fanon, *Black Skins, White Masks*, trans. Charles Lam Markmann (Paris: 1952; repr. New York: Grove Press, 1967), pp. 83–108, esp. p. 108.

52 Mason, *Prospero's Magic*, p. 96. For a thoughtful exploration of some recent literature on this theme, see Thomas Cartelli, "Prospero in Africa: *The Tempest* as Colonialist Text and Pretext," in Jean E. Howard and Marion F. O'Connor, eds., *Shakespeare Reproduced: The Text in History and Ideology* (London: Methuen, 1987), pp. 99–115.

53 S. Belhassen, "Aimé Césaire's *A Tempest*," in Lee Baxandall, ed., *Radical Perspectives in the Arts* (Middlesex, U.K.: Penguin, 1972), p. 176. See also Thomas A. Hale, "Sur *Une Tempête* d'Aimé Césaire," *Etudes Littéraires*, VI (1973): 21–34; Roger Toumson, *Trois Calibans* (Habana: Casa de las Américas, 1981), pp. 301–486; and Nixon, "Appropriations of *The Tempest*," pp. 570–73.

to such a variety of non-English ethnic groups and nationalities? Part of the explanation is certainly Shakespeare's international fame: His plays and characters are almost as familiar to people from the Third World as to those from western nations. An authority on Nigeria reported in 1958 that "it is not uncommon to find a semi-educated Nigerian . . . who can . . . quote the Bible, and recite Hamlet."[54] Moreover, for Africans especially, a close knowledge of Shakespeare often is a mark of superior training and wisdom. As one black scholar observes, among Africans the ability to quote abundantly from Shakespeare is both a sign of a cultured mind and an eloquent refutation of the white-racist assumption that blacks are intellectually inferior.[55] And perhaps, an authority on African literature suggests, Shakespearean rhythms fit especially well with the cadences and tones of African linguistic traditions and with a widespread affinity for proverbs; Shakespeare is accordingly quoted often in African political and cultural dialogue.[56] Thus, African writers readily employ Caliban as an effective rhetorical device, though usually – unlike some Caribbean authors – with profound undercurrents of ambivalence toward an alien symbol.[57]

Perhaps too – and this is more speculative – Caliban is attractive to some authors because of the etymological identification of Shakespeare's savage with Caribbean or African settings through his supposed derivation from "cannibal." The evidence for that etymology is unproven at best, but it is widely held (as we suggested in Chapter 2) and even stated as a truism by scores of Shakespearean specialists.[58] Again, however, the connection is ironic, for the image it calls up is surely pejorative. Third World authors, of course, rarely take the cannibal connection literally.[59] Rather, they find

54 Ali A. Mazrui, "Some Sociopolitical Functions of English Literature in Africa," in Joshua A. Fishman, Charles A. Ferguson, and Jyotirinda Das Gupta, eds., Language Problems of Developing Nations (New York: Wiley, 1968), pp. 183–97, esp. pp. 185–86, 190 (quotation), 193; Bruner, "Meaning of Caliban," pp. 240–41.

55 Mazrui, "Some Sociopolitical Functions," pp. 185–87.

56 Bruner, "Meaning of Caliban," p. 241; Mazrui, "Some Sociopolitical Functions," pp. 187–90.

57 We are indebted to Lemuel A. Johnson for pointing out the variety of ironies that pervades African uses of Caliban.

58 See especially Chapter 5.

59 Cf. the discussion of Oswald de Andrade in Rodríguez Monegal, "Metamorphoses of Caliban," pp. 82–83.

in Caliban's possible etymology further evidence of the imperialist mentality that let Prospero seize the island, enslave Caliban, and announce (through Miranda) that the native is immune to "any print of goodness" (I.ii.351).

Perhaps these are adequate justifications for the Caliban metaphor's popularity among African writers. But a more basic reason is undoubtedly its typification of a major phase of their modern history. If Caribbeans could see in Prospero the embodiment of European and North American imperialism, and could see in Caliban a symbol of themselves, Africans were likely to make comparable identifications. From the dawn of Europe's overseas expansion in the sixteenth century (even earlier in North Africa, of course), Africans suffered a host of invasions, initially economic but increasingly political, military, and cultural. The slave trade was only the most obvious and traumatic of European assaults on Africa. By the end of the nineteenth century, western Europe controlled most of the African continent. Foreigners ran the governments, the industries, the churches, the schools; natives worked the mines, tilled the fields, fetched the wood. The African liberation movements of recent decades ended European hegemony and revived indigenous cultures; they also fostered open resentment of the former "masters" and the alien literatures imposed by the imperialists on the native populations. Many African writers, not surprisingly, adopted the anticolonial *Tempest* metaphors that were gaining currency in the West Indies and Latin America and that Mannoni had applied so forcefully to neighboring Madagascar.

For a variety of reasons, then, Caliban has been prominent in African prose and poetry, especially in the third quarter of the twentieth century. For example, Raphael E. G. Armattoe of Ghana includes in his collection of poems, *Deep down the Blackman's Mind,* these sentiments:

> We have a new freedom, a new mistress
> Not with lines nor with curves nor symmetry
> Nor with brains nor great talents encumbered:
> She is Africa with her terror and her norms.
> All that in Hades or in Inferno lives
> Which Caliban has made his own beneath the seas

Plainness beyond despair, folly to the *nth*,
All these are found in our Hesperides.[60]

A second example: In the early 1970s, Lemuel Johnson of Sierra Leone titled his collected poems *Highlife for Caliban*. Several of the poems have Shakespearean motifs, but they scarcely mention Shakespeare's savage; even "Calipso for Caliban" never uses the name, although it mentions "papa prospero." Johnson clearly expected his readers – Africans and others – to recognize his emblemization of Caliban nonetheless.[61]

A final example: Taban lo Liyong of Uganda, also writing in the early 1970s, applied *The Tempest* metaphor explicitly and ironically:

> Bill Shakespeare
> Did create a character called Caliban
> The unwilling servant of Prospero,
>
> . . . .
> One thing about Caliban: he was taught language
> And what a potful of curses he contained!
> . . . .
> (By the way,
> I am also called Taban
> Very near to Caliban
> And was taught language
> And what do I do with it
> But to curse, in my own way?)[62]

---

60 Raphael E. G. Armattoe, *Deep down the Blackman's Mind* (North Devon, U.K.: 1954; repr. Nendeln, Netherlands: Kraus, 1973), p. 59.

61 Lemuel A. Johnson, *Highlife for Caliban* (Ann Arbor, Mich.: Ardis, 1973), pp. 33–35, with an Afterword by Sylvia Wynter, pp. 129–56, that underscores the ambiguity of the Caliban symbol in Johnson's poetry. See also Bruner, "Meaning of Caliban," pp. 248–49. Johnson further explicates and undermines the symbol in a manu-script essay entitled "Shoeing the Mule: Caliban as Genderized Response." For additional comments on Johnson, see Chapter 10.

62 Taban lo Liyong, *Frantz Fanon's Uneven Ribs: With Poems More and More* (London: Heinemann, 1971), p. 41; another reference to Caliban is on p. 68. For other in-vocations of Caliban by African writers contemporary with the three quoted here, see Ngugi Wa Thiong'o (of Kenya), *Homecoming: Essays on African and Caribbean Literature, Culture and Politics* (New York: Lawrence Hill, 1973), pp. 7–9; and especially David Wallace (of Zambia), *Do You Love Me Master?* (Lusaka, Zambia: National Educational Company, 1977). The latter work, a play that draws exten-sively on *The Tempest*, was first performed in 1971.

Taban lo Liyong's final lines are, of course, a paraphrase of Caliban's "You taught me language; and my profit on't / Is know how to curse. The red plague rid you / For learning me your language!" (I.ii.362–64). The irony and poignancy of that passage has intrigued many critics: Prospero's legacy to Caliban is not a glorious new way to express his finest thoughts but merely the means to curse his own fate and his oppressor's power. Civilization's most basic cultural tool is no gift at all. (Some of Caliban's subsequent lines arguably are among Shakespeare's most eloquent. But on balance, Caliban insists, he gained little from Prospero's language.) Until the middle of the twentieth century, most Shakespearean critics implicitly sided with Prospero on this issue, blaming Caliban for his own linguistic limitations: His warped nature was impervious to nurture's lessons.[63] Even the early-twentieth-century advocates of the Caliban metaphor at least implied that Caliban was a linguistic boor when they chose him to symbolize imperialistic Anglo-Americans or overbearing Afrikaners.

But language as a key to the special relationship between Prospero and Caliban took a new turn in 1960 when the Barbadian novelist and poet George Lamming, in a largely autobiographical reassessment of Caliban as the victim of cultural imperialism, suggested that language was Caliban's "prison." Through language, Prospero controls the monster's present and limits his future – "the first important achievement of the colonising process." "This gift of Language meant not English, in particular, but speech and concept as a way, a method, a necessary avenue towards areas of the self which could not be reached in any other way." Language is necessary to expression, and expression is essential to change, but it is Prospero's language and therefore largely Prospero's vision of the future that Caliban must accept. And yet language is always problematic, giving voice unexpectedly to hidden hopes. As John Pepper Clark observed a decade after Lamming first raised the issue, Caliban "is as much drunk with his second language [before Prospero's arrival he presumably communicated well enough with

63 See, for example, Edmond Malone, ed. *The Plays and Poems of William Shakspeare,* Vol. XV (London: Rivington et al., 1821), pp. 13–14.

Sycorax] ... as he is with the heady wine Stephano serves him."[64] Caliban, in short, is victimized both physically and culturally, yet he has a new weapon of resistance. This privileging of language as a crucial form of Prospero's control over the native – a theme reiterated in Lamming's novel *Water with Berries* (1971) and in several subsequent Caribbean and African works – led critics to broaden their understanding of the colonial process and of indigenous responses. For all victims of cultural imperialism, but especially for societies without a common language, "language is power" had particular poignancy.

The German authority on "neo-African" literature, Janheinz Jahn, added an important codicil to the trend by interpreting Prospero's gift of language as liberating rather than confining. Jahn, like Philip Mason, is wary of reading too much into an early Jacobean play; he is unwilling "to drag Shakespeare into modern controversies or credit him with ideas some way ahead of his time!" Still, Jahn finds the Prospero-Caliban "parallel" irresistible, and he readily follows the lead of the African writers he studies by applying *Tempest* metaphors to modern conflicts between oppressors and oppressed.[65] Prospero's language, he suggests, provides Caliban with a medium of expression for *Caliban's* culture. Prospero, of course, thinks the monster has no culture, but Caliban possesses

a culture Prospero did not create and cannot control, which he, Caliban, has recognized as his own. But in the process [of recognition] the language is transformed, acquiring different meanings which Prospero never expected. Caliban becomes "bilingual." That language he shares with Prospero and

64 George Lamming, *The Pleasures of Exile* (London: Michael Joseph, 1960), pp. 109–10; John Pepper Clark, *The Example of Shakespeare* (Evanston, Ill.: Northwestern University Press, 1970), ch. 1 ("The Legacy of Caliban"), p. 3, previously published in *Black Orpheus*, II (1968); 16–39, esp. p. 17. On Lamming and his context, see Nixon, "Appropriations of *The Tempest*," pp. 566–70; on Lamming and the Caliban metaphor, see Elizabeth Nuñez Harrell, "*The Tempest* and the Works of Two Caribbean Novelists: Pitfalls in the Way of Seeing Caliban" (Ph.D. dissertation, New York University, 1977), esp. ch. 4.
65 Janheinz Jahn, *Neo-African Literature: A History of Black Writing*, trans. Oliver Coburn and Ursala Lehrburger (Düsseldorf-Köln: 1966; repr. New York: Grove Press, 1968), p. 239.

the language he has minted from it are no longer identical. Caliban breaks out of the prison of Prospero's language.[66]

Jahn even suggests a rough date for Caliban's linguistic jailbreak: Between 1934 and 1948 the literature of "Negritude," initiated by Leopold Sedar Senghor of Senegal and others, staged "the successful revolt in which Caliban broke out of the prison of Prospero's language, by converting that language to his own needs for self-expression."[67] To distance themselves still further from Prospero's colonialist clutches, some African and Caribbean writers employ dialectical English, as in Lemuel Johnson's calypso rhythms; going a giant step further, the distinguished Kenyan author Ngugi Wa Thiong'o now writes in Gikuyu.[68]

Jahn's analysis, like the writings (implicitly, at least) of the negritude authors he praises, elevates Caliban from a symbol of the politically oppressed and culturally stunted native to a symbol of the temporarily inarticulate yet culturally rich native. Whereas Mannoni's Caliban was inferior because Prospero destroyed his culture and never fully replaced it with another, Jahn's Caliban has a valuable heritage that finds expression through Prospero's language, even though Prospero is deaf to the message.[69] In sum, Jahn shifts the focus from despair over the deprivation of native culture to pride

---

66 Jahn, *Neo-African Literature*, p. 242.

67 Jahn, *Neo-African Literature*, p. 242.

68 See, for example, Ngugi Wa Thiong'o, *Ngaahita Ndeenda* (1980), reissued in English as *I will Marry When I Want* (London: Heinemann, 1982); and *Matigari* (Kenya: 1987; repr. Oxford: Heinemann, 1989). For a brief but useful discussion of Ngugi's position, see David Hart, "Worlds Apart," *New Socialist*, XLIV (December 1986): 33, and, more extensively, Cartelli, "Prospero in Africa"; and Bill Ashcroft, Gareth Griffiths, and Helen Tiffin, *The Empire Writes Back: Theory and Practice in Post-colonial Literatures* (London: Routledge, 1989), pp. 123–32.

69 Jahn, *Neo-African Literature*, pp. 241–69. See also Bernth Lindfors, "The Rise of African Pornography," *Transition*, No. 42 (1973): 65–71. Caliban's language is considered from a broader perspective by Stephen Greenblatt, "Learning to Curse: Aspects of Linguistic Colonialism in the Sixteenth Century," in Fredi Chiappelli, ed., *First Images of America: The Impact of the New World on the Old*, 2 vols. (Berkeley: University of California Press, 1976), Vol. II, pp. 561–80, esp. pp. 568–75. See also Houston A. Baker, Jr., "Caliban's Triple Play," in Henry Louis Gates, Jr., ed., *"Race," Writing, and Difference* (University of Chicago Press, 1986), pp. 381–95; Patrick Taylor, *The Narrative of Liberation: Perspectives on Afro-Caribbean Literature, Popular Culture, and Politics* (Ithaca, N.Y.: Cornell University Press, 1989).

Colonial metaphors

in its tenacity. But in either case, Caliban is a paradigm for the oppressed, not the oppressors. Since 1950, no prominent author – from Europe or America or the Third World – has identified Caliban with the imperialists, as did Darío, Rodó, Barnes, and others in the first half of the century. Rather, as John Wain summarized the situation in 1964, Caliban "has the pathos of the exploited peoples everywhere, poignantly expressed at the beginning of a three-hundred-year wave of European colonization."[70] Caliban's trans-formation, for the time being at least, is diametric and virtually unanimous.

V

The universality of the new Caliban metaphor is aptly illustrated by two works that explore late-twentieth-century themes: apartheid in South Africa and French nationalism in Canada. Sibnarayan Ray's essay on "Shylock, Othello and Caliban" finds important parallels between certain Shakespearean characters and the victims of "ethnic-cultural superiority" – Ray's universalization of "apartheid." "Broadly speaking, the dominant community holds in arrogant contempt the one that is dominated; the latter, on its part, is driven to reluctant subservience, smouldering hatred and fear, and clandestine schemes of revenge." Thus defined, apartheid appeared in ancient Greece and China as well as in Europe, India, and else-where. Not that Shakespeare had any such applications in mind. Rather, because "a work of art, once completed, may communicate meanings which were outside the conscious intentions of the artist," Caliban effectively represents native populations almost every-where, especially in Africa, the United States, and Australia.[71]

70 John Wain, *The Living World of Shakespeare: A Playgoer's Guide* (London: Macmillan, 1964), pp. 226–27.
71 Sibnarayan Ray, "Shylock, Othello and Caliban: Shakespearean Variations on the Theme of Apartheid," in Amalendu Bose, ed., *Calcutta Essays on Shakespeare* (Calcutta University, 1966), pp. 1–16, esp. pp. 2–3, 10–13. For an explanation of why *The Tempest* has had relatively little reassessment in India and a provocative discussion of several aspects of Caliban's metamorphosis, see Ania Loomba, *Gender, Race, Renaissance Drama* (Manchester University Press, 1989), pp. 142–58. Useful too are Jyotsna Singh, "Different Shakespeares: The Bard in Colonial/Postcolonial India," *Theatre Journal*, XLI (1989): 445–58, and Gauri Viswanathan, *Masks of Con-*

In 1974, the Haitian-born Max Dorsinville's *Caliban withou Prospero: Essay on Quebec and Black Literature* carried the Caliban metaphor to Canada, one of the few regions of the globe not touched specifically by Ray or his numerous predecessors. Simultaneously, the book gave new emphasis to Caliban's cultural tenacity. As Ronald Sutherland notes in the Preface, Dorsinville goes beyond an analysis of the parallels between French-Canadian and African-American literature – both are colonial, in a sense, but irrepressible and newly vigorous – to formulate "a new concept [for] ... the literatures of all emerging national or ethnic groups." In the Caliban-Prospero metaphor, Dorsinville finds ready-made "an instrument of insight into the complexities of cultural confrontation in a colonial context." Through a provocative blend of psychoanalytic theory and literary analysis, Dorsinville traces the evolution of two minority literatures in North America from their early dependence on the dominant culture to their recent emergence as literatures in their own right: Caliban *without* Prospero.[72]

Dorsinville is not reluctant, as were Rodó and Barnes much earlier and others more recently, to make *Tempest* metaphors explicit and emphatic. His book bristles with references to "Calibanic literature," "Calibanic culture," "a Calibanic search," "a strictly Calibanic viewpoint," "[t]he Calibanic man," and "the Calibanic writer."[73] All such phrases refer, in Dorsinville's lexicon, to the literature that emerged at various times in various parts of the world where Europeans once settled, imposed their culture, were soon (sometimes not so soon) imitated by their colonial descendants, and eventually were rejected by culturally independent "post-European" authors. Dorsinville's story, in short, is Caliban's cultural emancipation. That Dorsinville invokes not only Quebecois and African-American literature but also, at least briefly, the literatures of Anglo-Saxon Americans, English-Canadians, Haitians, Argentinians, Brazilians,

quest: *Literary Study and British Rule in India* (New York: Columbia University Press, 1989).
72 Dorsinville, *Caliban without Prospero*, passim. On Caliban in Canadian literature, see also Chantal Zabus, "A Calibanic *Tempest* in Anglophone & Francophone New World Writing," *Canadian Literature*, No. 104 (Spring 1985): 35–50, esp. pp. 42–49; and Diana Brydon, "Re-writing *The Tempest*," *World Literature Written in English*, XXIII (1984): 75–88.
73 Dorsinville, *Caliban without Prospero*, pp. 15, 33, 78, 206.

and Senegalese suggests the remarkable versatility of the Caliban metaphor.

There are, however, limits to the metaphor's attraction. As Chantal Zabus points out, "In English Canada, Caliban is artfully relegated to the wings of the literary scene and such topics as language and rape receive no attention. Unlike the Black writer, the English-Canadian writer privileges Miranda over Caliban and appears to dwell more on the Prospero/Miranda or Miranda/Ferdinand relationships." English-Canadians, with few exceptions, identify with Prospero's daughter rather than with his slave; they seek independence from parental control rather than freedom from bondage; they assert their individuality rather than rebel against their mentors.[74] *Tempest* metaphors, it seems, are situational as well as ubiquitous.

Still, there is no denying the power of the Caliban metaphor on the Third World, even if its impact on political and cultural consciousness defies precise measurement. The frequency and poignancy with which Caliban has been invoked for nearly a century and the variety of authors who have enlisted him in ideological causes suggest that Shakespeare's savage and deformed slave met exceptionally well the needs of Third World authors and readers for a literary metaphor that was both readily identifiable and emotionally acceptable. That Caliban served so many masters surely reflects Shakespeare's unmatched universality and *The Tempest*'s adaptability to colonial contexts, whether seen from the imperialists' or the natives' perspective.

74 Zabus, "Anglophone & Francophone New World Writing," p. 42; Brydon, "Rewriting *The Tempest*," pp. 77–84.

Chapter 7
Stage history

These our actors, / As I foretold you, were all spirits,
and / Are melted into air, into thin air.

The Tempest (IV.i.148–50)

We all dupe ourselves in the theatre because we
have been sold a bill of goods for a good quarter of a
century before we enter.

Charles Marowitz (1978)

Speaking as guru to the 1970s avant-garde theatre, Charles Marowitz
criticized traditional Shakespearean productions for being too staid,
reactionary, and boring. Some of his critique is appropriate; the
theatre has always been a conservative institution. As a collective
organization of actors, writers, singers, dancers, scene painters,
costumiers, designers, and other craftsmen, it usually has handed
down stage business from one generation to the next; innovation, at
least before World War II and the development of instantaneous
communications systems, came gradually.

In the past two decades, academic Shakespeareans have sat
eagerly at directors' and actors' feet, acceding to their demands that
Shakespeare's plays be considered and taught as dramatic scripts.
Major Shakespearean journals now regularly contain reviews of
recent productions, and performance criticism is a respectable literary
genre. The road separating acting houses and academic institutions
is not always a two-way street, however. Although many academics

hunger for tidbits of stage business and bring actors to their class-rooms, few thespians actively study literary criticism. Even in the postmodern era, a decade sometimes passes before a new critical interpretation affects performance. Consequently, whereas Caliban's stage career has followed the same path as the interpretations by litterateurs, adaptors, and political writers outlined in the foregoing chapters, it has lagged somewhat behind. Until quite recently there has been a generation gap, a thirty-year hiatus between views of Caliban in print and his representation in the theatre.

Moreover, performances are texts in themselves, subject to inter-pretation and appropriation by the reviewers who describe them and the theatre historians who attempt to reconstruct them. Some-times a stage production breaks the bonds of tradition and, in turn, inspires new views of a character or a play. More often, a per-formance is assessed according to the audience's expectations and values. The theatre, far more than the study, is a social space where substantial numbers of people enjoy a shared experience. Examination of Caliban on stage indicates more clearly how he was conceived by each generation as a whole, not just by editors and scholars.

I

The Davenant-Dryden-Shadwell *The Tempest: Or, The Enchanted Island* was so popular with Restoration audiences that it quickly became the established stage version and persevered for a century and a half. Except for Garrick's brief restoration of Shakespeare's text in the middle of the eighteenth century, the Restoration *Tempest* held the boards until 1838. While eighteenth-century editors and literary critics worked with Shakespeare's text, audiences saw only the radical adaptation.[1]

From all accounts, Caliban in the Dryden-Davenant version was subordinated to "Duke" Trinculo, whose expanded role in Davenant's script made the jester's part a prize for leading comedians like Cave Underhill. No eyewitness accounts survive of Caliban's portrayal,

1 Stephen Orgel, ed., *The Tempest*, "The Oxford Shakespeare" (Oxford University Press, 1987), Introduction, p. 69.

but it is clear that along with the seamen – Stephano, Mustacho, Trinculo, and Ventoso – and his sister Sycorax, he served to burlesque commonwealth politics. The result seems to have been a memorable scene of bawdy humor, song, and dance. When Pepys first saw *The Enchanted Isle* (7 November 1667), he described it as "the most innocent play that I ever saw" and praised the echo song between Ferdinand and Ariel. A week later (13 November 1667) he saw the production a second time. His diary entry observes that it is "full of so good variety that I cannot be more pleased almost in a comedy, only the seamen's part a little too tedious." Pepys returned to the Dryden-Davenant *The Tempest* on 12 December, 6 January (1668), and 3 February. After the latter performance, he confessed, "this day I took pleasure to learn the time of the seaman's dance, which I have much desired to be perfect in, and have made myself so." All in all, Pepys saw *The Tempest* nine times, but only after the eighth performance did he refer to Caliban. His diary for 11 May 1668 reports that he went backstage between the acts to write down the words of the echo song and "had the pleasure to see the actors in their several dresses especially the seamen and monster, which were very droll."[2] Pepys's description of Caliban as "the monster" accords with the Dryden-Davenant cast list and suggests that he was represented as physically deformed.

Caliban's role remained sadly diminished in Shadwell's operatic *Tempest* (1673). This spectacle cut the Dryden-Davenant text to add extravagant musical numbers and elaborate scenic designs. The opening stage directions indicate that no expense was spared to delight the audience's appetite for spectacle:

The Front of the Stage is open'd, and the Band of 24 Violins, with the Harpsicals and Theorbo's which accompany the Voices, are plac'd between the Pit and the Stage. While the Overture is playing, the Curtain rises, and discovers a new Frontispiece, joyn'd to the great Pylasters, on each side of the Stage. . . . In the middle of the Arch are several Angels, holding the Kings Arms, as if they were placing them in the midst of that Compass-pediment. Behind this is the Scene, which represents a thick Cloudy Sky, a very Rocky Coast, and a Tempestuous Sea in perpetual Agitation. This

2 Quoted from Helen McAfee, *Pepys on the Restoration Stage* (New Haven, Conn.: Yale University Press, 1916), pp. 75–77.

Tempest (suppos'd to be rais'd by Magick) has many dreadful Objects in it, as several Spirits in horrid shapes flying down amongst the Sailers, then rising and crossing in the Air. And when the Ship is sinking, the whole House is darken'd, and a shower of Fire falls upon 'em. This is accompanied with Lightning, and several Claps of Thunder to the end of the Storm.[3]

Caliban, his sister Sycorax, and the seamen are relegated to the forestage in what is described as "the wilder part of the Island, 'tis composed of divers sorts of Trees, and barren places, with a prospect of the Sea at a great distance." This wild area contrasted sharply with Prospero's symmetrical, carefully ordered cyprus groves. "The Wild Island" is the scene of Trinculo and Caliban's drunken antics in Act IV. Caliban sings:

> We want Musick, we want Mirth,
> Up, Dam, and cleave the Earth:
> We have now no Lords that wrong us,
> Send thy merry Sprights among us.

This catch is followed by a spectacle: "A Table rises, and four Spirits with Wine and Meat enter, placing it, as they dance, on the Table: the Dance ended, the Bottles vanish, and the Table sinks agen."[4]

This scene succeeded, for in his 1708 memoir of the stage, John Downes selected it for praise:

... in 1673. The Tempest, or the Inchanted Island, made into an Opera by *Mr. Shadwell*, having all New in it; as Scenes, Machines; particularly, one Scene Painted with *Myriads* of *Ariel* Spirits; and another flying away, with a Table Furnisht out with Fruits, Sweet meats, and all sorts of Viands; just

---

3 Reproduced in facsimile in George Robert Guffey, *After The Tempest* (Los Angeles: William Andrews Clark Library, Augustan Reprint Society, Special Series No. 4, 1969), sig. B1r. We have changed the original italicized text to roman type for the readers' convenience. For an explanation of the mechanisms behind these special effects, see Jocelyn Powell, *Restoration Theatre Production* (London: Routledge & Kegan Paul, 1984), ch. 4. For discussion of the libretto for this operatic version and for the King's Company burlesque, *The Mock Tempest*, see James G. McManaway, "Songs and Masques in *The Tempest*," in *Theatre Miscellany: Six Pieces Connected with the Seventeenth-Century Stage* (Oxford: Basil Blackwell, 1953), pp. 69–96; and Charles Haywood, "*The Songs & Masque in the New Tempest*: An Incident in the Battle of the Two Theatres, 1674," *Huntington Library Quarterly*, XIX (1955): 39–55.
4 Reproduced in Guffey, *After the Tempest*, sig. I2r.

when Duke *Trinculo* and his Companions were going to Dinner; all was things perform'd in it so Admirably well, that not any succeeding Opera got more Money.[5]

Again, there is no specific reference to how Caliban was performed. But this operatic *Tempest* was produced at the Theatre Royal, Drury Lane, almost every year from 1702 to 1756, its popularity unabated.

In March 1756, David Garrick, actor-manager for the Drury Lane, experimented with a new operatic *Tempest*. Garrick pruned Shakespeare's lines, incorporated Dryden-Davenant material, and added thirty-two songs by John Christopher Smith. So larded with arias were the major characters that Caliban had even less prominence than before, though he did sing this lovely air:

> The owl is abroad, the bat, and the toad,
> And so is the cat-a-mountain.
> The ant and the mole fit both in a hole,
> And frog peeps out of the fountain.

In an early scene, Trinculo refers to Caliban as an amphibious monster, but no sooner is the "dear tortoise" introduced than he is forgotten. The opera contains no resolution to the Stephano-Trinculo subplot, except a drinking song in Act III.[6] This opera, not surprisingly, failed. After a short run and discouraging reviews, Garrick admitted defeat and closed it.

The following year (1757), Garrick offered a new version, billed as "written by Shakespeare." It returned to the First Folio, minus 432 lines and with 14 added. This phase of Garrick's growing effort to restore Shakespeare's original text was successful.[7] It ran nearly every year until 1787, when John Philip Kemble substituted his own acting text. Kemble reintroduced Dorinda and Hippolito from the Dryden-Davenant version, but he eliminated Sycorax, Ventoso,

---

5 John Downes, *Roscius Anglicanus, or an Historical Review of the Stage* (London: H. Playford, 1708), pp. 34–35.

6 See David Garrick, *The Tempest: An Opera* (London, 1756), reproduced in Guffey, *After the Tempest*. The song quoted is from sig. E3v.

7 Charles Beecher Hogan, *Shakespeare in the Theatre, 1701–1800*, Vol. II (Oxford: Clarendon Press, 1952), pp. 636–38. See also George Winchester Stone, "Shakespeare's *Tempest* at Drury Lane During Garrick's Management," *Shakespeare Quarterly*, VII (1956): 1–7.

and Mustacho. His Caliban had Shakespeare's original lines.[8] This hodgepodge persisted until 1838, when William Charles Macready returned to Shakespeare's text.

II

Despite the paucity of details about the actors who played Caliban during the Restoration and the early eighteenth century, it is clear that Caliban was a minor role. Actors were selected for a voice and figure that could easily portray the monster's grotesque qualities. Between 1710 and 1733, Ben Johnson performed Caliban at Drury Lane. William Cooke described him as a superb comedian: "His *forte* was in the grave, dry, humorous parts of comedy. . . . He was always in *earnest* with his part."[9] Charles Macklin, known for his bulbous nose and awkward figure, is mentioned as having played Caliban as well. Presumably this was during his apprenticeship, before he made his name with an innovative Shylock.[10] Edward Machan, a lame actor who failed as Richard III, performed Caliban at Phillips's Booth in Bartholomew Fair during 1749.[11] Edward Berry (1700–60), Caliban in Garrick's restoration of the original text, was notable for his huge body and booming voice and was accused of howling on all occasions.[12] *The Theatrical Review* praised Berry's Caliban, "where his art seems to vye with that of Shakespear, to make that out-of-the-way character look probable, natural, and pleasing, in spight of nature, probability, and the most hideous shape."[13] James Dance, also known as James Love (1721–24), acted

---

8 See *John Philip Kemble Promptbooks*, Vol. VIII, ed. Charles H. Shattuck (Charlottesville, Va.: Folger Shakespeare Library, 1974).

9 William Cooke, *Memoirs of Charles Macklin, Comedian* (London: Printed for James Asperne, 1804), p. 67.

10 His biographer, James Thompson Kirkman, lists Caliban among Macklin's roles. See *Memoirs of the Life of Charles Macklin, Esq.*, Vol. II (London: Lackington, Allen, 1799), p. 445.

11 Philip Highfill, Jr., Kalman A. Burnim, and Edward A. Langhans, *A Biographical Dictionary of Actors, Actresses, Musicians, Dancers, Managers, & other Stage Personnel in London, 1660–1800*, Vol. IX (Carbondale: Southern Illinois University Press, 1982), p. 402 (henceforth cited as Highfill, *Biographical Dictionary*).

12 Highfill, *Biographical Dictionary*, Vol. II, p. 64.

13 *The Theatrical Review for the Year 1757, and Beginning 1758* (London: Printed for J. Coote, 1758), p. 13.

Caliban at Drury Lane from 1765 to 1769. As one commentator notes, "Roles like Jacques, Sir Toby Belch, Caliban, Jobson, and Falstaff were suited to his manner, his unwieldy figure, and a voice described . . . as 'somewhat asthmatical, and abounding with many inharmonious tones'."[14]

Not surprisingly, during the years of the operatic *Tempest*, Caliban was also played by comedians with musical talent. Charles Bannister, Drury Lane's Caliban for nearly thirty years (1777 into the 1800s), was praised for a voice "which he used . . . both as a tool of the mimic's trade and with near-operatic skill in dramatic singing." He also boasted a "Herculean figure."[15] Another comedian, Charles Blakes, portrayed Caliban from 1759 to 1763. Blakes also sang sea songs during most intervals. In *Tempest* productions, this must have seemed an appropriate pastime for the fishy monster.[16]

Caliban's relative insignificance to eighteenth-century productions is understandable. Though audiences enjoyed the seamen's music and antics, Caliban did not fit well with the age's notions of comedy. As early as Shadwell, theatre critics had eliminated natural imperfections as suitable topics for satire. Caliban's grotesque deformities were not the proper vehicle for good-natured wit; his natural folly was inappropriate to an art form that dealt with manners and artificial follies.[17]

As argued in Chapter 4, critical interpretations of Caliban were bound to change in response to cultural shifts. On stage the changes took longer. John Philip Kemble, in many ways a transitional figure looking back to Garrick as well as ahead to the age of Kean, illustrates this lag. While Kemble produced *The Tempest* on stage in 1806, in the study Coleridge was rediscovering Caliban's poetic qualities. Kemble's stage *Tempest* reverted to the eighteenth century by re-introducing Dorinda and Hippolito; Kemble left Caliban as he found him, so that the role became more desirable and provided more room for interpretation. With Shakespeare's original lines restored, Caliban could be more than a drunken buffoon, but by sharing

14 Highfill, *Biographical Dictionary*, Vol. IX, p. 360.
15 Highfill, *Biographical Dictionary*, Vol. I, p. 262.
16 Highfill, *Biographical Dictionary*, Vol. II, p. 150.
17 For discussion of Restoration and eighteenth-century conceptions of humor, see Stuart M. Tave, *The Amiable Humorist* (University of Chicago Press, 1960).

the play with Hippolito, the "natural man," he could not signify humanity in a state of nature. In sum, Caliban on stage was not what Coleridge imagined him in the study.

Still, the actor who portrayed Caliban in Kemble's production could bring a new dimension to the role. According to Leigh Hunt, an eyewitness to early-nineteenth-century *Tempest* productions, John Emery's performance was a wonderful combination of the pathetic and the coarse:

this roughness as well as awe MR. EMERY most inimitably displays, particularly in the vehement manner and high voice with which he curses *Prospero* and the thoughtful lowness of tone, softened from it's [*sic*] usual hoarse brutality, with which he worships his new deity. . . . [He] approaches to terrific tragedy, when he describes the various tortures inflicted on him by the magician and the surrounding snakes that "stare and hiss him into madness." . . . [T]he monster hugs and shrinks into himself, grows louder and more shuddering as he proceeds, and when he pictures the torment that almost turns his brain, glares with his eyes and gnashes his teeth with an impatient impotence of revenge.[18]

Kemble's biographer, James Boaden, was less favorably impressed. He wrote that Emery's

Caliban was a brute, it is true, and what he should not have been, a Yorkshire one; but there was no poetry in his conception of the character. It has always been *roared* down the throats of the vulgar; but Caliban is not a vulgar creation. It is of "imagination all compact."[19]

Hazlitt, too, disliked Mr. Emery, snidely remarking that "MR. EMERY had nothing of Caliban but his gaberdine, which did not become him."[20] Still, Emery's dramatic interpretation invoked tragic elements of Caliban that had been neglected in earlier productions. Now there was scope for Caliban's poetic sensibilities and suffering as well as his grotesquerie.

18 Leigh Hunt, *Critical Essays on the Performers of the London Theatres* (London: John Hunt, 1807), pp. 110–11.
19 James Boaden, *Memoirs of the Life of John Philip Kemble, Esq.* (London: Longman, Hurst, Rees, Orme, Brown, & Green, 1825), pp. 224–25.
20 William Hazlitt, *A View of the English Stage* (London: Robert Stodart, 1818), p. 131.

III

During the first third of the nineteenth century, both at Drury Lane and Covent Garden, the Kemble-Dryden-Davenant version persisted. William Charles Macready played Prospero in 1821, 1824, and again in 1833, but he did so unhappily. Later he described the acting version he was forced to use as a *"melange* that was called Shakespeare's *Tempest*, with songs interpolated by Reynolds among the mutilations and barbarous ingraftings of Dryden and Davenant." Macready found the performances tedious and lamented that his role was a "stupid old proser of commonplace which the acted piece calls Prospero."[21] Subordinate to Macready's Prospero was a bestial Caliban. A description of Caliban's costume at Drury Lane (1824) and Covent Garden (1827) in a contemporary acting edition reads, "Entire dress of goat's skin; long claws on the fingers; very dark flesh legs; the hair long, wild, and ragged."[22] Given Macready's disgust with these productions, it is not surprising that when, in 1838, he revived *The Tempest* as Shakespeare had originally conceived it, minus Dorinda and Hippolito, the new production confirmed the romantic critics' more sympathetic conceptions of Caliban.

Caliban was by then a more important character, played by George Bennett, an actor who excelled in tragic as well as comic roles. Besides Caliban, he was remembered for performances of Sir Toby Belch in *Twelfth Night*, Pistol in *Henry V*, Enobarbus in *Antony and Cleopatra*, Bosola in *The Duchess of Malfi*, and Apemantus in *Timon of Athens*. Bennett began the stage tradition of lunging at Prospero during the opening confrontation, then recoiling from a wave of the magic wand, finally writhing in helpless fury.[23] Reviewer John Forster described this scene in the 21 October 1838 *Examiner*:

21 *The Journal of William Charles Macready, 1832–1851*, abr. and ed. by J. C. Trewin (London: Longmans Green, 1967), pp. 15–16.
22 William Shakespeare, *The Tempest . . . as Performed at the Theatres Royal, London* (London: John Cumberland, n.d.), p. 10.
23 See Arthur Colby Sprague, *Shakespeare and the Actors: The Stage Business in his Plays, 1660–1905* (Cambridge, Mass.: Harvard University Press, 1944), p. 41.

His first discovery in the hole where he is "styed" was singularly picturesque, nor less so was his manner of grabbing out of it to fly on Prospero,
whose wand in a moment flung the danger of his fury down, and left him
merely *dancing mad* with impotent rage.[24]

Here the modern Caliban, victim of oppression, was born.

Macready's *Tempest* ran for fifty-five performances, netting an
average income of £230 per night. Macready's journal confesses his
pleasure: "I look back upon its production with satisfaction, for it
has given to the public a play of Shakspeare which had never been
seen before, and it has proved the charm of simplicity and poetry."
The journal reveals that even when Macready felt he had been
"cold" or "indifferent" in the part, he was well received and
generally was called back by the audience.[25] Macready's innovative
Tempest was soon followed by rival versions.

Two promptbooks provide valuable insights into Caliban's new
role. The first was for Samuel Phelps (1804–78) at Sadler's Wells
Theatre in 1847. Phelps had performed with Macready at Covent
Garden and portrayed Antonio in the 1838 *Tempest*. When Parliament withdrew the exclusive privileges of Drury Lane and Covent
Garden in 1844, Phelps formed a company that specialized in
higher drama. Phelps acted Prospero in 1847; George Bennett again
portrayed Caliban.

According to the promptbook, Caliban was still fairly bestial, but
he was a man-beast, not simply a monster. His first entrance is
carefully described: "Enter Caliban. Opening L of Flat / Crawling
out on all fours as a Beast, rises & threatens Prospero, who raises
his wand & checks him. Caliban recoils as if spell struck." As he
describes the fresh springs and brine pits, Caliban is to be "stamp-
ing and gabbling with fury." (Much of this stage business was
to become standard, repeated in promptbooks throughout the
century.) Prospero's reminders of his magical power make Caliban
afraid, and he exits "tremblingly." He rebels (in II.ii), indignantly

24 John Forster, *Dramatic Essays* (London: Walter Scott, 1896), pp. 70–71.
25 *The Diaries of William Charles Macready, 1833–1851*, 2 vols., ed. William Toynbee
(London: Chapman & Hall, 1912), Vol. I, pp. 474–504; Vol. II, pp. 5–9; quotation
from Vol. II, p. 5.

discarding his burden of wood. He drinks thirstily throughout the scene, while crawling and kneeling at Stephano's feet. In Act III, scene ii, Caliban, like Stephano and Trinculo, is literally falling-down drunk. Says the promptbook: "Caliban speaks his other speeches either kneeling, sitting, or on all fours like a beast." When Ariel mischievously causes Stephano to strike Trinculo, "Caliban shows a strong and savage expression of joy."[26] This Caliban's bestiality may be a throwback to the eighteenth century, but his defiance smacks of the age of revolution and romanticism.

By the middle of the nineteenth century, Shakespearean drama was being acted regularly in America as well as in England.[27] On 11 April 1854, the comedian William Burton portrayed Caliban at his own theatre in New York, where visitors from the northeastern states had thronged to see Burton impersonate Dickensian characters. They expected broad and coarse humor, but his Caliban was more than comic. Like George Bennett's earlier representation, he was a combination of eighteenth-century monster and nineteenth-century rebel, mixed this time with traces of the mythic wodewose. Burton's friend and biographer W. L. Keese recalled that "His *Caliban* we have tried to forget rather than remember; it terrified us and made us dream bad dreams, but for all of that, we know that it was a surprising impersonation."[28] An anonymous author in the *New York Times*, on 20 June 1875, recalled Burton's Caliban:

A wild creature on all fours sprang upon the stage, with claws on his hands, and some weird animal arrangement about the head partly like a snail. It was an immense conception. Not the great God Pan himself was more the link between the man and beast than this thing. It was a creature of the woods, one of nature's spawns; it breathed of nuts and herbs, and rubbed itself against the back of trees.[29]

26 Folger *Tempest* promptbook No. 13, pp. 24, 25, 62, 64.
27 See Charles H. Shattuck, *Shakespeare on the American Stage; From the Hallams to Edwin Booth* (Washington, D.C.: Folger Shakespeare Library, 1976); and Lawrence W. Levine, "William Shakespeare and the American People: A Study in Cultural Transformation," *American Historical Review*, LXXXIX (1984): 34–66.
28 William L. Keese, *William E. Burton: Actor, Author, and Manager* (New York: Putnam, 1885), p. 175.
29 Quotation from John Russell Brown, *Shakespeare's Plays in Performance* (London: Edward Arnold, 1966), p. 109.

The stage directions from Burton's promptbook bear out this portrayal. Throughout his speech to Prospero (I.ii), Caliban "roars or yells with rage." His gaberdine is a large skin, not a cloak. Later he clings to Stephano's keg, growls when he loses it, and paws Stephano's leg to get it back again. Burton's Caliban was meant to be animal-like (though not necessarily Darwinian); his ferocity was awesome.[30]

Prompt copy for Charles Kean's extravagant 1857 production at the Princess Theatre is equally revealing. In accord with what had become standard stage business, John Ryder's Caliban flies at Prospero and shrinks back when he extends his magic wand. The gaberdine scene is milked for all its humor with the following interplay: "Trin nudges Steph not to give all the wine to Caliban and then goes round at back to RH. Cal takes a long pull at the bottle. Trin. looks at him in surprise. Cal turns and looks savagely at Trin."[31]

Ryder's costume (Figure 6) was later described in Thomas Barry's acting edition: "Brown fleshings, covered with hair, green nails, toes and fingers, fins on shoulders and arms, calf of legs, webbed fingers and toes, goggles on eyes, wolf skin shirt, wild wavy wig, beard, and moustache."[32] In the Kean costume book, Caliban has long toenails and fingernails and is covered with bushy brown fur.[33] His human form appears underneath. This may reflect the traditional animal-skin costume, but it also suggests the dawn of the apish Caliban.

IV

During the middle of the nineteenth century, costumes such as John Ryder's emphasized Caliban's animal characteristics. Occasionally, however, the costumier went to extremes. Dutton Cook insisted in an 1871 review that George Rignold's Caliban was "perhaps needlessly repulsive of aspect, and the tusks and pasteboard jaws worn by the actor have the disadvantage of hindering his articulation."[34] Despite

30 Folger *Tempest* promptbook No. 12.
31 Charles Kean's promptbook, Folger *Tempest* promptbook No. 10, p. 37.
32 Folger *Tempest* promptbook No. 4.
33 Charles Kean's costume book, Folger art volume d 49, dated 1853.
34 From a clipping inserted in Folger *Tempest* promptbook No. 4. Source unknown.

6. The costume sketches for John Ryder as Caliban in Charles Kean's
production (1857).

such difficulties, from Emery's performance on, actors conveyed
not only Caliban's savagery but also his tragic sense of Prospero's
injustice. The result was performances human in their emotional
power, animal in appearance and behavior.

The conception of Caliban as an amphibian, somewhere between
brute animal and human being, was made more explicit and timely
in Daniel Wilson's *Caliban: The Missing Link* (1873), as discussed in
Chapter 4. Despite considerable scholarly interest in Darwinism,
it did not dominate stage versions until late in the century.[35]

35 See Trevor R. Griffiths, "'This Island's Mine': Caliban and Colonialism," *The
Yearbook of English Studies*, XIII (1983): 159–80, for a discussion of Darwinian
approaches to Caliban that complements ours.

7. Frank Benson carrying a fish and clad, according to his wife, as "half
monkey, half coco-nut" (ca. 1895).

Lady Benson recalled in her memoirs that in preparation for acting
Caliban in the 1890s, F. R. Benson "spent many hours watching
monkeys and baboons in the Zoo, in order to get the movements
and postures in keeping with his 'make-up'." She described his
costume as "half monkey, half coco-nut" and noted that he "de-
lighted in swarming up a tree on the stage and hanging from
the branches head downwards while he gibbered at 'Trinculo'."[36]
Edward Gordon Craig, who thought Benson (Figure 7) a second-rate
actor, observed that "Benson's idea of Caliban was to come on stage

36 Lady Benson, *Mainly Players: Bensonian Memoirs* (London: Thornton Butterworth,
1926), p. 179. For an interesting discussion of spectacle in both Benson's and
Tree's productions of *The Tempest*, see Mary M. Nilan, "'The Tempest' at the Turn
of the Century: Cross-Currents in Production," *Shakespeare Survey*, XXV (1972):
113–23.

8. Tyrone Power as Caliban in Augustin Daly's production of *The Tempest* (1897).

with a fish between his teeth," a bit of stage business adopted later by Beerbohm Tree.[37]

Tyrone Power's costume for the 1897 Augustin Daly production was similarly apish. The color sketch in Daly's souvenir album shows a human form covered with brown fur. He wears a green tunic (shades of Tarzan) and sports metallic scales around his calves. His long nails and hairy face bespeak his animal qualities; his erect posture and expression suggest the human.[38]

Power's costume, according to a *New York Times* critic (7 April 1897), is conventional, but his mask and wig are "most unhappy,

37 Edward Gordon Craig, *Index to the Story of My Days* (London: 1957; repr. Cambridge University Press, 1981), p. 221.
38 Augustin Daly's souvenir album, Folger art volume b 31, includes color drawings for each character in addition to photographs, playbills, and clippings from *The Tempest*'s stage history.

while his delivery of the poetry lacks melody." To William Winter, reviewer for the *New York Daily Tribune* (also 7 April 1897), Caliban represented a "brutish creature, the hideous, malignant clod of evil, in whom, nevertheless, the germs of intelligence, feeling and fanciful perception are beginning to stir." Winter praised Power's "half-bestial, half-human aspect, the rude, grisly strength, the intense, sustained savage fury and the startling gleams of thought and feeling." However one judges Power's performance, it is clear that he – and Daly – saw Caliban as a precivilized missing link (Figure 8). Caliban the ape-man had crossed the Atlantic.

Beerbohm Tree also stressed Caliban's humanity in his production of 1904. In the Preface to his acting edition, Tree argued that Caliban had a human shape and that "in his love of music and his affinity with the unseen world, we discern in the soul which inhabits the brutish body of this elemental man the germs of a sense of beauty, the dawn of art."[39] Tree's costume consisted of fur and seaweed; he also, significantly, wore a necklace of shells and coral. When this Caliban hears the island's music, he dances and tries to sing. At the beginning of Act III, scene ii, he listens to the isle's sweet music while weaving a wreath of flowers for Stephano: *"Placing the wreath on his head, he looks at himself in the pool."*[40] The most famous scene of this production was a final tableau that shows the Neapolitans sailing home:

Caliban *creeps from his cave and watches. . . .* Caliban *listens for the last time to the sweet air* [Ariel's song], *then turns sadly in the direction of the departing ship. The play is ended. As the curtain rises again, the ship is seen on the horizon,* Caliban *stretching out his arms toward it in mute despair. The night falls,* and Caliban *is left on the lonely rock. He is king once more.*[41]

Tree noted that at this moment "we feel that from the conception of sorrow in solitude may spring the birth of a higher civilization."[42] Despite his primitive origins, Tree's Caliban expressed deep human

39 *Shakespeare's The Tempest As Arranged for the Stage by Herbert Beerbohm Tree* (London: J. Miles, 1904), p. xi. The ensuing stage directions are cited from this edition.
40 Tree, *Tempest*, p. 42.
41 Tree, *Tempest*, p. 63.
42 Tree, *Tempest*, p. xi.

9. Beerbohm Tree in fur, seaweed, and shells (1904), painted by
Charles A. Buchel.

sensibilities and aspirations. Perhaps this "deformed savage" –
image of humanity's earliest ancestors – could evolve into civilized
man (Figure 9).

The Darwinian Caliban persisted well into the twentieth century.
Gordon Crosse praised Robert Atkins's Caliban at the Old Vic
(1920–25) because "he showed with superlative art the malevolent
brute nature with the dim, half-formed, human intellect just breaking
through."[43] G. Wilson Knight records that he played Caliban at
Toronto (1938) wearing heavy gray furs over a complete covering of
green greasepaint with purple variations that blended "the slimy

43 Gordon Crosse, *Shakespearean Playgoing, 1890–1952* (London: A. R. Mowbray,
1953), p. 58.

reptilian and savagely human."[44] In 1938, Robert Atkins again depicted Caliban, this time as an aspiring and frustrated Neanderthal. English productions of 1940 and 1951 presented Caliban as a prehistoric figure, emerging from the slime of his bestial origins.[45]

V

Darwinian conceptions of Caliban continued to dominate the stage until the 1950s, when literary critics and intelligentsia in the Third World began to see him in a different context. The stage followed suit fairly rapidly. Colonial interpretations of Caliban flourished during the 1960s and into the 1980s. By then, Caliban had become a role often reserved for black actors.

This, too, was a gradual process. Trevor R. Griffiths notes in his study of colonial and antislavery interpretations that Roger Livesey's hairy and scaly Caliban at the Old Vic in 1934 "appears to have been the first Caliban to have actually blacked up, but this excited virtually no critical comment."[46] Blackness could indicate Caliban's alienness, not necessarily an awareness of racial conflicts. In the all-white theatrical world of the 1940s and '50s, few parts had been open to members of minority groups. Caliban could be played by a black man; the strangeness, seemingly part of the costume, need not startle the predominantly white audience.

Canada Lee first broke the color barrier. In 1945 he portrayed Caliban in Margaret Webster's New York *Tempest*. Lee wore a scaly costume and grotesque mask, moved with an animal-like crouch, and emphasized Caliban's monstrousness. The *Saturday Review* noted that "Canada Lee's Caliban is a monster; earth-sprung; fearsome, badgered, and pathetic. His only trouble is that he keeps all of Caliban's poetry earth-sprung, too."[47] Lee's widow, Frances, described her husband's performance to Glenda E. Gill in 1980: "In a costume of fish scales and long fingernails, Lee first appeared onstage bent over in a humpback position akin to Richard III; the

44 G. Wilson Knight, *Shakespearian Production* (London: Routledge & Kegan Paul, 1968), p. 164.
45 See William Babula, *Shakespeare in Production, 1935–1978; A Selective Catalogue* (New York: Garland Publishing, 1981), pp. 307–21.
46 Griffiths, "'This Island's Mine'," p. 175.
47 *Saturday Review*, 10 February 1945, p. 29.

audience subsequently thought of him only in that curved position, even when he stood tall."[48] Lee's performance won modest praise and opened the role of Caliban to blacks, but the transformation to an essentially "black" part was still in the future. Critics of the 1945 production gave no hint of Caliban as colonial victim.

Earle Hyman essayed the part in 1960 at the American Shakespeare Festival in Connecticut. Hyman, too, played up Caliban's monstrosity, wearing inflated belly and legs and a grotesque headpiece. The photograph in *Shakespeare Quarterly* makes him look scarcely human.[49] In 1962, James Earl Jones used a similar costume, though his interpretation was more reptilian. Alice Griffin described Jones's Caliban as "a savage, green-faced lizard darting his red tongue in and out, lunging clumsily at what he wanted, and yelping when he was denied it."[50]

Jones's and Hyman's Calibans looked to the past. For the rest of the 1960s and beyond, Caliban evolved from quasi-bestial monster to a wholly human vehicle for contemporary ideas. The following survey is far from comprehensive, but it reflects the breadth of Caliban's politicization during the 1960s and 1970s.

Influenced by Jan Kott's harsh interpretation of the play as a study in violence, Peter Brook directed a production in 1963 at Stratford-upon-Avon in which Roy Dotrice played Caliban as a Java man who represented "emergent humanity."[51] His phallic gestures conveyed primitive man's raw sexuality. Brook continued this motif in 1968 with an experimental rendition of *The Tempest* at the Round House in London. Brook used Caliban and his hypothetical mother Sycorax to

represent those evil and violent forces that rise from man himself regardless of his environment. The monster-mother is portrayed by an enormous

---

48 Glenda E. Gill, "The Mercurial Canada Lee," *White Grease Paint on Black Performers* (New York: Peter Lang, 1988), pp. 21–66, esp. p. 41. Gill includes a photograph of Lee in costume.

49 Claire McGlinchee, "Stratford, Connecticut, Shakespeare Festival 1960," *Shakespeare Quarterly*, XI (1960): 469–72.

50 Alice Griffin, "The New York Season, 1961–1962," *Shakespeare Quarterly*, XIII (1962): 553–57, esp. p. 555.

51 Robert Speaight, "Shakespeare in Britain," *Shakespeare Quarterly*, XIV (1963): 419–32.

woman able to expand her face and body to still larger proportions. . . . Suddenly, she gives a horrendous yell, and Caliban, with black sweater over his head, emerges from between her legs: Evil is born.

As the action proceeds, Caliban rapes Miranda, escapes from Prospero, and takes over the island. The play continues in a mime of homosexual rape, Caliban on Prospero, ending with broken voices intoning Prospero's epilogue.[52]

Brook's experiment clearly differed from Shakespeare's original, but it charted the way to new stage interpretations of Caliban. The role now represented power more than subjugation. Henry Baker, for example, embodied Caliban's violence in the 1970 Washington Summer Festival Shakespeare production. Jeanne Addison Roberts described Baker as "darkly beautiful in his glistening fish scales" and "powerful and intractable from beginning to end." Baker never obeyed Stephano's command to kiss his foot, never cowered, never uttered the final resolve to be wise and sue for grace. To Roberts, "Baker's black skin, his somewhat flawed enunciation, a minstrel-show mouth painted grotesquely in a greenish face, and the use of the word 'slave' evoked instantly for the Washington audience the American Negro."[53] Caliban was now a black militant, angry and recalcitrant.

Jonathan Miller used similar dynamics in his 1970 production at the Mermaid Theatre. Miller had studied Mannoni's *Prospero and Caliban*,[54] and he interpreted *The Tempest* as a play about England's colonial experience.[55] In an interview with David Hirst, Miller observed that

You get two forms of tribal response to the white colonials – either a detribalised, broken-down, shuffling, disinherited feeling – which is what Caliban represents – or, on the other hand, a sophisticated technologically-capable, fast-learning response which was represented by the Ibos in

52 Margaret Croyden, "Peter Brook's *Tempest*," *The Drama Review*, III (1968–69): 125–28; quotation from p. 127.
53 Jeanne Addison Roberts, "The Washington Summer Festival, 1970," *Shakespeare Quarterly*, XXI (1970): 481–82.
54 See Chapter 6, Section IV.
55 See Griffiths, "'This Island's Mine'," pp. 177–78, and David L. Hirst, *The Tempest: Text and Performance* (London: Macmillan, 1984), pp. 43–60.

191

Nigeria who were capable of picking up all the administrative skills whilst still pressing for their liberty.[56]

Miller's Caliban, Rudolph Walker, was described by one reviewer as an uneducated field Negro, "in contrast to Ariel, a competent, educated 'houseboy'." Set in the world of Cortez and Pizarro, Miller's version reflected the complex interrelations of colonial masters and their subjugated natives.[57]

Variations on the colonial theme persisted through the 1970s. The New York Shakespeare Festival presented Jaime Sanchez as a Puerto Rican Caliban in 1974,[58] and in the same year Denis Quilley's Caliban at London's National Theatre was likened by reviewers to James Fenimore Cooper's Chingachgook. David Hirst described Quilley's bisected makeup:

one half of his face presented the ugly deformed monster, the other an image of the noble savage. This meant that, in visual terms, by turning his profile to the audience he could change his appearance in a moment. . . . The rich associations of Hiawatha and the Last of the Mohicans were thus able to force the central issue of the conflict of nature and nurture firmly into the audience's visual and intellectual perception.[59]

Quilley's Caliban was the noble savage "with one side of him as a man, and the other side half emerging from animality."[60]

In 1978, David Suchet portrayed Caliban for the Royal Shakespeare Company; his representation of Caliban as native is, perhaps, the culmination of colonial interpretations. Suchet prepared for the role by reading promptbooks and reviews at the Shakespeare Centre in Stratford. To his chagrin, he found that "Caliban had been played as: (1) a fish, (2) a dog with one and/or two heads, (3) a lizard, (4) a monkey, (5) a snake, (6) half-ape, half-man, with fins for arms,

---

56 Hirst, *The Tempest*, p. 50.
57 Robert Speaight, "Shakespeare in Britain," *Shakespeare Quarterly*, XXI (1970): 439–40.
58 M. E. Comtois, "New York Shakespeare Festival, Lincoln Center, 1973–74," *Shakespeare Quarterly*, XXV (1974): 405–06.
59 Hirst, *The Tempest*, p. 48.
60 Robert Speaight, "Shakespeare in Britain, 1974," *Shakespeare Quarterly*, XXV (1974): 389–94; quotation from p. 394.

(7) a tortoise. . . . One overall feeling came over me – that of being totally miscast."[61] After studying the text, Suchet concluded that Caliban did indeed have a human shape and that "Shakespeare had obviously gone to great pains (not without tongue in cheek) to describe the popular concept of the 'native'."[62] Suchet wanted to convey his concept by becoming a composite version of Third World peoples, a generalized "primitive man." Working with costume designer Brenda Leedham, he decided

I didn't want to be instantly recognizable as being obviously an African native or an Indian or an Eskimo or an Aborigine. . . . Brenda . . . made two rubber prosthetics which covered my eyebrows and gave me a prehistoric-looking forehead. Then she made me an African nose but we decided against frizzy, tightly matted hair and instead she made the top of my head appear bald and lumpy by placing dollops of porridge on it and covering the whole top of my head with latex. The result was unbelievably effective. Then I put on two layers of dark brown make-up all over my body and then sprayed it pewter-coloured. Under the stage lighting the effect was that sometimes I would look black, sometimes pewter, and sometimes I even took on a greenish hue.[63]

Suchet's costume worked (Figure 10). Reviewer John Velz reported that Suchet's Caliban combined both West Indian and African characteristics.[64] Another reviewer described Suchet's Caliban as a "naked, dark-skinned primitive, with a bald head and bloodshot eyes; . . . his exploitation was strongly emphasised."[65]

VI

The climax of Caliban's politicization came, perhaps, during 1980–82, when productions around the world emphasized what had become the standard interpretation. In the popular imagination,

61 David Suchet, "Caliban in *The Tempest*," in *Players of Shakespeare*, ed. Philip Brockbank (Cambridge University Press, 1985), pp. 167–79; quotation from p. 169.
62 Suchet, "Caliban," p. 171.
63 Suchet, "Caliban," p. 179.
64 John Velz, "*The Tempest*," *Cahiers Elisabethains*, XIV (1978): 104–06.
65 Roger Warren, "A Year of Comedies: Stratford 1978," *Shakespeare Survey*, XXI (1979): 201–09, esp. p. 203.

10. David Suchet's composite "Third World" Caliban (Stratford, 1978).

Caliban now represented any group that felt itself oppressed. In New York, he appeared as a punk-rocker, complete with cropped hair, sunglasses, and cockney accent.[66] In Augsburg, Germany, Caliban continued as a black slave, who performed African dances and rituals during the Stephano-Trinculo scenes.[67] In Connecticut, director Gerald Freedman viewed Caliban as an aspect of Prospero's character – the libido that cannot be controlled. He cast Joe Morton, a black actor, in the part and had him sing his freedom catch to jazz tunes. Libido or no, this Caliban still symbolized a repressed

66 Maurice Charney and Arthur Ganz, "Shakespeare in New York City," *Shakespeare Quarterly*, XXXIII (1982): 218–22.
67 Werner Habicht, "Shakespeare in 'Provincial' West Germany," *Shakespeare Quarterly*, XXXI (1980): 413–15.

minority.[68] The Globe Playhouse of Los Angeles, using a cast of mixed nationalities, assigned Caliban to Mark Del Castillo-Morante, who portrayed Caliban as an American Indian. The *Shakespeare Quarterly* review suggests that Del Castillo-Morante's interpretation reflected Montaigne's essay and the historical background of the American Indian circa 1610.[69]

Although 1981 may have marked the apogee of Caliban's colonial image, it also indicated the shape of things to come. Whereas the colonial theme usually is considered essential to contemporary *Tempests*, Caliban's monstrosity is reemphasized. Joe Morton, the black actor who played Caliban for Gerald Freedman in Connecticut, performed the role a second time at The Mount, a summer theatre in Lenox, Massachusetts. This time the actor's blackness was insignificant. Peter Erickson described the effect:

Caliban's costume consisted of a narrow, flared leather cape as a tail; a daggerless scabbard dangling from his waist; leather gloves, which, blended in with his blackened skin, gave the illusion of enormous hands; a mask of light brown body paint which . . . left large circles around the eyes. . . . This Caliban was typically on or near the ground – he walked bent over at the waist, torso swaying up and down or shaking vigorously in an animal-like posture. . . . An assortment of convincing groans and growls served as background, imbuing his language with striking visceral impact.[70]

This Caliban had returned to his monstrous origins.

Ralph Berry wrote in 1983 that "Nowadays, directors have gone off Caliban: I suspect that they are bored with symbols of colonial oppression, and have wrung all the changes they can on Red Indians and Rastafarians."[71] Berry's observation seemed apt enough during the 1982 production by the Trinity Repertory Company (Providence, Rhode Island). To convey Caliban's monstrousness, Adrian Hall

---

68 For a description of Morton's performance, see Errol G. Hill, "Caliban and Ariel: A Study in Black and White in American Productions of *The Tempest* from 1945–1981," *Theatre History Studies*, IV (1984): 1–10.

69 Joseph H. Stodder and Lillian Wilds, "Shakespeare in Southern California and Visalia," *Shakespeare Quarterly*, XXXI (1980): 254–74.

70 Peter Erickson, "A *Tempest* at the Mount," *Shakespeare Quarterly*, XXXII (1981): 188–90; quotation from p. 189.

71 Ralph Berry, "Stratford Festival Canada, 1982," *Shakespeare Quarterly*, XXXIV (1983): 93–96, esp. p. 95.

strapped Richard Kneeland's feet to three-foot stools. As Caliban clomped across the stage, he was grotesque indeed. Some in the audience worried more about how Caliban would fall to his hands and knees than about his lines or characterization. The production suggested that even for Caliban, there are limits to innovation.

The Tempest continued to be popular through the 1980s. During 1988 alone, Londoners could see three major productions. Peter Hall's rendition at the National Theatre revealed Caliban's monstrosity in exaggerated bestiality. Tony Haygarth appeared, according to reviewer Jill Pearce, "almost naked, covered with blood and slime and with Frankenstein-like teeth."[72] When the "costumed" Haygarth greeted Queen Elizabeth II backstage, newpapers around the world featured photographs of the encounter: In a royal confrontation of "beauty" and "beast" the queen was elegantly gowned, while Haygarth was nude except for a large artificial phallus.

Nicholas Hytner's Royal Shakespeare Company *Tempest* expressed monstrosity in a milder way. John Kane's Caliban was human in appearance, except for skin like the underbelly of a dalmatian – black splotches stenciled over pink body paint. He sported long nails, presumably to dig pignuts. On his head, hands, wrists, and feet was a shiny gravelly substance, suggesting aquatic origins and the cave from which he appeared.

Kane took pride in his Caliban's "unique servility"; his monster did not aspire to freedom or to hegemony over the island. Rather, he wanted a master who would love him. He wanted to return to the golden age before he was cast out from the family circle; he hoped through Stephano and Trinculo to re-create that golden world. He would be happy as a servant if only he were not pinched. And he loved the island, which, in some mysterious sense, spoke through him. Caliban, according to director Hytner, was necessary to Prospero as an object on which he could project that part of himself with which he felt uncomfortable, particularly sexual desire. Caliban, in turn, did not fathom his own misdeeds. He inherited evil from his mother – natural evil that was inextricable from his character despite Prospero's efforts to civilize him. Even so, he

---

72 Jill Pearce, "*The Tempest*," *Cahiers Elisabethains*, XXXV (1989): 88–89; quotation from p. 89.

longed for Prospero to take him back and love him again. In the final scene, Caliban fell prostrate at Prospero's feet, fully expecting that he would be whipped or pinched. John Wood's Prospero reached down, gently patted the monster's head, and uttered the magic word "pardon." Caliban looked up, astonished, and grateful that at long last he was forgiven.[73]

Some productions in 1988 revealed that the colonial theme was still viable, though it no longer dominated *The Tempest*. Jonathan Miller's Old Vic *Tempest* represented Prospero's island as a Third World colony. The Neapolitan visitors were white actors in Jacobean costume; in contrast, Ariel, Caliban, and three islanders were played by black actors. The islanders carried spears and dressed in loincloths; Caliban, performed by Rudolph Walker, wore torn trousers. According to reviewer Patricia E. Tatspaugh, "a calypso beat [gave] a West Indian flavor to 'Ban, Ban, Ca Caliban'" and challenged Stephano and Trinculo "to move in rhythm to the strange music." At the finale, Miller followed in Herbert Beerbohm Tree's footsteps by providing a vignette of the island after Prospero's departure, but his focus was Ariel, not Caliban. In a postcolonial twist, Ariel, who seemed complacent through most of the play, took over the island. Tatspaugh described the action:

Ariel picks up the pieces of Prospero's broken staff, holds them together, and points them theatrically at Caliban, whose face falls, for he has just examined Prospero's cave as a potential home. The three islanders stand obediently to the side.[74]

Whereas one native (Caliban) has been humanized by his colonial experience, the other (Ariel) is suddenly transformed to a dictator. This may reflect Miller's awareness that the breakdown of European imperialism had mixed results, occasionally producing totalitarian regimes as repressive as any foreign rule.

The 1990 *Tempest* at the Folger Shakespeare Theatre was less intellectual than either Hytner's or Miller's, relying mostly on elab-

---

73 Based on comments by Nicholas Hytner at the Shakespeare Institute, August 1988, and an interview between Virginia Vaughan and John Kane, August 1988. See her review in *Shakespeare Bulletin*, VII (January/February 1989): 11.
74 Patricia E. Tatspaugh, "The Old Vic *Tempest*," *Shakespeare Bulletin*, VII (1989): 8–9.

orate special effects for audience appeal: a tumultuous storm scene, rock music, and an MTV masque with life-size videos. But even there *The Tempest*'s colonial overtones were not entirely muffled. Caliban was straightforwardly acted by the simply clad black actor Raphael Nash, whose magnificent physique towered over the rest of the cast. For the most part, Nash stood erect, and his only deformity was the sandy grit in his hair. Because there was nothing particularly monstrous about him, the only apparent reason for Prospero's disgust seemed to be veiled racism. Whether it was intentional or not, the facts of director Richard E. T. White's casting implied the dominance of a white power structure.

Judging from productions over the past ten years, it is difficult to predict where Caliban will travel. During the next decade, the Royal Shakespeare Company probably will remain the most popular and influential producer of Shakespeare, despite its financial difficulties. Whatever tack it takes, however, the abundance of Shakespeare festivals in the United States and elsewhere in the world guarantees that no stage view of Caliban will monopolize turn-of-the-century productions. From the rich history of theatrical innovation surveyed here, it seems safe to predict that there may still be some surprises in store for Caliban watchers.

Chapter 8
Screen history

Such shapes, such gesture, and such sound, expressing . . . a kind / Of excellent dumb discourse.
                                        The Tempest (III.iii.37–39)

Film is no enemy to Shakespeare, and Shakespeare no enemy to film.
                                        Jack Jorgens (1977)

As the chorus proclaims in *Henry V*, Shakespeare was frustrated by the limits of his wooden O:

> O for a Muse of fire, that would ascend
> The brightest heaven of invention:
> A kingdom for a stage, princes to act,
> And monarchs to behold the swelling scene! . . .
>   Can this cockpit hold
> The vasty fields of France? Or may we cram
> Within this wooden O the very casques
> That did affright the air at Agincourt?
>   (Chorus I.1–18)

In 1944 Laurence Olivier and in 1989 Kenneth Branagh demonstrated in films of *Henry V* that the movie camera can indeed represent "the swelling scene" and "the vasty fields of France" in exciting and realistic detail as Shakespeare's theatre could not. Shakespeare on film can be compelling popular theatre.

What now seems obvious for *Henry V* is not true of *The Tempest*. Though it has been presented repeatedly on film throughout the twentieth century, no director of Olivier's or Branagh's stature has attempted a popular cinematic version. Instead, *Tempest* films are roughly divided between low-budget television presentations and more expensive adaptations that abandon Shakespeare's text altogether.

The single large-screen interpretation of *The Tempest* was directed by avant-garde filmmaker Derek Jarman in 1979, but it never gained the popular appeal of Roman Polanski's *Macbeth* or Franco Zeffirelli's *Romeo and Juliet*. Jarman used Shakespeare's text and characters, so technically his film was not an adaptation. But he transposed so many scenes and cut so many lines that the final product seemed little akin to Shakespeare's drama. Rather, it was a remaking of Shakespeare's script into a commentary on the 1970s counterculture movement.

Adaptation seems to have been the key to successful cinematic representations of *The Tempest*. As one of Shakespeare's most un-realistic plays, *The Tempest* is not suited to Zeffirelli's evocations of local color or Peter Brook's harsh documentary style.[1] Prospero's magic, Ariel's invisibility, the island's mystery, and the spectacles of disappearing banquet and masque all conspire to create an atmosphere of fantasy. No wonder that the most successful screen version of *The Tempest*, at least in terms of popular appeal and longevity, is the science-fiction film *Forbidden Planet*. Although it abandons Shakespeare's language entirely, its central conflict be-tween the conveniences of technology and the terror of science's destructive power captures the serious elements of Prospero's magic in ways the television presentations of the British Broadcasting Corporation (BBC) and the Bard do not.

Our focus, of course, is not *The Tempest* as a whole but Caliban. In the chronological survey that follows, we highlight how Shakespeare's savage slave was costumed and performed within each production's overall design. We relate him to the director's

---

1 For a discussion of screen realism, see Jack J. Jorgens, *Shakespeare on Film* (Bloomington: Indiana University Press, 1977), pp. 8–9. Our use of the terms "presentation," "interpretation," and "adaptation" also comes from Jorgens (pp. 12–14).

artistic vision and assess his impact on a particular audience. In the process, we find, as we have found elsewhere, a broad range of characterizations and interpretations.

I

The first *Tempest* film appeared in 1905. Frustratingly little is known about that production or the half dozen that followed in the next twenty-two years. Robert Hamilton Ball's exhaustive research into silent films has uncovered only scattered references and reviews. Few, if any, of the films survive; we know of them through reviews and advertisements.

In 1905, with moving pictures in their infancy, British pioneer Charles Urban filmed (in America) the shipwreck scene from Herbert Beerbohm Tree's *Tempest*. The film's purpose was not so much audience entertainment as stage manager's prop. According to *The Optical Lantern and Cinematic Journal*, "As the [acting] company now tour[s] the country, there will be no need to carry the cumbersome property belonging to the scene. The Bioscope will do the work of depicting the scene by projections from behind the screen." The film was "tinted to the suitable weird moonlight color." Caliban (played by Tree) obviously did not benefit directly from the new technology, which, in any event, lasted less than two minutes.[2] In 1908, a much longer British film (780 feet, compared with Tree's 100 feet) apparently tried to capture a truncated version of the whole *Tempest*. It was, the absence of evidence suggests, neither advertised nor reviewed. The only surviving clues are brief notices in trade journals. They do not mention Caliban.[3]

Another *Tempest*, which may be the lost Clarendon film,[4] is extant at London's National Film Archives. Directed by Percy Stow, this short 35 mm film cuts most of Caliban's role and focuses mainly on Prospero's plans for Miranda's marriage.

Slightly more is known about a 1911 production. Edwin Thanhouser, an American stage actor and entrepreneur (and the

2 Quotations from Robert Hamilton Ball, *Shakespeare on Silent Film: A Strange Eventful History* (London: Allen & Unwin, 1968), pp. 30–32, 306.
3 Ball, *Silent Film*, pp. 76–77, 318.
4 Ball, *Silent Film*, p. 76.

most seriously committed of American *auteurs* of Shakespearean silent films), created successful films of *Richard III*, *King Lear*, and *The Winter's Tale* (1910); his *Tempest*, however, apparently flopped, ostensibly because, according to the *Moving Picture World*, "Ariel is . . . the only truly well acted part in the picture."[5] Again, no mention of Caliban.

Caliban seems scarcely to have existed in a French version of *The Tempest* in 1912. The twenty-minute production drastically altered Shakespeare's original, especially by conflating the details of the story and privileging the opening and closing scenes, which left Caliban without a significant role. But however slight his part, he was at least seen in France, Germany, England, and the United States, where thirty copyrighted prints circulated among exhibitors.[6]

Caliban enjoyed no such exposure in the 1914 British film, which, like Beerbohm Tree's earlier production, took *The Tempest* to mean a storm, nothing more.[7] More comprehensive was the Pathé production of 1921, but it was a modernization remote from Shakespeare's text. Little is known about this 2,000-foot film, in which Caliban apparently was again barely represented.[8] Comparably insignificant and now obscure – Ball calls them "quite irrelevant" – were silent *Tempest*s in 1927 and 1929. The former, starring John Barrymore, was described as a "Romantic drama of the Russian Revolution."[9]

II

With the development of talking pictures and television, *The Tempest* has been appropriated with surprising frequency. Britain's rich theatrical heritage almost guaranteed that as television became more readily available, the BBC would bring legitimate theatre, particularly Shakespeare, to a mass audience. The BBC/Time-Life television production (discussed later) is but the most recent of several BBC versions of *The Tempest*. The first was transmitted on 5 February 1939 from London. Produced and directed by Dallas

5 Ball, *Silent Film*, pp. 70, 317.
6 Ball, *Silent Film*, pp. 150–51, 341.
7 Ball, *Silent Film*, pp. 201, 353.
8 Ball, *Silent Film*, pp. 266–67, 372.
9 Ball, *Silent Film*, pp. 264, 370.

Bower, this television version featured Peggy Ashcroft as Miranda, John Abbott as Prospero, and George Devine as Caliban. The earliest postwar television broadcast occurred on 12 October 1956, again from the BBC. Caliban was acted by Robert Atkins, Prospero by Robert Eddison. In a comprehensive filmography, Kenneth S. Rothwell describes Atkins's Caliban as "a truly horrible, misshapen figure, ape-like with long hair."[10] This, not surprisingly, coincides with Atkins's stage interpretations at the Old Vic in the 1920s and again in 1938, which embodied turn-of-the-century conceptions of Caliban as a missing link.[11]

A third BBC television *Tempest*, produced by Cedric Messina, was broadcast on 12 May 1968. Caliban was portrayed by Keith Michell, Prospero by Michael Redgrave. Program notes for the 9 May 1968 *Radio Times* describe the Neapolitans as "washed up on an island on which the only inhabitant was Caliban – the primitive creature with no sense of right or wrong and without the powers of speech. Prospero has, using his magical powers, overthrown him, taught him speech, but has kept him subjugated." A photograph shows Michell with long hair and beard. Though power seems to have been the issue between Prospero and Caliban, this production apparently was not set in a colonial context. Caliban continued to be what he had been for Beerbohm Tree, a primitive but sympathetic ape-man.

III

Six other cinematic versions of *The Tempest* have appeared in England and the United States since World War II. Unlike the versions described earlier, which are available only in film archives, these *Tempests* are for public sale through video catalogues and are widely dispersed in England and the United States. They are part of the general public's exposure to Shakespeare's play and to impressions of Caliban and hence warrant more extensive comment than we have accorded the older, obscure films. Each recent film

10 Kenneth S. Rothwell and Annabelle Melzer, *Shakespeare on Screen: An International Filmography and Videography* (New York: Neal Schuman, 1990), p. 284.
11 See Chapter 7, Section IV, for discussion of Atkins's stage Caliban.

reappropriates Caliban to suit its particular purpose: Sometimes he relates to trends we have already discussed in critical and theatre history; sometimes he seems sui generis.

The earliest *Tempest* in the postwar period appropriates Shakespeare's plot to the fantasy world of science fiction. Set in 2257 AD on the planet Altair IV, *Forbidden Planet* (1956) projects Prospero's island far into the future. Prospero, played by Walter Pidgeon, is Dr. Morbius, a philologist who had arrived on Altair IV twenty years before the film begins. He was accompanied by his wife, who later died, presumably during the birth of their daughter Altaira (the Miranda figure, acted by Anne Francis). His original shipmates mysteriously died early on; Morbius reports that they were all torn limb from limb by "some terrible incomprehensible force," a "devilish thing that never once showed itself." The spaceship vaporized as the three remaining Earthmen tried to take off. In contrast to his fellow crew members, Morbius wanted to investigate the new world's wonders, particularly the ancient civilization of the Krell, now extinct, that had thrived on Altair IV thousands of years earlier.

In many respects *Forbidden Planet* follows Shakespeare's original pattern: Commander Adams (the Ferdinand figure, played by Leslie Nielsen) meets and falls in love with Altaira; the cook (Earl Holliman as a sort of Trinculo) gets drunk on Tennessee bourbon manufactured by Robby the Robot (the film's Ariel); Morbius's magic, which comes from his study of the Krell, makes him superior in knowledge and wisdom to the men from Earth; Altaira is now past puberty and ready for sex and marriage. There the similarities end.

Forbidden Planet's Morbius is quite different from Shakespeare's Prospero. As Joseph Milicia observes, Prospero is not as self-deluding as Morbius; he "is never in real danger of losing control to Caliban, unlike the case of Morbius and his monster."[12] In contrast to Prospero, Morbius does not want to return to Earth, nor does he want visitors. He discourages their arrival and soon orders the rescue party to leave. But Commander Adams is undeterred; he wants to investigate the planet and to retrieve, if possible, Altaira and her father.

12 Joseph Milicia, "Introduction" to W. J. Stuart's novel *Forbidden Planet* (New York: 1956; repr. Boston: Gregg Press, 1978), p. viii.

The longer the intruders stay, the more frustrated Morbius becomes. He shows them the secrets of the Krell – his particular masque – but only after they have invaded his study and insisted on some answers. The Krell were, he claims, an ethically and technologically superior race who thrived a million years before humanity crawled out of the slime. At the apogee of their civilization they created a huge thermonuclear power plant with 7,800 levels and 9,200 reactors to power the planet and remove all need for physical instrumentality. Then, in a single night, they vanished.

Where does Caliban fit into this sci-fi drama? In one sense, he is not a character in the film; in another sense, he is ever-present, though visible only through special effects. His shape, a Grendel-like monster, is revealed by electromagnetic currents as he crosses the spaceship's electrical fence and tears several spacemen apart (again, in Grendel fashion). He is also revealed through his footprints (measuring 37 × 19 inches), characteristic, we are told, of a four-footed arboreal creature, though he is instead a biped. His shape, speculates the spaceship's resident scientist, "runs counter to every known law of adaptive evolution."

Caliban's successful depredations on the spaceship accelerate in the spectacular but eerie fashion appropriate to science fiction until the denouement: the discovery that this flesh-tearing monster is the electrical projection of Morbius's own mind, the id within him that seeks to destroy and kill. Morbius accepts that the id may have destroyed the Krell, that despite their advanced stage of evolution they could not escape "the elementary beast within." He has more difficulty acknowledging the id within himself. Commander Adams rejoins: "We're all part monster in our subconscious, so we have laws and religion." He admonishes Morbius: "You sent your secret id out to murder your colleagues who wanted to return to Earth. Even in you there still exists the mindless primitive who wants to punish your daughter for her disloyalty and disobedience." As the destructive force pulsates around them, Morbius finally cries out: "Guilty, guilty! My evil self is at that door and I have no power to stop it." He sacrifices his life to thwart the monster and orders the captain to throw the switch that will destroy the planet in a giant thermonuclear reaction. Commander Adams and Altaira escape in the spaceship, sadly observing, as they watch from afar the destruction of Altair IV, "it will remind us that we are after all not God."

The creators of *Forbidden Planet* seem to have projected post–World War II terrors onto Shakespeare's original savage. Their interpretation of Caliban as the id, the thing of darkness within us that we must acknowledge as ours, is patently Freudian in an era groping to understand the senseless cruelties of the 1930s and '40s.

However educated or civilized humans think they are, *Forbidden Planet* suggests, this beast lurks within, ready to pounce and destroy. Morbius endures Prospero's timeless problem of maintaining order and decency without himself being transformed into an evil monster who abuses power and authority. The film is also postwar in its emphasis on nuclear power as a potential source of destruction – of civilization and of the planet itself. Though set in 2257 AD, *Forbidden Planet*'s concerns, particularly in its portrayal of Caliban (Figure 11), were especially appropriate for the 1950s.[13]

The second cinematic version of *The Tempest* in the postwar period is a relic of the 1960s live television drama. George Schaefer's Hallmark Hall of Fame rendition adapted Shakespeare's play to the requirements of television programming, cutting Shakespeare's text to suit its ninety-minute format but keeping the plot, characters, and language fairly true to the original. And yet his conception of the play as a "soufflé," something light and airy,[14] made this video production far less serious, and for many viewers probably less interesting, than *Forbidden Planet*.

Schaefer cast celebrities in the title roles: Maurice Evans as Prospero, Roddy McDowall as Ariel, and Lee Remick as Miranda. Richard Burton enacted Caliban; Schaefer presumably chose him for his magnificent voice. Burton's renditions of Caliban's poetic passages were set pieces: The other actors stood almost entranced at the fusion of voice and poetic phrase. His costume was less memorable. Burton wore the almost predictable fins, puppy-dog ears, and huge

---

13 For a modern travesty of *Forbidden Planet* and Shakespeare's *Tempest*, see Bob Carlton's rock-and-roll musical, *Return to the Forbidden Planet*, "A Methuen New Theatrescript" (London: Methuen, 1985). In this multimedia spoof, Ariel the Robot has several of Caliban's lines; Cookie's desire for Miranda also links him with Shakespeare's monster.

14 See Bernice Kliman's interview with Schaefer in *Film Criticism*, VII (1983): 29–37.

11. Dr. Morbius's id (implicitly Caliban) attacks Captain Adams (Ferdinand) and his men in this touched-up frame from *Forbidden Planet* (1956).

primordial nose common to stage productions. In a green-and-brown body stocking covered with scales, he was neither fish nor ape, but a strange cross between them. Although he often hunched over, he still seemed more erect, more intellectual, and vastly more cultured than most Calibans.

Given the production's soufflé quality, it is not surprising that Caliban's conspiracy against Prospero is not taken seriously by Prospero or the audience. Trinculo, played by man-in-the-street Tom Poston, and Stephano (Liam Redmond) are particularly preposterous. Caliban admits his foolishness in serving them and ends the video with new respect for a rather authoritarian, fatherly Prospero.

This production, in accord with Hallmark Hall of Fame practice, was Schaefer's attempt to present a live play on the television screen. His *Tempest* was thus a "presentation," an effort "to convey the original with as little alteration and distortion as possible."[15] Film critic Anthony Davies argues that presentations are based on "the contention that a play produced on the theatre stage is essentially complete, and that cinema is simply a medium for its transmission and preservation."[16] Though electronic tricks made Ariel six inches or six feet high as circumstances dictated, Schaefer's was a *Tempest* straight from the Old Vic.

In 1979, television audiences were offered a new presentation of *The Tempest* in the BBC/Time-Life series. This video, directed by John Gorrie, is even more literal than Schaefer's version; it retains most of Shakespeare's language and is faithful to the text's scenic structure. Michael Hordern plays a somewhat bemused but stern Prospero. Caliban, acted by Warren Clarke, seems something of a throwback to the ape-man of Herbert Beerbohm Tree, with long hair covering his body and jutting brows over his eyes. Ariel, by contrast, is fairylike, with no body hair at all. Gorrie uses his television camera to make Ariel appear and disappear. No such tricks are needed, however, to convey Caliban's earthiness. He first appears hunched over his stack of wood. In the gaberdine he truly seems to be a monster. In contrast to Richard Burton's intellectual Caliban, Clarke's monster is a brute, a sort of high-grade moron, who delivers his lines with the accents of Lenny in *Of Mice and Men*. He has some perception of Miranda's beauty, but for the most part he is simpleminded. When he sues Prospero for grace at the play's conclusion, he falls on his knees in teary-eyed remorse. Clarke's Caliban is a brute for whom we feel pity but little respect. As reviewer Dominick Grundy observes, in this rendition Caliban and Ariel, rather than Miranda and Ferdinand, "round out the island family by being its indispensable, sulky teenagers."[17]

England offered another cinematic *Tempest* the same year, but instead of simply presenting Shakespeare's text, this version

---

15 Jorgens, *Shakespeare on Film*, p. 12.
16 Anthony Davies, *Filming Shakespeare's Plays: The Adaptations of Laurence Olivier, Orson Welles, Peter Brook and Akira Kurosawa* (Cambridge University Press, 1988), p. 9.
17 Dominick Grundy, "The Shakespeare Plays on TV," *Shakespeare on Film Newsletter*, V, No. 2 (1981): 3.

Screen history

rearranged the speeches and the sequence of events. Derek Jarman's ninety-minute movie, like the BBC television version, was a low-budget production. A fortyish Prospero was depicted by Heathcote Williams, while Jack Birkett enacted another brutish, moronic Caliban. There the similarity to the BBC/Time-Life version abruptly ends.

Jarman's films usually were statements of the late-1970s and early-1980s British counterculture, intended for punk and gay audiences. His *Tempest* is no exception. Its freedom with the text, fresh and imaginative to some reviewers, struck others as bizarre. Jack Birkett, a blind mime-actor, portrays an effeminate but physical Caliban. He first appears in the mansion's kitchen (the bulk of the film was shot at the Palladian Stoneleigh Abbey in Warwickshire), eating a raw egg. He is middle-aged, bald, and, in David Hirst's words, "shambling, displaying in grisly close-up his ugly teeth set in a permanent grimace of hatred."[18] He jumps at Miranda, laughs, shakes his fly at her, and returns to his eggs. This initial visual image of Caliban suggests appetite in its rawest form – hunger and lust – and Miranda could easily be consumed like an egg. In his 1984 autobiography, Jarman described the filming of this scene:

We rehearsed slowly, arm in arm, often no more than twice, and he always hit the mark. His laughter echoed through Stoneleigh. "This island's mine by Sycorax, my muvver" in his North Country brogue brought spontaneous applause from the crew. He ate the raw eggs with a wicked relish, and every so often sat in the corner in a fit of melancholy. It is seventeen years since he went blind, but during that time has turned himself into a great harlequin.[19]

To control Caliban's appetite, Prospero deliberately steps on his fingers, suggesting that communication with a retarded monster requires force more than language. (The emphasis on physicality also enables Birkett to use his miming skills to great advantage.) Birkett plays his childlike Caliban with a high-pitched, whiny voice. Caliban brings his logs in a wheelbarrow, chortles and scratches himself. Both Miranda and Prospero show physical disgust when-

18 David Hirst, *The Tempest: Text and Performance* (London: Macmillan, 1984), p. 49.
19 Derek Jarman, *Dancing Ledge* (London: Quartet Books, 1984), pp. 202–03.

ever he appears. Caliban, in turn, continually laughs and leers. He watches Miranda voyeuristically in her bath and lurks around the corners of the mansion.

Jarman is particularly outrageous in a mimed flashback to twelve years before the film begins: An adult Caliban nurses at Sycorax's pendulous breast. She is fat and repulsive – an "obese, naked sorceress, heavily made up and smoking a hookah."[20] A chained Ariel is forced to participate in Sycorax's obscene rites, to Caliban's sadistic pleasure.

The film contains no gaberdine scene, per se. Caliban falls on the beach, where Stephano and Trinculo find him. He gladly shares their bottle, and the three dance a jig, then sneak toward the mansion to kill Prospero. In a bizarre finale, they find the house full of sailors, who dance a hornpipe reminiscent of *H.M.S. Pinafore*. Trinculo dresses up as a female impersonator, and Caliban dances with him. The sailors look on, making catcalls, while Caliban grins with pleasure. All action ceases when Prospero appears. The film concludes with Ceres (soul singer Elisabeth Welch) performing a Busby Berkeley rendition of "Stormy Weather." When she disappears, so does everyone else. We see a brief shot of Prospero dreaming and hear a voice-over of the "revels now are ended" speech.

Jarman expressed in his autobiography the desire for a set that could represent "an island of the mind, that opened mysteriously like Chinese boxes."[21] Deep inside this puzzle (inside the Chinese box formed by Stoneleigh Abbey) Prospero could practice his magic using the formulae of Cornelius Agrippa. As a Renaissance magus, Heathcote Williams remains firmly in control. Because he never relinquishes his magic, Caliban can never be a threat. Jack Birkett's rendition, in turn, is more mooncalf than monster; he is neither frightening nor particularly angry. He is primarily a harlequin – a grotesque and sometimes obscene figure of fun.

Three years later, Paul Mazursky's adaptation *Tempest* (1982) sported a Caliban with vigorous, heterosexual appetites, coupled with a healthy dose of cupidity. Raul Julia's wide-eyed Kalibanos

---

20 Hirst, *Text and Performance*, p. 55.
21 Jarman, *Dancing Ledge*, p. 186.

joins lust for Miranda with a colonial's desire to make a fast buck off his gullible masters. Mazursky modernizes Shakespeare's plot to depict an eminent Manhattan architect in his fifties, caught in a midlife crisis. John Cassavetes plays Phillip Dimitrious, who flees his job and his wife (Antonia, played by Gena Rowlands) and takes his daughter, Miranda (Molly Ringwald), with him to an abandoned Greek island. He is also accompanied by his mistress, a delightfully sexy young woman named Aretha (Ariel, acted by Susan Sarandon), whom he had acquired en route. They and the island's single native, Kalibanos, live in relative harmony for a year, spending their working hours rebuilding an ancient outdoor amphitheatre. Phillip practices celibacy, much to Aretha's frustration, while Kalibanos hopes that tourist boats will arrive so he can barter for goods, such as the Sony television set he uses to lure Miranda into his cave. Miranda exhibits typical teenage sullenness and longs for her friends and New York life-style.

This comic idyll comes to an end when a tempest, ostensibly called up by Phillip, washes ashore the motorboat that contains Antonia and her lover, Phillip's former boss, Alonso (Vittorio Gassman). Phillip accedes to Aretha's plea to forgive everyone and kills a goat in ritual sacrifice. With a tango playing sensually in the background, each of the characters forgives the others, even Phillip, who stops dancing with Antonia to ask Kalibanos to forgive him. Kalibanos is preoccupied in his dance with Dolores (who speaks in the idealistic platitudes of Gonzalo), a blonde from the shipwrecked boaters, and merely says, "OK, OK." The final scene shows Phillip, Antonia, and Miranda returning to Manhattan, a reconciled family about to resume its life in New York.

Raul Julia's Kalibanos is throughout more a figure of fun and sexuality than menace. A goatherd by trade, he controls his flock by playing "New York, New York" on the clarinet. He is a native of the remote island (a Third World prototype, if you will) who is fascinated by western goods and culture. When Phillip first arrives, Kalibanos introduces himself: "I am the big guy on this island. I am the boss." But in the next breath, he begins to call Phillip "Boss." He bums a cigarette and intuitively carries Phillip's suitcase.

The central conflict between Phillip and Kalibanos is over Miranda. In contrast to Shakespeare's play, where the attempted rape is

211

well in the past, this Kalibanos is persistent. The first view of him is behind a portable bush, where he leers at the skinny-dipping Miranda. He mutters "Some body!" and moves his bush closer. His antics are humorous, especially in contrast to Phillip's self-absorbed angst. However appealing, Kalibanos's physicality represents a threat to Phillip's world, especially his control of Miranda. Later, Phillip shouts: "If you touch my daughter, I'll kill you."

When Aretha informs Phillip that Miranda visited Kalibanos's cave to see the television and that he made a pass at her, Phillip is furious. He challenges Kalibanos: "Did you touch her?" When Kalibanos admits, "I kiss her. It was beautiful," Phillip knocks him from a rowboat into the sea. From the water Kalibanos cries, "I was boss before you show up." Phillip replies, "You are ignorant. I taught you how to count." Kalibanos shouts in return, "I show you the sweet water and now you prance because my bonnie johnny dance in my pants." Kalibanos forces Phillip to recognize that Miranda is no longer a child and that if he stays on the island, Kalibanos must have her or there will be an incestuous relationship with her father. As the scene ends, Phillip jumps in the water to rescue Kalibanos, who cries, "You are a god." Pulling Kalibanos toward the boat, Phillip replies, "No, I'm a monkey just like you."

In Mazursky's *Tempest*, the Caliban figure embodies sexuality in an uncultured life-style. Phillip tells Alonso to be nice to Kalibanos, for, after all, "he's your long lost ancestor." But Kalibanos also balances the figure of the colonized native with the indigenous inhabitant who exploits the naive tourists on his island. As Stephano and Trinculo comment in his cave, "He's attractive in a Third World sort of a way." Kalibanos, in turn, tries to sell them phony Greek statuettes. At the end, Phillip recognizes his link with Kalibanos: The concluding tango symbolizes the common humanity of all the characters gathered on the island. Kalibanos is never shown, however, anywhere but on his island. Presumably he would be out of place on the streets of Manhattan.

The most recent *Tempest* is as far from Jarman and Mazursky as one can travel. Produced in Hollywood during 1983 as an American low-budget competitor to England's BBC/Time-Life video, Bard Productions' telegenic *Tempest* may be the ultimate in literal presentation of Shakespeare's text. Not a word is cut. The set is a bare,

Elizabethan platform stage with two side doors, a curtain at the rear, and an upper balcony. Even the storm is created as it might be in the theatre: Ariel's spirits shake lengths of blue cloth in billowy waves, accompanied by sounds of thunder and lightning. Costumes are standard Elizabethan dress (for most of the men, doublet and hose), and the masque features Elizabethan recorder music, song, and dance. The only filmic techniques are changing camera angles and tracking that highlight soliloquies and character interaction. While the actors remain fairly static, the camera moves, bringing them to life.

In contrast to Mazursky's and Jarman's obsession with post-modernist anxieties, the Bard *Tempest* is unfailingly wholesome. The Prospero of Efrem Zimbalist, Jr., is wise and benign – the kind of father Robert Young played in the 1950s television series *Father Knows Best*. Ariel (Duane Black) in silver body paint is smooth and sinuous. Caliban (William Hootkins), by contrast, is short and fleshy, a sort of Anglicized Danny de Vito. Except for long nails painted black, he is entirely human and in no way deformed. He goes bare-chested for the most part (though his torso is draped with fishnet and rags); he wears ragged cloth breeches, leather wristlets decked with shells, and frayed leather anklets. His hair and beard are long and disheveled. He walks a bit apishly, stamps his feet when angry, and throws his logs about like a wrestler. This Caliban is, in sum, a throwback to the wild man. He is a slob, a creature of appetite – a drunk and a lech. He is capable of mystical wonder (almost a trance) as he describes the island's music, but he conveys no smoldering resentment. This is no victim of colonial oppression. He is angry when he does not get what he wants (Miranda), or sullen when he is made to work, but he is not political. At the finale, for example, Hootkins's Caliban falls flat on the stage, fearful of being pinched, to grovel at Prospero's feet. He is pathetic rather than defiant. Pardoned, he kicks Stephano and gleefully drags Trinculo off stage.

Perhaps the Bard *Tempest* is an aberration, an overly conservative rendition spawned by the complacency of the Reagan era and geared to the school video market. Or perhaps William Hootkins's cuddly Caliban is a harbinger of a new trend – reaction against angst and political posturing. In either case, it rounds out the current

213

spectrum of cinematic experimentation with Shakespeare's *Tempest*.

One hopes that someday a director of stature and popular appeal – Kenneth Branagh, perhaps – will film Shakespeare's *Tempest* with imagination and technical innovation as well as fidelity to the text. As perhaps the dramatist's most spectacular play, *The Tempest* is ripe for film's fluidity of visual image. When that happens, Caliban will continue to reflect the forces society fears as well as the bestial, sexual side of human nature. As the films already produced reveal, Caliban may be a terrifying presence or a comic buffoon, but he remains a rich, multivalent symbol.

Chapter 9
Artists' renditions

This is a strange thing as e'er I looked on.
The Tempest (V.i.289)

"[V]isual criticism," that body of latent critical interpretation found in the total work undertaken in any
age by its artists and designers, validly supplements
our more customary verbal criticism.
W. Moelwyn Merchant (1959)

Caliban's ambiguity in Shakespeare's text attracted a wide range of
visual representations, in addition to disparate critical and dramatic
interpretations and sociopolitical appropriations. Sometimes the
artists served a role similar to the photographer's: faithful renderings
of scenes from current stage performances. At other times, artists
were themselves interpreters or adapters, conveying through line
and color their own impressions of Caliban's shape, character, and
place in *The Tempest*. Our concern in this chapter is with the latter
type of aesthetic endeavor, though the distinction between the categories is occasionally obscured by a lack of information about a
craftsman's source of inspiration; he may have been more influenced
by stage performances than his rendition suggests. But whatever the
artistic purposes, the number and variety of Caliban images were
impressive, especially in the late eighteenth century and much of
the nineteenth century. Thereafter, film – at first as still lifes, then as
moving pictures – largely preempted the realm of Shakespearean
illustration.

215

I

The earliest illustrations of Shakespearean characters appeared in the first collected edition of the eighteenth century, Nicholas Rowe's seven-volume set, published in 1709 by Jacob Tonson. Each play had only one illustration, a frontispiece representing the whole text. *The Tempest's* illustration by François Boitard depicts the storm of Act I, scene i. Hobgoblins fly across a tempestuous sky as the ship founders below.[1] None of the play's dramatis personae appear.

Caliban's artistic debut – so far as we can ascertain – occurred in the mid-1730s in a *Tempest* illustration by William Hogarth (1697–1764). Already well known for multiple paintings of "A Harlot's Progress" and "A Rake's Progress," and for several major individual works, including "The Beggar's Opera," Hogarth in about 1736 tried his hand for the second time on an illustration of a Shakespearean play. In the late 1720s, he had painted "Falstaff Examining his Recruits," a composition that followed closely the staging and actors' faces in productions he had seen of *Henry IV, Part 2*. According to art historian Ronald Paulson, Hogarth treated his subjects as if they were dramatic characters. "[M]y picture is my stage," Hogarth wrote, "and men and women my players, who by means of certain actions and gestures exhibit a dumb show." His portrayal of Falstaff selecting a motley army was such a "dumb show." Not so his scene from *The Tempest* nearly a decade later. It portrays the play's major figures in a grouping gathered loosely but directly from Shakespeare's text rather than stage productions.[2] Prospero and Miranda sit outside the cave; Ferdinand bows reverently

---

1 T. S. R. Boase argues that this engraving owes nothing to Continental models and that because it cannot be based on stage effect (as the other Rowe engravings seem to be), it must derive from some unknown popular source. See "Illustrations of Shakespeare's Plays in the Seventeenth and Eighteenth Centuries," *Journal of the Warburg and Courtauld Institutes*, X (1947): 83–108. For a more recent discussion of the Rowe engravings, see H. A. Hammelmann, "Shakespeare's First Illustrators," *Apollo*, LXXXVIII, Suppl. No. 11 (August 1968): 1–4.

2 Robin Simon, "Hogarth's Shakespeare," *Apollo*, CIX (March 1979): 213–20; Ronald Paulson, *Book and Painting: Shakespeare, Milton and the Bible – Literary Texts and the Emergence of English Painting* (Knoxville: University of Tennessee Press, 1982), pp. 38–39, 48; quotation from p. 38; *Dictionary of National Biography*, 21 vols. and supplements (Oxford University Press, 1917–91), Vol. IX, pp. 977–91 (henceforth cited as *DNB*).

12. William Hogarth's scene from *The Tempest* (ca. 1736), the first known illustration of Caliban.

toward Miranda from the left; Ariel plucks a lute above them; and Caliban enters far right with a bundle of wood. His toes are webbed; his legs are scaly; his shoulders sprout finlike appendages in addition to arms. This could not be the Dryden-Davenant-Shadwell version of *The Tempest* (the only version staged in the 1720s and '30s), which has no such scene, but is instead a slightly modified rendition of the First Folio's Act I, scene ii. Although in Shakespeare's text Caliban has exited before Ferdinand's entrance, here he appears gratuitously yet not implausibly as a silent witness to Miranda and Ferdinand's first meeting (Figure 12).

As Paulson and Robin Simon have pointed out, Hogarth's painting abounds with biblical iconography: Innocent Miranda is accompanied by a lamb, her coloring is reminiscent of the Virgin Mary's in High Renaissance art, her posture proclaims that she is "No wonder sir, / But certainly a maid." Ferdinand's bent knees and his hands

217

pressed prayerfully together suggest a magus paying hommage. Caliban contrasts strikingly with Ariel – the latter angelic, the former devilish.[3] His right foot crushes two linked doves, symbols of the intended marriage that Caliban will attempt to destroy. He is, in sum, fiendish, monstrous, menacing – a fitting reflection of mid-eighteenth-century perceptions of Prospero's slave.[4]

A few years after Hogarth's introduction of Caliban to the world of illustration, Francis Hayman (1708–76) designed and Francis Gravelot engraved illustrations for Thomas Hanmer's six-volume edition of Shakespeare's plays (1744). Hayman was immersed in London's theatrical world. Before he became a book illustrator, he worked as a scene painter at the Drury Lane Theatre. He was a member of the Beefsteak Club, where theatrical matters were often discussed, and associated with Hogarth and David Garrick.[5] Hayman was regarded as the first historical painter of the time; in 1768, he was a founding member of the Royal Academy of Arts.[6]

Hayman's portrayal of Act I, scene ii, of *The Tempest* foregrounds Prospero and Miranda, while Caliban lurks dimly near the mouth of a cave in the background. We see only his face and torso, which are darker than his master's. His features are irregular, but too little of his body shows to tell if it is deformed (Figure 13). Caliban's marginal position in the background reflects, perhaps, his marginality in the mid-eighteenth-century productions, where Caliban's role was subordinate even to Trinculo's.

T. S. R. Boase, an authority on early Shakespeare illustrations, argues that "Hayman marks the meetingplace of two schools, the continental and the English."[7] From Hogarth, Hayman borrowed dramatic figures whose facial expressions and gestures imitated contemporary acting styles. The French influence came from François Boitard, working with Louis du Guernier, the principal engraver in

3 Simon, "Hogarth's Shakespeare," pp. 217–19; Paulson, *Book and Painting*, p. 49.
4 Paulson, *Book and Painting*, pp. 51–52. For a possible "subliminal reference" to Caliban in another Hogarth painting, see David Dabydeen, *Hogarth's Blacks: Images of Blacks in Eighteenth Century English Art* (Athens: University of Georgia Press, 1987), pp. 80–81.
5 *DNB*, Vol. IX, pp. 296–97.
6 For a full account of Hayman's life and oeuvre, see Brian Allen, *Francis Hayman* (New Haven, Conn.: Yale University Press, 1987).
7 Boase, "Illustrations of Shakespeare's Plays," p. 91.

13. Francis Gravelot's engraving of Francis Hayman's romanticized scene from *The Tempest* (1744).

Jacob Tonson's team for the 1709 edition. These two streams – imported and indigenous – influenced British artists to the end of the eighteenth century.

Our third Caliban is a watercolor from 1770 (Figure 14) by Samuel Hieronymous Grimm (1734–94). Known chiefly for his skill and accuracy as a topographical painter, Grimm was also noted for caricatures of humorous subjects.[8] His Caliban, like Hayman's, may reflect contemporary theatrical practice – though not necessarily a particular production – for the painting depicts a human form underneath a bear's head and skin.[9] The head signifies a truly animal Caliban, not human at all. It also signals the actor's impersonation by showing clear evidence of the human form underneath the animal skin, a metadramatic technique, intentional or not, that reminded its viewers that they were watching a fiction. Grimm's was the bestial Caliban common to eighteenth-century critical discourse.

John Bell's edition of Shakespeare's plays, published in 1773, featured numerous illustrations by Edward Edwards (1738–1806). An associate of the Royal Academy, Edwards specialized in portraits, landscapes, and Shakespeare subjects, including scenes for John Boydell's Shakespeare Gallery during the 1790s.[10] Edwards's Caliban of 1773 gulps eagerly from a cask of wine while Stephano and Trinculo gaze at him with amusement and awe. Their focus draws attention to Caliban's figure in the foreground; he dominates the picture. His muscular nudity (covered by a simple loincloth) contrasts with their ragged but "civilized" European garments. He appears darker and more rugged than they; his feet and hands seem oversized and perhaps webbed. He is, apparently, a blend of man and beast, but clearly more human than animal (Figure 15). Here again, the pictorial representation coincided with critical commentary: The approaching romantic movement had begun to soften Caliban's image, to emphasize his human shape, and to narrow the cultural gap between the monster and the island's other inhabitants.

8 *DNB*, Vol. VIII, p. 697.
9 As mentioned in Chapter 3, Malone recorded in the 1821 variorum the practice of playing Caliban in a bear or animal skin.
10 Samuel Redgrave, *A Dictionary of Artists of the English School* (London: George Bell & Sons, 1878), p. 138.

14. Caliban under an animal skin in Samuel H. Grimm's watercolor (1770).

In the same vein is John Hamilton Mortimer's (1741–79) head of Caliban, composed in 1775 for a series of twelve plates of Shakespearean characters. Mortimer, a historical painter who was known also for his personal excesses and wild living, created etchings full of picturesque romance and terror. His specialty was ferocious banditti.[11] Mortimer's puppy-headed Caliban seems more pathetic than ferocious, however. The lines quoted beneath the portrait, "Do not torment me . . . ," suggest his fear of Prospero's power to punish. This Caliban's form, except for his floppy ears, doglike whiskers, and long pointed fingernails, is essentially a human being (Figure 16). Mortimer, like Edwards two years earlier, anticipated the sympathetic Caliban of romantic writers such as Hazlitt and Coleridge.

If a new trend in Caliban portraiture was under way, it was far from universal. In sharp contrast with Mortimer's conception were

11 *DNB*, Vol. XIII, p. 1026.

15. Caliban encounters "celestial liquor" in Edward Edwards's illustration
for John Bell's edition of *The Tempest* (1773).

the engravings of the German artist Daniel Nicolaus Chodowiecki
(1726–1801). Born in Danzig into a distinguished family that included at least two other artists, Chodowiecki studied several artistic
media, including engraving, calendar and almanac illustration, and
especially book illustration. In the latter medium he was noted for
his illustrations of works by Goethe, Cervantes, Smollett, and other
major authors. So respected were his abundant illustrations that
Chodowiecki became secretary and subsequently director of the
prestigious Berlin Academy.[12] Yet his plates for *The Tempest* (ca.

12 *Neue deutsche Biographie*, Vol. III (Berlin: Dunker & Humbolt, 1957), pp. 212–13;
cf. George C. Williamson, ed., *Bryan's Dictionary of Painters and Engravers*, rev. ed.,
5 vols. (London: George Bell & Sons, 1926–30), Vol. I, p. 291.

16. John Hamilton Mortimer's portrait of Caliban as a "puppy-headed monster" (painted in 1775, engraved in 1820).

1780) are relatively unheralded, perhaps because they epitomize too starkly the early-eighteenth-century view of Ariel and Caliban as polar opposites: Ariel is a feminine angel hovering daintily over the other characters; Caliban is a giant tortoise, human only in his upright stature and genitalia and to some extent in his face. Lumpy and deformed, he embodies Caliban's supposed bestiality. Chodowiecki has taken Prospero's command, "Come, thou tortoise," quite literally.[13] This Caliban is not a man but a monster from the deep (Figure 17).

13 Another tortoiselike Caliban is featured in an undated (probably late-eighteenth-century) painting; see Folger Library, art box R 167, no. 23.

17. Caliban as a monstrous tortoise in Daniel Nicolaus Chodowiecki's *Tempest* illustration (ca. 1780).

II

While Chodowiecki worked on his bookplates in Germany, the great age of Shakespeare illustration was under way in England. International peace and the ensuing renewed contact between Great Britain and the Netherlands allowed the importation of new ideas and techniques from the Continent and the production of superior artwork. No sooner had London alderman John Boydell established his business in the engraving trade than he turned England from an importer to an exporter of fine prints.[14] Boydell's and others' commercial successes, the establishment of the Royal Academy, and Joshua Reynolds's *Discourses* all fostered an expansion in the

14 For biographical and critical information on John Boydell, see Sven H. A. Bruntjen, *John Boydell, 1719–1804: A Study of Art Patronage and Publishing in Georgian London* (New York: Garland Publishing, 1985). An illustrated overview of "the Boydell venture" is provided by W. Moelwyn Merchant, *Shakespeare and the Artist* (Oxford University Press, 1959), pp. 66–76.

number of English artists and improvements in the quality of their products.

Boydell is best known to Shakespeareans for his Shakespeare Gallery, an elaborate scheme first announced in 1786. Boydell's proposal – pay English artists to paint Shakespearean scenes, then sell engravings of those paintings at home and abroad – was based, aside from the profit motive, upon a sincere nationalistic desire to honor English painters and to provide them with native subjects. Since the Reformation, English artists had ignored the religious themes treated so successfully by the Italian masters: Religious representation smacked of popery, so English artists concentrated on portraiture. But in Shakespeare, England had a secular subject nearly as fertile and uplifting as scripture. After the mid-eighteenth-century exaltation of Shakespeare as "The National Poet" (culminating in David Garrick's Shakespeare Jubilee of 1769), it was perhaps inevitable that Boydell and his associates would urge English artists to find proper subjects in Shakespearean texts. And as cultural historian Richard D. Altick observes, the popularity of theatrical painting after the middle of the eighteenth century "was due partly to Garrick's shrewd recognition of its publicity value."[15] Spurred by Garrick's entrepreneurship and a coalescence of chauvinistic forces, Shakespeare became a visual as well as a verbal cultural icon.

Boydell's scheme was designed for maximum publicity and profit. The best English artists were to be hired and their works hung in a public gallery. After viewers gazed their fill at full-color originals, they could buy engravings of their favorite scenes at modest prices. To top it off, Boydell hired textual critic George Steevens to edit a nine-volume edition of the plays that would include illustrations from the gallery. Sold by subscription, printed by Englishmen for Englishmen on English paper, the Boydell-Steevens Shakespeare was a mammoth expression of late-eighteenth-century English cultural nationalism.

Although the whole enterprise took much longer than originally anticipated and lost rather than made money for the Boydell firm,

---

15 Richard D. Altick, *Paintings From Books: Art and Literature in Britain, 1760–1900* (Columbus: Ohio State University Press, 1985), p. 13; see also pages 43–50 for analysis of the Boydell gallery and its impact.

it accomplished some of its goals, especially the employment of thirty-three artists and the reproduction of scores of Shakespearean scenes. Four of the many scenes from *The Tempest*, each painted by a different artist, included Caliban. Collectively those representations reflect the disparate styles of the gallery as a whole, for Boydell's artists were heterogeneous. T. S. R. Boase divides them into two broad schools: the Italian, influenced by Sir Joshua Reynolds's theories on historical painting and by their own studies in Italy, and the English school, which stemmed from Hogarth. The latter school, claims Boase, consisted of men "who had worked at Vauxhall or done interior decorations for the Adam brothers or other fashionable architects, who were supplying the ever growing demand for book illustrations, who never had the means of foreign travel, humbler men whose works could be obtained for smaller prices."[16]

The first depiction of Caliban in Boydell's gallery appeared in 1789 in a work by Joseph Wright of Derby, a painter of some distinction. His "Prospero in his cell" foregrounds Prospero, Miranda, and Ferdinand; Caliban is a tiny figure in the distant background, cavorting with Trinculo and Stephano.[17] Because Caliban's features are difficult to distinguish, thus precluding meaningful analysis, we have not reproduced Wright's painting here.

The second Caliban in the Boydell gallery was the work of Reverend Matthew William Peters (1742–1814), a member of the Royal Academy who had studied in Italy. Although he attained modest success as an artist, Peters took religious orders in 1783; he continued to paint, but by the late 1790s he had resigned from the academy.[18] His Caliban is remarkably human in form and figure, kneeling before Prospero and Miranda in Act I, scene ii. He appears frightened, afraid of Prospero's wrath, seeming to cry for sympathy (Figure 18). Perhaps in crafting a supremely human and vulnerable Caliban, Peters was displaying the Christian teaching that had

16 Boase, "Illustrations of Shakespeare's Plays," p. 96.
17 For a black-and-white reproduction of this painting, see Merchant, *Shakespeare and the Artist*, plate 16b; Merchant assesses Wright's talents on page 73.
18 *DNB*, Vol. XV, p. 964. Robin Hamlyn argues that Peters painted more actively in the 1790s than art historians have realized, particularly for James Woodmason's Irish Shakespeare Gallery. See Hamlyn, "An Irish Shakespeare Gallery," *Burlington Magazine*, CXX, No. 905 (1978): 515–29.

18. A very human Caliban, painted for the Boydell gallery (ca. 1789; engraved 1802) by the Reverend Matthew William Peters.

become the central focus of his life. In accord with eighteenth-century critical interpretations of *The Tempest*, Prospero the magus dominates the scene: His uplifted wand and upright posture ensure his control of the monster.

The Boydell gallery's third Caliban, by Henry Fuseli (1741–1825), is in sharp contrast. Fuseli, a prime exemplar of the Italian school, was born in Zurich and nursed in the atmosphere of German romanticism. In 1763 he was introduced to Sir Joshua Reynolds, who encouraged Fuseli to become a painter. Between 1770 and 1778 Fuseli studied in Rome, where he made sketches for a Shakespearean ceiling in imitation of Michelangelo's Sistine Chapel. Winifred H. Friedman argues that Fuseli absorbed the mannerism of Michelangelo; Fuseli's muscular figures clearly derive from his experiences in Rome.[19] His Shakespeare ceiling sketch includes a figure of Caliban – muscular, devilish, with prominent genitals.[20] Fuseli's depiction of *The Tempest*'s Act I, scene ii, for the Boydell gallery is even more mannerist. Caliban looks more sinister, more devilish than in his earlier depiction, and less human; and though snakelike branches hide his private parts, he appears more lustful. Prospero in the gallery version (based on portraits of Leonardo da Vinci, as Stephen Orgel has shown[21]) acts as a shield, placing himself firmly between the defiant monster and his innocent daughter. The magus's outstretched arm and pointed finger signify his dominance; Caliban responds with a defiant glare but cannot resist Prospero's power. Above flies a seraphic Ariel, further insurance of Prospero's control. Fuseli's *Sturm und Drang* romanticism appears in the stormy sky, gnarled woods, eerie creatures, and Caliban's anger (Figure 19). The entire composition embodies the conflict between Enlightenment reason and romantic rebellion that shaped much of Fuseli's thinking.[22]

The final Boydell gallery Caliban was painted by Robert Smirke (1752–1845), also a member of the Royal Academy, who fits the criteria for Boase's "English" school. According to Friedman, Smirke was "most at home with common humanity, while Fuseli was without equal in the realm of the supernatural."[23] Smirke's 1798 Caliban

19 Winifred H. Friedman, *Boydell's Shakespeare Gallery* (New York: Garland Publishing, 1976), pp. 203–10.
20 Reproduced in *Henry Fuseli, 1741–1825*, trans. Sarah Twohig (London: The Tate Gallery, 1975).
21 *The Tempest*, ed. Stephen Orgel (Oxford University Press, 1987), pp. 7–9.
22 For Fuseli's responses to the Enlightenment and romanticism, and especially to Rousseau, see Eudo C. Mason, ed., *The Mind of Henry Fuseli* (London: Routledge & Kegan Paul, 1951), esp. pp. 121–36.
23 Friedman, *Boydell's Shakespeare Gallery*, p. 203.

19. Henry Fuseli's first portrayal of Caliban (1789).

is fully human in appearance and, apparently, in sensibilities. He
emerges from his gaberdine in fearful agony that Stephano and
Trinculo will torment him as Prospero does. His drooping mustache
and hair style create an exotic appearance, suggesting the stereo-
typical nineteenth-century view of Orientals. But, insofar as his
body can be seen, he is neither monstrous nor deformed (Figure 20).
In this rendition he is not under Prospero's control but Stephano's:
The drunken butler stands over him with the celestial liquor that
will capture Caliban's allegiance.

In the same year as Smirke's painting for Boydell, another member of the Royal Academy, Thomas Stothard (1755–1834), published
an engraving of Caliban. Stothard began his career as a book illustrator for John Bell; in 1783 he illustrated *The Picturesque Beauties of
Shakespeare* with Robert Smirke. Stothard also painted three scenes
for Boydell's gallery – from *Two Gentlemen of Verona*, *Henry VIII*, and

20. Robert Smirke's first Caliban (1798).

21. Caliban with snakes and porcupine, by Thomas Stothard (1798).

Othello.[24] Though Stothard excelled in scenes of "tender pathos and gentle humor,"[25] his Caliban is neither gentle nor humorous. The savage's fanged mouth opens in a snarl, his head tilts defiantly back, and his arms are half raised as if to ward off punishment or a harsh command; one foot is lifted in response, perhaps, to the porcupine below. Beside him are two coiled snakes, Caliban's conventional companions in many eighteenth- and nineteenth-century drawings. Whether the snakes here suggest Caliban's satanic origins, his phallic propensities, or his murky dwelling place, they lurk sinuously around him and prejudice the viewer's response (Figure 21).

24 Friedman, *Boydell's Shakespeare Gallery*, pp. 183–85.
25 *DNB*, Vol. XVIII, pp. 1320–24.

22. Henry Fuseli's second Caliban for the Boydell gallery (1803).

When the Boydell-Steevens edition of Shakespeare's works appeared in 1791–1805, it included a second Fuseli engraving of Caliban (1803).[26] Fuseli's interpretation of Caliban, however, has softened since his gallery version. This Caliban is much tamer. He is smaller, less muscular, less fiendish, less threatening. He ogles Miranda with a devilish leer, but his menacing posture and formidable glare of a decade earlier are gone (Figure 22). Prospero is even

26 For the confusing printing history of the Boydell-Steevens volumes, see Bruntjen, *Boydell*, p. 112.

23. Robert Smirke's second Caliban (1821).

more dominant than he was in the 1798 engraving. He towers over both Caliban and Miranda.

Smirke's nineteenth-century Caliban (1821) is also less threatening than his earlier portrayal. Here Caliban is alone; his body is upright, bare-chested, and comparatively hairless. This Caliban still scowls, still sports a mustache and long nails, but his physique and physiognomy are not deformed (Figure 23). One suspects that Smirke and his contemporaries had read or heard about Coleridge and Hazlitt's textual comments on Caliban or that they had been influenced by the same broad cultural trends. Artists' renditions of Caliban were now decidedly more human and more sympathetic than they had been a generation earlier.

III

Illustrated editions of Shakespeare's plays appeared periodically throughout the nineteenth century, but the outbreak of war between

England and France early in the century disrupted the trade in larger engravings. In 1804, Boydell was forced to auction off the paintings from his Shakespeare Gallery to pay debts and avoid bankruptcy.[27] A great age of Shakespeare illustration had ended, although artists continued to produce Shakespearean scenes for the next half-century and beyond. But gradually, as photography overtook painting in the late nineteenth century and moving film gained ground in the twentieth, portrayals of Shakespearean scenes and characters on canvas or copper declined. Some artists continued to be intrigued by Shakespeare's savage, of course; their representations, though fewer and further between, are found well into the late twentieth century.

Such images are most readily available in nineteenth-century editions of the plays. As the century progressed, the book trade expanded to the growing middle class. Inexpensive editions of Shakespeare appealed to families interested in moral education, not just in theatre. A good example of a Shakespeare text geared to a mass audience is Dolby's British Theatre edition of *The Tempest* in 1824. On the frontispiece is an engraving of Caliban, Ariel, Stephano, and Trinculo. The caption reads "Act V, Scene 2," but the action seems more appropriate for Act III, when the three drunks sing their catch. Trinculo plays a fife and drum; Caliban dances. The artist, Isaac Robert Cruikshank (1789–1856), was the elder brother of George Cruikshank, an illustrator of Charles Dickens's works. Robert (as the younger Cruikshank was called), like his sibling, made his living from caricatures, humorous sketches, and book illustrations. He was also a devotee of the theatre and an intimate of actor Edmund Kean.[28] Robert Cruikshank's Caliban, shaggy-haired and fur-clad, may be a representation of current stage practice. In contrast to the angry Calibans of the Boydell gallery, this smiling figure seems content with Stephano and Trinculo's liquor and companionship (Figure 24).

John Orrin Smith's (1799–1843) drawing of Caliban (one of nearly 1,000 designs he created for Joseph Kenny Meadows between 1839 and 1843)[29] also caricatures Shakespeare's monster – somberly rather

27 Friedman, *Boydell's Shakespeare Gallery*, pp. 88–93, offers an account of the lottery.
28 *DNB*, Vol. V, pp. 259–60.
29 *DNB*, Vol. XVIII, p. 493; Redgrave, *Dictionary of Artists*, p. 404.

24. The Dolby edition of *The Tempest* (1824), featuring Robert Cruikshank's
jovial Caliban.

than comically. Caliban emerges from his cave with a sly, angry
look. His huge nose, fanged lower lip, and crawling posture do not
make him sympathetic, but the exaggerated features seem more a
caricature of malign humanity than an attempt to portray realis-
tically a literary or stage character (Figure 25). Yet Smith's Caliban,
like Smirke's and Cruikshank's, is human and, compared with
eighteenth-century depictions, relatively docile.

A reversion to the bestial Caliban appears in the extensive book
illustrations by the German artist Friedrich August Moritz Retzsch
(1779–1857), whose reptilian monster contrasts starkly with most
nineteenth-century portrayals. Retzsch was one of the most prominent artists of his time: a star student at the Academy of Art in
Dresden and later a professor there; a widely admired painter of
mythological scenes and portraits; illustrator of books by Goethe and
Schiller. By the time he retired from teaching in 1828 to concentrate
on drawing and painting, he had gained public praise and royal

25. A malicious but human Caliban by John Orrin Smith (ca. 1840).

honors. He was especially noted for line drawings (often subsequently engraved on copper), most notably for an edition of *Faust*, which had "a rare sharpness, fineness, and elegance."[30] This eschewing of color and shading produced a stark but highly distinctive style – called "outlines" in English – that served well the current technology of book illustration.

Between 1828 and 1845, Retzsch used that sparse technique to illustrate eight of Shakespeare's plays. They appeared initially in separate bilingual (German and English, in parallel columns) volumes and were later combined into a single-volume *Gallery to Shakspeare's Dramatic Works*. Retzsch's *Tempest* volume, published in 1841, included twelve scenes from the play and an "Explanation" of each

30 For biographical information on Retzsch, see *Outlines to Shakespeare's Dramatic Works. Designed and Engraved by Moritz Retzsch*, 4th ed. (Boston: Roberts Brothers, 1878), [I]–IV; and Williamson, ed., *Bryan's Dictionary*, Vol. IV, p. 215.

Artists' renditions

drawing by Dr. Hermann Ulrici, a German authority on Shakespeare. His description of Caliban is worth quoting at length because presumably it speaks for the artist and thus is a rare instance of detailed insight into an illustrator's perception of his subject:

Caliban is manifestly the half devil [Ulrici wrote], as Shakspeare describes him. His head, with the low, almost vanishing forehead and short chin, is akin to that of a beast, the expression of which is still heightened by the hideous, open jaws; his large eyes, flashing hatred and malice, betray his devilish origin. The ear is in form of a winding horn; his thighs and the lower part of his body are covered with finny scales, one of which extends over the back part of the skull. Shaggy hair covers his hips and some of the joints. His hands and feet end in unwieldy claws. The feet are short and thick, the upper part of the body is long and broadshouldered, to show manifestly his heavy, earthy nature and to mark the contrast with Ariel.

As important as Ulrici's description of Caliban's body was his assessment of its meaning:

His attitude and manner express suppressed rage and powerless spite, brutal obstinacy and disobedience. His whole appearance is fantastically ugly, without exciting disgust and aversion. It is the Fantastic which attracting rather than repelling, gives him that poetical impress, which the poet has diffused over his whole figure.[31]

This Caliban was clearly – in Ulrici's text and Retzsch's drawing – the most thoroughly bestial monster since Chodowiecki's tortoise. Retzsch has obviously derived his interpretation from Shakespeare's text rather than stage performances. His curious combination of fish, dog, and fiend seems to meld textual references to a "strange fish," a "puppy-headed monster," and "a born devil" into a fearsome, quasi-human shape (Figure 26).[32]

31 Moritz Retzsch, *Gallery to Shakspeare's Dramatic Works, in Outlines* (New York: G. & B. Westermann Brothers, 1849). The volume is unpaginated; the quoted passages appear as commentary on *The Tempest*, plate IV. See also *Retzsch's Outlines to Shakspeare. The Tempest* (Leipsic: Published by Ernest Fleischer; London: Sold by Black & Armstrong, 1841), Preface, for comments by Ulrici on his involvement in the project.
32 For a brief summary of Retzsch's career and a long list of his works, see *Allegemeines Lexikon der bildenden Künstler*, 37 vols., ed. Ulrich Thieme et al. (Leipzig: W.

237

26. F. A. M. Retzsch's "outline" of Caliban in Act I, scene i (1841).

IV

By the middle of the nineteenth century, Caliban was viewed in a new light. Although Daniel Wilson's *Caliban: The Missing Link* was not published until 1873, Darwinism had already affected literary interpretation and artistic modes of representation.[33] Occasionally in the 1850s, and increasingly thereafter, artists' renditions reflected Caliban's newly assigned role in human evolution. Frequently he is depicted as apish or amphibian. Sir John Gilbert's (1817–97) illus-

Englemann [vols. 1–4], E. A. Seemann [vols. 5–37], 1907–50), Vol. XXVIII, pp. 193–94. For an illustration that portrays Caliban as a frightful batlike creature, see James Ward's "Miranda and Caliban" (1837), reproduced in Merchant, *Shakespeare and the Artist*, plate 37b.
33 See Chapter 4, Section IV, for a discussion of Darwinism's influence on scholarly conceptions of Caliban and Chapter 7, Section IV, for its influence on stage productions.

27. Sir John Gilbert's Darwinian Caliban (ca. 1856).

trations for Howard Staunton's three-volume edition (1856–60) are cases in point. Caliban's facial features are more apelike than in eighteenth-century engravings. His long hair and jutting eyebrows suggest the African gorilla. In a crowning Darwinian touch, a monkey clambers above him, suggesting Caliban's close kinship to lower forms of life (Figure 27).

Another Caliban that may reflect a Darwinian influence appears in a representation of Act II, scene i, by Thomas Henry Nicholson (d. 1870). This versatile artist – draughtsman, illustrator, engraver, and sculptor – was the principal artist from 1853 to 1857 for *Cassell's Illustrated Family Paper*. His engravings for an edition of the *Works of Shakespeare* (n.d.) are busy and mannered. More important for our purposes is his reptilian Caliban, who sports, along with scales and a large back fin, pointed ears and an animalistic face (Figure 28). His

239

28. Caliban as part human, part reptile in Thomas Henry Nicholson's
engraving (ca. 1856).

posture and physique imply a lower form of human evolution,
although – in the absence of other evidence – Nicholson may have
attempted, as had Retzsch a couple of decades earlier, merely to
show Caliban as a fusion of the epithets hurled at him in *The
Tempest*'s text.

Similarly, Wilhelm von Kaulbach's (1805–74) illustration for his
Shakspeare-Album (1855–58) is more amphibian than ape. He has
fins, scales, and webbed feet, yet his head is human and hairy, and
he has a tail. His crouched position further emphasizes a crawling
animal, lower in the evolutionary scale than the upright Stephano
and Trinculo. That this is an artist's interpretation of the text rather
than a stage illustration is clear from the winged Ariel and numerous
cherubim hovering overhead (Figure 29).

The evolutionary motif is suggested also, but less starkly, in Walter

240

29. Wilhelm von Kaulbach's amphibian Caliban, with Trinculo, Stephano, and Ariel's minions (ca. 1858).

Crane's portrayals of Caliban. One of the most prolific and popular book illustrators of his day, Crane (1845–1915) was also a pioneer in woodcut designs. His early work was influenced by John Gilbert; he later shared the "new Hellenism" of his friend Oscar Wilde. Uneasy with what they saw as the Victorian era's lack of aesthetic standards, the new Hellenists studied – and often imitated – the art of ancient Greece, but also borrowed from medieval, Japanese, moresque, and Renaissance styles. Crane and his like-minded English contemporaries were thus highly conscious of their technique and composition and were determined to elevate English art to a new plateau. In the words of one of his biographers, Crane "sought a design of ordered spacings and graphic patterns to illustrate a story, with equally balanced areas of light and dark. More importantly, he used the element of line, either firm or dotted, and emphasized by

241

CALIBAN:- AS I TOLD THEE BEFORE I AM
SUBJECT TO A TYRANT: A SORCERER- (ACT III

30. Caliban as emaciated missing link in Walter Crane's engraving (1893).

colour, to unify a design and give it its expression of style." Before Crane and Aubrey Beardsley (perhaps his only peer as an illustrator), "the Pre-Raphaelite engravers believed that every square inch of their wood-engraved designs should be worked with a jewel-like effect."[34]

Caliban appears in two of Crane's eight scenes from *The Tempest* (1893).[35] His body is almost wholly human, except for the usual clawlike fingers and toes, but his head is somewhat apish in features, and his ears are pointed. His hair is long, and his only garment is an animal skin (Figure 30). Crane's selection may have been influenced by his own reading of Darwin and the evolutionary theories of Herbert Spencer. That Crane and the other Caliban artists of the preceding half-century chose certain facial features, body appendages, and postures hints strongly that they sought to portray Caliban in illustrations, as Daniel Wilson had in print, as "the missing link."

In a unique departure from the usual purposes of Shakespeare pictures – book illustration or gallery display – Paul Vincent Woodroffe (1875–1945) may originally have designed his Caliban for stained glass, the medium in which he specialized. In 1908, Woodroffe illustrated *The Tempest*; the painting reproduced here dates from 1910 (Figure 31). Woodroffe's representation of a wholly human Caliban bent under a burden of wood and a scarcely visible fairylike Ariel peeking from the woods may owe much to the pre-Raphaelite movement of the late-Victorian period. The artist's use of vivid colors divided by black lines suggests a stained-glass design; its clear colors, its realism, and its attention to detail are reminiscent of works by the leading pre-Raphaelite painters, Dante Gabriel Rossetti and John Everett Millais.[36]

Of a slightly later date than Woodroffe is an engraving of Caliban by the German artist Rudolf Grossman (1882–1941). This widely

34 Rodney K. Engen, *Walter Crane as a Book Illustrator* (London: Academy Editions; New York, St. Martin's Press, 1975), esp. pp. 6–11, quotations from pp. 9, 11; Isobel Spencer, *Walter Crane* (London: Studio Vista, 1975), passim.

35 *Eight Illustrations to Shakespeare's Tempest: Designed by Walter Crane* (boxed portfolio), engraved and printed by Duncan C. Dallas (London: J. M. Dent, 1893).

36 *The Dictionary of British Book Illustrators and Caricaturists, 1800–1914*, rev. ed. (Woodbridge, Suffolk: Antique Collectors Club, 1981), pp. 503–04.

31. Caliban in stained glass by Paul Vincent Woodroffe (1910).

32. Rudolf Grossman's lithograph of Caliban as brute (ca. 1916).

traveled painter, engraver, and lithographer was a member of the German Society of Artists and part of the art nouveau movement, which emphasized spontaneity, simplicity, and the use of new materials. His exhibited works, including illustrations of books by Goethe and Dostoyevski, combined impressionism and expressionism. Grossman did few Shakespearean scenes, but in about 1916 he executed two lithographs of Caliban. One of them (Figure 32) depicts a raw, naked, large-skulled Caliban; his single visible eye has a malicious stare, and his grin reflects cupidity and anger. Grossman's Caliban is apish in form and facial features, though not without a touch of human pathos.[37] His upright form, in contrast

37 Renate Brosch, Joachim Möller, and Gertel Wagner, *Shakespeare: Buch und Bühne* (Berlin: Staatliche Museen Preussischer Kulturbesitz, 1986), pp. 74–75; *Allgemeines Lexikon*, Vol. XV, p. 106, and Supplementary Vol. II, pp. 319–20; *Encyclopedia of World Art*, 17 vols. (1959–87), Vol. V, p. 206.

33. A low-browed, defiant Caliban, by Alfred Kubin (ca. 1918).

to the cowering Calibans of many previous artists, suggests the twentieth century's empowerment of Prospero's slave.

More human, but still partly anthropoid, is Alfred Kubin's portrait of Caliban alone on the beach. At first glance he seems to wear an American Indian headdress, but on closer inspection it is seen to be the top half of his load of wood. Caliban's skull is abnormally low and flat, suggesting stupidity; his baggy eyes bulge; his bulbous nose protrudes; his expression is dull and stubborn. His left hand grasps a rock, presumably as a weapon. He is naked and hairy (Figure 33). Kubin (1877–1959), himself an author, a cartographer, and an illustrator of the work of Sir Arthur Conan Doyle, among others, created in his Caliban (ca. 1918) a unique mix of wodewose and ape: less of a human than most nineteenth- and twentieth-century portrayals, and more of a figure from fairy tales. Kubin, noted for "sinister and fantastic line illustrations," seems to mark

246

34. Caliban (center rear) as orangutan in Felix Meseck's 1922 illustration.

the beginning of a new trend in Caliban depictions – away from the literal readings of the text and toward imaginative, even "fabulous," renditions.[38]

More explicitly apish than Grossman's or Kubin's Caliban – in fact, more truly an ape than any pictorial representation we have seen – is Felix Meseck's illustration for Shakespeare's *Der Sturm* (1922). Meseck (1883–1955) had studied art in several German institutions and exhibited in major galleries in the 1920s and '30s. His book illustrations graced works by Goethe (*Prometheus*), Swift (*Gulliver's Travels*), E. T. A. Hoffmann, and others. His Shakespeare illustrations number twenty-nine: fifteen for *Hamlet* (1920) and fourteen for *The Tempest*. In size, shape, face, and posture, Meseck's

38 *Shakespeare: Buch und Bühne*, pp. 74, 76; *Allegemeines Lexikon*, Supplementary Vol. III, pp. 130–31; David Bland, *A History of Book Illustration: The Illuminated Manuscript and the Printed Book* (Berkeley: University of California Press, 1969), pp. 408–09.

Shakespeare's Caliban

35. Caliban as grotesque man/toad, by Werner Pelzer (1959).

Caliban (Figure 34) is an orangutan – a complete denial of Prospero's testimony that he was "honored with a human shape" but very much in accord with notions, still prevalent in the early twentieth century, that Caliban somehow represented humankind's anthropoid ancestry.[39]

The trend toward abstract Calibans is more clearly reflected in Werner Pelzer's illustrations for Rudolf Alexander Schröder's German translation of *Sturm* (1959). Caliban is beastly, misshapen, and amorphous, a crouching figure with a reptilian head and apish arms, yet so imprecise as to be almost anything the viewer imagines (Figure 35).[40] Even less precise is László Lakner's 1985 Caliban. Lakner (b. 1936) has received numerous awards and honors since his graduation in 1960 from the Budapest Academy of Art, includ-

39 *Shakespeare: Buch und Bühne*, pp. 45–46. For information on Meseck, see *Allegemeines Lexikon*, Supplementary Vol. III, p. 377.
40 *Shakespeare: Buch und Bühne*, p. 47.

248

36. A largely abstract Caliban, painted by László Lakner (1985).

ing several fellowships, awards, and an honorary professorship at the University of Essen; his work has been shown in galleries, museums, and special collections throughout the world. In Lakner's painting of Caliban, no true shape can be discerned; the monster is delineated by splashes of black against a blue/gray/white/burnt-umber background, with his name scrawled in bold brush strokes across the top of the canvas (Figure 36). Caliban is an idea more than a form; a mood more than a creature.[41]

41 [Renate Brosch], *Images of Shakespeare* (Berlin: Deutsche Shakespeare Gesellschaft West e V, 1986), s.v. László Lakner.

V

The preceding discussion and accompanying pictures demonstrate a rough correlation between the interpretive trends in artistic portrayals of Caliban and simultaneous trends in Shakespeare performance, criticism, and adaptation. That is true not only of general notions about Caliban's shape and character but also about the artist's positioning of Caliban in relation to Prospero, Miranda, Stephano, and Trinculo, which tends to follow contemporary attitudes toward issues of dominance and control embedded in the play.

Two exceptions to the parallel interpretations stand out. First, artists have been more likely than literary critics, actors, and appropriators to emphasize Caliban's bestial characteristics – especially evident in Chodowiecki's, Retzsch's, and Meseck's works but noticeable too in renditions by Fuseli, Kubin, and others. Second, art diverges from acting, scholarship, and adaptation in the former's paucity of portrayals of Caliban as an American Indian or palpable victim of colonialism, though there may be a hint of the latter in recent abstract works.

Why artists have occasionally diverged from the mainstreams of literary and (to a lesser degree) stage interpretation is difficult to say. Part of the explanation probably is artistic license: Painters can emphasize exotic characteristics of Caliban's appearance without incurring the scorn of their peers; they take more pride in aesthetic execution than in conformity to an orthodox reading of the text. Thus the artist's interpretation may be as much a search for vibrant visual signifiers as for a holistic understanding of the play – as Chodowiecki's tortoise and Meseck's ape imply. And surely *The Tempest's* ambiguity – not to say contradictoriness – about Caliban's shape invites artists to magnify certain verbal clues, at the expense of other evidence, to a far greater degree than have, by and large, literary critics or even actors and adapters.

Probably, too, artists are less cumulative in their work than are academics (and hence are more like performers), whose interpretations usually build upon earlier critical judgments – as much reactions to others' work as they are fresh readings of the text. An artist's line or color portrayal of Caliban, by contrast, is likely to be freer, more original, more idiosyncratic than is the scholar's or political spokesperson's verbal rendition. Yet as members of the same broad cultural environment with actors, critical scholars, and sociopolitical appropriators, artists have generally portrayed Caliban in rough alignment with the other interpreters of *The Tempest*'s "savage and deformed slave."

Chapter 10
Modern poetic invocations

You taught me language.

The Tempest (I.ii.362)

[T]he greatest poets have aspects which do not come
to light at once; and by exercising a direct influence
on other poets centuries later, they continue to affect
the living language.

T. S. Eliot (1943)

Shakespeare's *Tempest* has long inspired creative writers, many of
whom have appropriated Caliban: Herman Melville's short story
"Hood Isle and the Hermit Oberlus" and Browning's dramatic
monologue "Caliban Upon Setebos" are but two renderings inspired
by Shakespeare's monster.[1] As Browning's work suggests, the
romantic poets were particularly attracted by Caliban's ability to
commune with nature and by the unusual language he uses to
describe his enchanted island. And as our preceding chapters indicate, by World War I Caliban had become a rich cultural signifier
in several literary genres. Thus it is hardly surprising that Caliban
should have appealed to modern poets, who saw in him a multivalent, readily recognizable symbol.

During the twentieth century, poets have appropriated Caliban

---

1 See Chapter 1, footnote 2, for a list of novels that allude to Caliban in the title or
otherwise use the *Tempest* story.

for a variety of purposes, some political, some aesthetic. Understandably, Caliban's efforts to learn a foreign idiom and to articulate what he thinks and feels have been a major issue and challenge for modern writers who are especially attuned to rhythms of speech and precise selections of words and images. Like Browning, some try to provide Shakespeare's monster with the speeches the dramatist left out, speeches that explain his anger, wonder, and resentment. Others use his speech to embody a particular ideological stance. And some simply use his name as a literary allusion that enriches a new poetic context.

Not every modern poet who alludes to Caliban does battle with Shakespeare, but some demonstrate what Harold Bloom described as the "anxiety of influence." According to Bloom, a poet antithetically " 'completes' his precursor, by so reading the parent-poem as to retain its terms but to mean them in another sense, as though the precursor had failed to go far enough."[2] The Tempest raises issues concerning the use and abuse of power, the anger of the oppressed, and the role played by control in our personal and political lives. In the play these issues are resolved – on the surface, at least – by Prospero's abandonment of his books and departure from the island. For the most part, twentieth-century poets who allude to Caliban imply, in Bloom's view, that Shakespeare failed to go far enough. Although their appropriations of The Tempest are not unanimously pessimistic about human nature, one might agree with Bloom that "as the poets swerve downward in time, they deceive themselves into believing they are tougher-minded than their precursors."[3] For many modern poets, The Tempest is not finished; its characters live on, their problems unresolved.

The best-known modern appropriation of The Tempest is W. H. Auden's lengthy poem The Sea and the Mirror (discussed in Chapter 4). Our focus here is on lesser-known short lyric poems written since World War I that in some way exploit Caliban as an allusion or an extended metaphor for their own creative purposes. Our treatment of the poems is basically chronological; within that frame-

2 Harold Bloom, The Anxiety of Influence: A Theory of Poetry (Oxford University Press, 1973), p. 14.
3 Bloom, Anxiety of Influence, p. 69.

work, several trends emerge that, not surprisingly, parallel schools of thought we have traced elsewhere. In several instances, however, Caliban appears in guises unique to poetry. During the Depression, for example, Caliban became for many poets a symbol of economic oppression, something we did not find in criticism, art, or the theatre. Yet after World War II he emerged – as he did in other genres – as an emblem of newly enfranchised colonial peoples. In both contexts his language often makes Caliban seem distant and strange, but it can also make him seem to be one of us.

We make no claim to have discovered every *Tempest* poem written since World War I, but the fourteen discussed here poignantly illustrate Caliban's continuing appeal as symbol and metaphor to imaginative artists.

I

In the earliest poems in this genre, Caliban represents the downtrodden laborer, doomed to meaningless, arduous, repetitive tasks. Edwin Markham is the first and perhaps the best exemplar. Well known for his poem of the same name as Millet's painting "The Man with the Hoe," written in 1899, Markham patronized various reform movements during his long career as teacher, lecturer, and poet. In 1906–07 he published in *Cosmopolitan* a series of essays on child workers. At some point in his career, he also became a disciple of the theories of Swedenborg. Markham, in short, was a radical reformer in his time, a crusader for the working man and against child labor. In August 1926, *The American Mercury Reader* published his "Ballad of the Gallows Bird." The narrator is hanged after killing an enemy in a family feud; the bulk of the poem describes the narrator's experiences – visions, if you will – after he has been hanged for his crime. One is a confrontation with Caliban, a laborer doomed to endure a life of endless work, like Sisyphus:

> At dawn I passed a tottering shape,
> Bent with a load of earth,
> A shape the lust of a dragon-man
> Might engender into birth.

"Caliban, where do you go?" I cried,
And the bent shape answered me:
"I go to pay an incredible debt:
I am doomed to fill the sea.

"The last load must be carried down,
The debt must all be paid:
All mountains, all must melt before
The pecking of one spade."

Caliban was Markham's symbol of generations who – in the words of Gerard Manley Hopkins – "have trod, have trod, have trod" under the burden of unending, meaningless physical labor.

Louis Untermeyer echoes this theme in his short poem "Caliban in the Coal Mines," first published in 1935:

God, we don't like to complain.
We know that the mine is no lark.
But – there's the pools from the rain;
But – there's the cold and the dark.

God, You don't know what it is –
You, in Your well-lighted sky,
Watching the meteors whizz;
Warm, with a sun always by.

God, if You had but the moon
Stuck in Your cap for a lamp,
Even You'd tire of it soon,
Down in the dark and the damp.

Nothing but blackness above,
And nothing that moves but the cars. . . .
God, if You wish for our love,
Fling us a handful of stars![4]

The poem's allusion to Caliban depends for its effectiveness on the reader's knowledge of Shakespeare's play. The narrator's mine

4 Louis Untermeyer, *Selected Poems and Parodies of Louis Untermeyer* (New York: Harcourt, Brace & Co., 1935), p. 9.

invokes Caliban's cave; his longing for light and warmth parallels Caliban's longing for Prospero's blessing. Caliban the coal miner yearns for light, but is condemned rarely to see or feel it.

Edwin Muir's "Sick Caliban"[5] also depends on allusion in the title. The poem describes a man's confrontation with a pathetic Caliban. The speaker forsakes the strange creature, but wonders if he should have stopped to help or call others to assist:

> Should he have cried
> On all the world to help that suffering thing,
> Man, beast, or bestial changeling,
> Or huge fish stranded choking in dry air
> Without the sense to die?
> Yet that great emerald blazing on its finger,
> The proud and sneaking malice in its eye
> That said, I suffer truly and yet malinger,
> Long for and hate the stupid remedy.
> Look: I am yourself for ever stuck half way.
>
> And then he knew
> Those he would summon were a multiplied
> Mere replica of himself, and all had thought
> Long since, No remedy here or anywhere
> For that poor bag of bone
> And hank of hair.[6]

The speaker returns to carry the creature down "the straight road to his death," hoping that somehow "time would devise / A meaning." The "hank of hair" and "bag of bone" traditionally represent elemental humanity, the dust that God used to make Adam, the bone he used to make Eve. The speaker, like Caliban and all humanity, is stuck halfway between the angels and the beasts. The speaker's examination of the "sick Caliban," a monstrous alter ego, may reflect Muir's experience with psychoanalysis at the end of World

5 The date for this poem is problematic, because it was found among Muir's papers after his death. It may have been published in a magazine somewhat earlier; it did not appear in a book until 1960, when his first *Collected Poems* was published. Muir could have composed it at any time in the 1930s, '40s, and '50s, but its tone suggests the earliest decade.
6 Edwin Muir, *Collected Poems* (Oxford University Press, 1965), pp. 276–77.

War I. In his autobiography, the poet reflected on what he had learned:

I saw that my lot was the human lot, that when I faced my own unvarnished likeness I was one among all men and women, all of whom had the same desires and thoughts, the same failures and frustrations, the same unacknowledged hatred of themselves and others, the same hidden shames and griefs, and that if they confronted these things they could win a certain liberation from them.[7]

The speaker's willingness to carry the carcass of "sick Caliban" may also mirror Muir's social concerns, for in describing his youthful commitment to socialism, he observed that "What claimed our love and compassion was misshapen humanity in all its forms."[8] Muir's poem uses a misshapen Caliban to address human animality and imperfection.

II

Whereas the Depression inspired a link between Caliban and the suffering laborer, World War II spawned a wider range of interpretations. Most cheerful are those from soldiers of Commonwealth countries who jokingly identify themselves with Shakespeare's monster. From New Zealand, for example, comes a chapbook of limericks and doggerel written by "Caliban." The last page notes that the poems were "Conjured up by 'Caliban' in his cups and done into a booklet by 'The Griffin' in sulky sobriety in his printing press by the park in Auckland." The poems are laments of army life from the soldier who serves far from home and hates washing dishes, chafes at being passed over for promotion, and resents the orders he receives from an unlikable superior officer. Although the poems are not particularly notable, *Live Rounds: Verses of Army Life* reveals the soldiers' awareness of Caliban and their adoption of him as a facetious mascot.[9]

A more serious version of the same theme is Robert Service's

7 Edwin Muir, *An Autobiography* (London: Hogarth Press, 1954), p. 158.
8 Muir, *Autobiography*, p. 234.
9 Caliban [pseud.], *Live Rounds: Verses of Army Life* (Auckland: Griffin Press, 1945).

257

"Fleurette," subtitled "(The Wounded Canadian Speaks)." Service spent two years during World War I as an ambulance driver and returned to Canada in 1940 as a war refugee. His narrator in "Fleurette" is a Canadian sergeant, injured when he threw his body over a bomb to save his men; he succeeded, but his face is now turned to "a hideous sight, / Hardly a thing in place; / Sort of a gargoyle, you'd say." He terms it his "Caliban mug." A kiss from Fleurette, sister of the wounded man who lies next to him, saves him from despair. Fleurette is Miranda: "As gay as a linnet, and yet / As tenderly sweet as a dove." Her chaste attentions turn his sorrow to such joy that he can joke about having cured the corn on his foot by amputation.[10]

If some soldiers used Caliban humorously, others saw him as a mirror of war's horrors. Michael Hamburger was serving in Britain's armed services in 1944 when he wrote " 'The Tempest': An Alternative." For Hamburger, born in Berlin in 1924, but raised and educated in England, the conflict between Axis and Allies was particularly wrenching. The poem depicts a world turned upside down. It begins after *The Tempest*'s harmonious conclusion and Prospero's triumph over his enemies. Something reverses the power relations: Caliban is now in control of the island, and Prospero is his slave.

> I, Prospero, stand on this island's shore,
> And from a distance vaguer and more dubious
> Than a dream I hear voices as of lovers
> Whispering in the night and courtiers jesting.
>
> I recall a tempest that created peace;
> But the power that brought forth storms and stillness
> Is quite decayed, so they have left me here,
> An old man with a bent back, who has outlived
> His death.
>   Yes, once they called me prince,
> (Though then my pride lay elsewhere) until I fled
> And made this isle my kingdom, ruling by magic.

---

10 Robert Service, *Collected Poems of Robert Service* (New York: Dodd, Mead, 1966), pp. 320–23.

I recall a tempest raised for the sake
Of a mortal throne, a night and a day
Of mortal music . . . and then this stillness.

Now I bear logs for Caliban whose lust
Has peopled the isle with monsters, begotten
On my daughter; sweet Miranda's grown a hag
With hatching of his slimy progeny.

Perhaps it was a dream (the human voices
And my hoping to follow them) – and a mere dream
Has made me weary – but my master calls, –
I'm coming Caliban. – One night, one day
Lost me my dukedom and my soul's wide realm,
Ariel deserted me and they left me here.

Prospero's dreams of the future have turned to a nightmare.[11]

Alexander Reid's "Twelve Variations on Caliban," written in 1947, returns to Caliban's viewpoint. The speaker's ability to articulate his feelings forces the reader to share his perspective of Prospero and the surrounding world. His voice is our voice, so he must be one of us. We see the monster crawling claustrophobically in his cave, imprisoned, angry, rebellious; his entrapped feeling represents western society's malaise. In the first variation, "The Days," each morning succeeds the last in an endless repetition of labor and boredom. Variation 2, "Caliban Worries About the Future," depicts Caliban tired, wondering if someday he might find contentment even in his enslavement. He concludes

Let me at least be tameless,
Not grow to love a cage.
Heart that has been so wild –
Never grow reconciled!

In "Caliban and Miranda" (variation 3) he reflects on Miranda's sweet beauty, with this bitter reflection:

11 Michael Hamburger, *Collected Poems, 1941–1983* (Manchester, U.K.: Carcanet Press, 1984), p. 24.

For all her beauty bright, and all her grace it seems
Spring from the rage of Caliban's blood
And the wreck of Caliban's dreams.

"Caliban in the Woods" (variation 4) presents the monster envying the birds their freedom:

You flit upon untrammeled wing
Through golden summers of delight.
No master tells *you* when to sing.

In the fifth variation, "Caliban Rejecting Heaven," he conceives of God as a larger version of Prospero who keeps 10 million Calibans in chains, ready to sing his praise on command. "Prospero's Bird" (variation 6) shows Caliban releasing Prospero's caged wild bird, who in recompense sits on the savage's "matted hair / Till its wild heart burst with singing."

The second half of the sequence repeats and intensifies Caliban's obsession with freedom. He dreams in variation 7 of the earth's tormented creatures and awakes with the cry, "Make Prospero die!" Variation 8, "Caliban Afraid," expresses his terror at the noises around him, and in "Caliban's Despair" (variation 9), the entire earth is full of chains and bars. In "Caliban in Revolt" (variation 10), he decides to make a league of Calibans and rise against Prospero; "Caliban and the Dead" (variation 11) is a fantasy of peaceful death, whose chief consolation will be that Prospero can no longer command him. The final poem, "Caliban Calls for the Release of All Prisoners," concludes: "Open all doors! Let every caged thing free! / Let there be nothing bound in earth or sea!"[12] The central issue in Reid's sequence, in sum, is freedom. Told from Caliban's perspective, the poems represent a slave who sees no justice in his plight, who hates his master, and who longs for release.

Entrapped in a body and a world he did not create, Caliban can be viewed as a postwar Everyman who represents the monstrousness of human moral deformity. Norman Rosten's 1965 "My Caliban Creature," like its predecessors, depends on the title's allusion

12 Alexander Reid, *Steps to a Viewpoint* (London: Andrew Dakers, 1947), pp. 28–39.

for its effectiveness. It asserts the fishlike creature's affinity to the speaker, a matter-of-fact urbanite:

> My Caliban creature, endearing monster,
> Come, give me your arm –
> Let's go to the opera,
> Confound the cops and those ladies
> Staring at your webbed feet,
> Then to a gala place to eat!
>
> No, no, your island's drowned,
> Along with your wild mother.
> The city zoo would take you,
> But I've filed the necessary papers.
> I'm adopting you, friend,
> Your name on my mailbox.
> I swear I'll protect you,
> Verminous and scaled,
> Roaring drunk,
> I know the slime,
> Clay and color,
> Whose shape I am,
>
> Caliban.[13]

We can easily adopt Caliban because despite his repulsive features, he is, in reality, ourselves.

Donald Davie also uses Caliban to reflect on a changing world. In "Shakespeare in the Atlantic," the speaker, apparently on a cruise ship to Bermuda, is confronted by a Viennese-American Jewish woman who wants to read his poems out loud. Her heavy accent "ravages" his nice English "hedgerow." In her the poet sees Sycorax, Caliban's mother. Like her uncivilized son, she has been taught language; she knows now how to curse. In the ship are many women like her.

> Their huge sons mean no harm
> either, although each
> New Adam's bruising heel

13 Norman Rosten, *Selected Poems* (New York: George Braziller, 1979), p. 121.

261

Shakespeare's Caliban

is shod from birth with horn
Against my flickering tongue.

The speaker's language, like Hero's in *Much Ado About Nothing,*
having become "everybody's," is now sullied. These Calibans will
murder the queen's English even as they seize it for their own.[14]

III

The postwar period engendered more than a babel of tongues,
however; it also spawned the cold war and fear of thermonuclear
destruction. Caliban was now appropriated by a Polish survivor
of the Resistance as a proletarian figure. Tadeusz Rozewicz's poem
"Nothing in Prospero's Cloak," translated from the original Polish
by Adam Czerniawski, is based on the repetition of the word
"nothing." Caliban waits for Prospero's magic, for the authority
represented by "magic robes," "streets and lips," "pulpits and
towers," and "loudspeakers." What he finds is nothing:

nothing condemns
nothing pardons.[15]

The repetitions of "nothing" reach beyond nihilism to a strange
dawn of hope, for in the death of expectation also dies disappoint-
ment and despair. According to critics Magnus Jan Krynski and
Robert A. Maguire, the poem presents the modern Caliban as a
symbol of the masses, "who presumably thirst for an inspiring
word from the humanist poet (a modern Prospero), but instead
hear only the empty verbiage of press, radio and television."[16]

Another consequence of World War II was the demise of colo-

14 Roger Pringle, ed., *Poems for Shakespeare,* 6 (London: Globe Playhouse Publications, 1977), p. 34.
15 Alan Sillitoe, ed., *Poems for Shakespeare,* 7 (London: The Bear Gardens Museum
and Arts Centre, 1979), p. 23.
16 Quoted from Magnus Jan Krynski and Robert A. Maguire in "Tadeusz Rozewicz,"
Sharon R. Gunton and Jean C. Stine, eds., *Contemporary Literary Criticism,* 100
vols. (Detroit: Gale Research, 1983) Vol. XXIII, pp. 358–63; quotation from p. 360.
Krynski and Maguire translate the poem's title as "Nothing in Prospero's Magic
Garment."

Modern poetic invocations

nialism as year by year more and more of Europe's former colonies in Africa and the Caribbean achieved independent nationhood. Many colonial poets (some of whom we cited in Chapter 6) now identified themselves with Caliban, the subjugated native, educated and still controlled by white Europeans. In 1969, Barbadian poet Edward Kamau Brathwaite published his first major book of poems, *Islands*. Brathwaite's "Caliban" depicts an islander descended from Africans who had suffered the hardships of the slave ships and labored endlessly in the cane fields. Shaped by this heritage, the poem's modern-day speaker has learned to limbo, defined in Brathwaite's glossary as

a dance in which the participants have to move, with their bodies thrown backwards and without any aid whatsoever under a stick which is lowered at every successfully completed passage under it, until the stick is practically touching the ground. It is said to have originated . . . after the experience of the cramped conditions between slave-ship decks of the Middle Passage. Now very popular as a performing act in Caribbean night clubs.[17]

Caliban begins with the realization that his people are poor and black. He looks at the nightclubs, "modern palaces" that "have grown out of the soil" as the "death / of suns, of songs, of sunshine." In the poem's middle sequence, he experiments like his Shakespearean original with the language Prospero taught him. Here his freedom song echoes the rhythms of the limbo:

> And
> Ban
> Ban
> Cal-
> iban
> like to play
> pan
> at the Car-
> nival;
> pran-

17 *Islands* was reprinted in Edward Kamau Brathwaite's *The Arrivants: A New World Trilogy* (Oxford University Press, 1969); quotation from p. 274.

Shakespeare's Caliban

cing to the lim-
bo silence
down
down
down
so the god won't drown
him
down
down
down
to the is-
land town[18]

As he sings, Caliban goes "down down down" as if under the limbo stick. His eyes are "shut tight / and the whip light / crawl- / ing round the ship / where his free- / dom drown." In the third movement he feels the

> long dark deck and the water surrounding me
> long dark deck and the silence is over me. . . .
> stick is the whip
> and the dark deck is slavery[19]

Still, Caliban limbos on; after sinking "down down down," he resurges. As the poem progresses, the sun comes up, the drummers praise his performance, and as he rises "up up up," the music saves him. After the waters of slavery have drowned him, he rises again. Out of the degradation of his slave heritage, he plucks a hard-won victory in the assertion of his indigenous culture.

Brathwaite's poem places Prospero's slave in a Caribbean context, but as indicated in Chapter 6, Caliban was adopted by African writers as well. Taban lo Liyong, born in Uganda in 1938, was the first African to receive a master of fine arts degree from the Writers Workshop at the University of Iowa. His collection of poems, *Frantz Fanon's Uneven Ribs* (1971), experiments intensely with language. Liyong – like Donald Davie – is particularly intrigued with Caliban's

18 Brathwaite, "Caliban," pp. 191–95; quotation from p. 192.
19 Brathwaite, "Caliban," p. 194.

264

line "You taught me language, and my profit on't is / I know how to curse." In "Uncle Tom's Black Humour" he writes:

> i was taught a tongue
> with which to curse prospero and woo miranda
> since ariel was so airy
> he had no room for a heart.

Liyong, as noted earlier, identifies his name, Taban, with Caliban, and like Shakespeare's monster, he "was taught language / And what do I do with it / But to curse, in my own way?"[20]

Ambivalence about language in particular, and European culture in general, is equally apparent in Lemuel Johnson's *Highlife for Caliban* (1973). The poems in this volume are autobiographical meditations on Johnson's experiences as a native of Freetown in Sierra Leone. They also reflect on the problems of cultural identity faced by all black Africans in the postcolonial era. The speaker in these poems is described in the accompanying commentary as Caliban Agonistes, the newly freed African who must find his own voice. Assuming Prospero's authority, the new black national government can no longer dream of revenge against Prospero, because it has become Prospero. Caliban must somehow incorporate his native tradition of voodoo and calypso with the education he has received from Europe. Johnson provides Caliban with strong musical rhythms that assert the speaker's independent status. Left on the island by himself, he must rediscover indigenous sounds and meanings:

> this is the place
> my inheritance.
> a chain of leached bones
> my inheritance
> mother
> this
> a chain of leached stones
> airless quays

---

20 Taban lo Liyong, *Frantz Fanon's Uneven Ribs* (London: Heinemann, 1971), pp. 66, 41. See Chapter 6 for further discussion of the colonial metaphor.

Shakespeare's Caliban

dust that rises
coasting on water

ah they walk on water
for you
they walk on water
papa prospero.[21]

IV

Although the colonial metaphor dominated perspectives of Caliban in literature and on stage during the 1970s and into the 1980s, there remained ample room for other interpretations. An idiosyncratic but nonetheless intriguing appropriation of Caliban appeared in 1976 in Walter McDonald's first poetry volume, *Caliban in Blue and other poems*. McDonald had served with the U.S. Air Force during the Vietnam War; his Caliban is a fighter pilot who loves the sensations of flight. In "Caliban on Spinning," the speaker compares flying to sexual orgasm:

> Spinning an airplane right
> is like a little death. . . .
> Throttled, the engine shudders
> like a lover bound. . . .
> Ride high with all your might upon the rudder
> surging under you –
> you must master it to spin well.

In "Caliban in Blue" the speaker contrasts the placid blue skies with the savage fury of a bombing mission. The skies, he says, "belong to Setebos." The pagan god directs the attack:

> His arms like radar
> point the spot.
> For this, I trained to salivate
> and tingle, target-diving,

21 Lemuel A. Johnson, *Highlife for Caliban* (Ann Arbor, Mich.: Ardis, 1973), p. 33. For further discussion of Lemuel Johnson and Raphael E. G. Armattoe, see Chapter 6, Section IV.

266

> hand enfolding hard throttle
> in solitary masculine delight.

The thrill is sexual. McDonald's Caliban allusion depends upon the monster's association with libido. Alone in flight, he acts out repressed violent and sexual urges, taking the sky by force as Shakespeare's original Caliban would have raped Miranda.

> Focused on cross hairs,
> eyes glazing, hand triggers switches in
> pulsing orgasm,
> savage release;
> pull out
> and off we go again
> thrusting deep
> into the martial lascivious blue
> of uncle's sky.[22]

Eleven years later (1987), Caliban returned to dramatic monologue in a poem reminiscent of Browning's "Caliban Upon Setebos" that is also strikingly modern: Theodore Weiss's "Caliban Remembers." Again Caliban is alone on the island, but now he wears Prospero's tattered robe. In Weiss's vision, Caliban's language is imperfect. Caliban's mind reveals itself in a stream of consciousness; the poem moves from one memory or association to another, with little logical progression. The reader feels the tortured subconscious workings of a nonnative speaker. Word orders are inverted, expressions are nonidiomatic. Weiss's Caliban is an alien in Prospero's orderly world. As the poem begins, Caliban stares at the ocean and remembers his joy at the ship's departure:

> At first I also, kicking up heels,
> scattered round their garments, linens,
> books. At first. But after – how find
> again that whole belonging mine
> before they came? – and worst those days

22 Walter McDonald, *Caliban in Blue and other poems* (Lubbock: Texas Tech University Press, 1976), pp. 3, 11.

267

when I, a smoke, fume through my hands,
loneliness whelms me.

He also recalls Miranda's beauty, his sexual awakening, and
Prospero's anger:

> Fear he had I'd fish
> his pond? Oh no, not fish it, stock it!
> Who else was there to do her turn,
> so save the day for the likes of me,
> and him as well, on the island?

In the poem's second section, Caliban asserts his synergistic relationship to Prospero:

> Master he may have been,
> yet could do nothing without me. Not,
> unless I, fetching sticks, patched fire,
> rouse his magic, its high-flown tricks.
> Whatever his flights, had to return
> to this island, his cell, me.
> Never could, whatever his flights,
> go back to his country till they came with
> that ship.
> I alone propped him, kept
> as earth does sky, else dropped in the sea.

As he fishes from the ocean, his rod, a fragment left from Prospero's
staff, reels in a book, the source of his former master's magic. He
ruminates on what the book meant to Prospero, how it kept him
isolated from the world of nature and made him wake from his
spells "ash-grey." Caliban's next thoughts turn to the effeminate
prince Ferdinand, "the feathery, ribboned thing" who stole his
place.

Caliban then recalls how Prospero had loved him, taught him
language, and shared his books. Among them was a traveler's
account of cannibals that used the metathesis "Caliban." Weiss's
Caliban flatly denies that his name originated from cannibals: There
were no men on the island to eat until Prospero came, and the

thought of human flesh disgusts him. His name came not from books but from his mother, who never bothered to explain its significance. Later, Caliban wonders

> Why, instead of all that work,
> those lessons, slow, dull, scratchy,
> did my master, worlds at hand,
> not turn me presto into prince?
> Sea, fire, sky he managed
> featly; but I too much for him,
> an earth magic alone could never change?
>
> Never, as he sought to stuff me
> with his learning asked he me
> my thought, my feeling. All I was
> was wrong, to change. All he wished
> was aping, my face wrought to look,
> a mirror, more and more like his.

Like the sorcerer's apprentice, Caliban plays with the magician's book, raising torrents of rain, thunder, and lightning. The howling wind frightens him until he cries:

> Off with the gown.
> Break the wand. Before this book,
> more than ever my master did,
> rules over me, ruins entirely,
> drown it again. Never wanted it
> in the first place. . . .
> Whatever his tempest brought
> about, this one washes me clean
> of them, blundering on their tottery
> two feet (upright they pride themselves
> on being!)

Caliban then wonders why Prospero drowned his book and returned to Milan to consort with devils like Antonio and Sebastian when he could have stayed on the island. Finally, the narrator envisions Prospero and Miranda surrounded by the magic and music that are now gone forever. He concludes:

269

Shakespeare's Caliban

How I long
to hear once more those me-completing
voices. Come back, would cast me
at their feet. And yet . . . alone, alone
as he must be, loathing, pitying, loving.[23]

Like many other appropriations of the *Tempest* story, Weiss's poem asserts Prospero and Caliban's mutual interdependence. As "this thing of darkness" Prospero must acknowledge, Caliban is Prospero's alter ego, the dark side of his soul that he can never entirely abandon. Even if we picture, as Weiss does, Caliban alone on his seaswept island, Prospero can never be far from his, and hence our, thoughts – a realization fitting for our century.

V

Unlike their predecessors in the eighteenth and nineteenth centuries, modern poets and fiction writers cannot subjugate Caliban into serving as a trivial, drunken buffoon, a vice figure, or a missing link. Prospero is no longer firmly in control. Solidly in the earth, Caliban is to the modern world a symbol of humanity, not simply bestiality. His difficulties in expressing his feelings, his ambivalence about language, his sense of being weighed down in a universe he does not understand, his aching desire, and his despair are foregrounded in twentieth-century poetry.

These poems indicate the extent to which Caliban has become a readily recognizable symbol in modern culture, a more important symbol, it appears, than Prospero. Until the twentieth century, Caliban was the outsider in Prospero's world; now their roles are largely reversed.

23 Theodore Weiss, *From Princeton One Afternoon: Collected Poems of Theodore Weiss* (New York: Collier Books, 1987), pp. 182–98.

Part IV
Conclusion

Chapter 11
Caliban's odyssey

I'll be wise hereafter, / And seek for grace.
The Tempest (V.i.294–95)

I took it for granted that Shakespeare's characters
were self-explanatory. Here [in Caliban's case] I was
mistaken.
Herbert Beerbohm Tree (1904)

The preceding ten chapters have demonstrated Caliban's remarkably
long and erratic journey through many lands and innumerable
minds. It remains only to summarize his odyssey and to add our
own conclusions to the two major sections of the book – conclusions
that have crept into the narrative from time to time but need explicit
expression and amplification here. In keeping with the book's separ-
ation of Caliban's story into his genesis in the mind of Shakespeare,
on the one hand, and his subsequent transformations in the minds
of interpreters, appropriators, and adapters, on the other hand, we
have divided this concluding chapter into the same two categories,
with a final brief section that looks to the future.

I

As we admitted in our Preface and tried to make clear in Chapters
2 and 3, no one knows or very likely will ever know just what
Shakespeare intended Caliban to be. The dramatist's possible sources

273

in history, literature, folklore, pageantry, iconography, and allegory are immense, and the range of suggested prototypes and influences is almost endless. Yet some conclusions from the welter of evidence seem clear.

The most obvious is that Shakespeare used no single idea or figure as Caliban's model. The strongest claim for a partial source, we believe, can be made for the English wild man, but only if he is seen as one among many – a primacy of influence, not a monopoly. We discussed at some length in Chapter 3 the wild man's deep roots in English literature and popular culture; Shakespeare and his audiences were, beyond a shadow of doubt, acutely aware of this paradigm of the sole inhabitant of a desolate environment – forest or island – who lacks all of society's refinements but is peculiarly adept at surviving in raw nature. And because England's wild-man lore encompassed a remarkable variety of types – from fully human to almost animal, from essentially moral to hopelessly corrupt, from gentle to ferocious – he was a suitable model for whatever kind of islander the playwright desired. Caliban's list of similarities to the wild man, we noted earlier, is substantial; but so, too, is the list of characteristics that Shakespeare must have drawn from other sources.

The American Indian has been the most frequently touted model, with more advocates, perhaps, than even the wild man, at least in the current century. In any case, the Indian has surely had the most avid advocates. Sidney Lee, Walter Raleigh, and Robert Cawley, among others, argued relentlessly that American natives were Caliban's sole prototype, though the American school could not agree on which Indian images influenced Shakespeare – noble, ignoble, or a blend of the two. And because Shakespeare's familiarity with the literature of exploration, indeed with its leading activists, is as undeniable as his familiarity with the wild-man motif, it is tempting to see Caliban as at least partly Shakespeare's emblemization of America's natives.

Here and there in The Tempest, Caliban does resemble the portrait of the Indians drawn in vivid prose by André Thevet and other early voyagers to America. Caliban's beastliness, for example, seems to mirror accounts of New World natives by a variety of Continental and English observers and secondary reporters, as do his suscep-

274

tibility to alcohol and his sexual appetite. Yet unless one assumes that Shakespeare wholly accepted the pejorative image in certain accounts and resisted the more benign and optimistic view that flourished during the late sixteenth century and the first decade of the seventeenth, Caliban is a curiously unrepresentative Indian. (We wonder, too, why Shakespeare, whose portrayals of outsiders had grown more sympathetic and sophisticated over the years – witness Shylock and Othello – would have been so hard on an Indian Caliban.)

Surely Caliban was not Indian in appearance. He is ugly, deformed, a monster – three terms almost never applied to American Indians, even by their severest critics. Rather, most European observers praised Indian physique and physiognomy. From Columbus on, reports from the New World insisted that virtually no Indians were misshapen and that most were tall, straight, well proportioned, vigorous, healthy, and attractive. They appear that way, too, in John White's and Jacques Le Moyne's paintings and in Inigo Jones's illustrations of Indian costumes for the English theatre. At the same time, Caliban wholly lacks the characteristics and accoutrements that the surviving pictorial and literary evidence presents as typically Indian: body paint, feathers, huts, canoes, tobacco, bows and arrows – minor signifiers that would have shouted "Indian" to a Jacobean audience. It is barely possible, of course, that in the early stage productions Caliban had one or more of these props. If so, there is not a hint of it in the First Folio text or in the scattered clues to Caliban's appearance and character in the earliest criticism and staging.

Those clues, to be sure, are frustratingly sparse and somewhat contradictory. Ben Jonson's reference (1614) to *The Tempest*'s servant-monster tells little about Caliban's ancestry or shape, but it does, perhaps, imply that Jonson did not see him as an Indian. Similarly, Samuel Pepys's description (1668) of Caliban's costume in the Dryden-Davenant recasting of *The Tempest* as "very droll" leaves a lot to be desired, but it, too, contains no suggestion of Indianness. Dryden's radical adaptation of *The Tempest* (1670) turns Caliban and Sycorax (his sister rather than his mother in this version) into "half-fish" monsters, but they are human enough to be, respectively, Trinculo's servant-pimp and the female he intends to marry.

Dryden's description of Shakespeare's Caliban (as distinct from Dryden's own portrayal of Caliban) emphasizes his grotesqueness and monstrosity. Still, Dryden is broadly in tune with Thomas Rymer's judgment (1677) that *The Tempest*'s monster was human despite his "awkward and ungainly" physique. If Dryden and Rymer are representative, Restoration readers of *The Tempest* saw Caliban as a rough-hewn creature, essentially human but grossly disfigured. We find no hint here of an American Indian and only a touch of the wild man. The latter source gains more credence if Edmond Malone's undocumented early-nineteenth-century claim is correct that Caliban's costume, "prescribed by the poet himself," consisted of a large animal skin with shaggy hair. But that costume, and many of Caliban's alleged shortcomings, could fit as well the Jacobean image of the Irishman: crude, malicious, rebellious, licentious, intoxicated, and verbally abusive. In the words of Philip Edwards, "The vagueness about what Caliban is, is important. . . . So, equally, he may be an Indian or an Irishman."[1]

Although there is often an element of monstrosity in the early references to Caliban, and although Caliban continued to bear that burden until the eve of the romantic era, monsters per se seem unlikely to have been Caliban's prototype. Attempts to link Prospero's slave to any single monster, or any category, or even to monsters in general, stumble on the evidence of *The Tempest*'s text that Caliban has a human shape, has human faculties – speech, thought, aspirations, to name a few – and performs exclusively human chores for Prospero and Miranda.

Shakespeare may have been well aware of the *commedia dell'arte*, but because the only written transcriptions of relevant *scenari* (those described in Chapter 3) date from periods much later than *The Tempest*, we cannot be sure – to borrow a phrase – what he knew and when he knew it. If *The Tempest* was influenced by *commedia* plots and characters, Caliban has more in common with the Italian *selvaggi* than with the harlequin. As the pastoral's wild man, he could well embody the physical appetites that often threaten to undermine the idylls of shepherds and shepherdesses. His physical

1 Philip Edwards, *Threshold of a Nation: A Study in English and Irish Drama* (Cambridge University Press, 1979), p. 108.

features and his lack of wordplay make him an unlikely clown. Besides, his appearance is far more akin to the wild man's furry countenance than to the harlequin's brightly colored motley.

Spenser may be a direct source for Shakespeare, but again, no words or phrases in *The Tempest* demonstrate specific borrowing. Spenser and Shakespeare shared a common literary tradition, particularly the pastoral and the "salvage man" who represents humanity in a state of nature. The Blatant Beast may be a literary ancestor, but any direct descent to Caliban seems improbable. Again, the physiognomy is wrong. The Blatant Beast is always just that, a beast. He is never drawn in human terms. He has canine and porcine characteristics; he never speaks for himself as Caliban does.

Given that *The Tempest* was performed for James's court and that Shakespeare was a member of the King's Company, the dramatist was aware of royal concerns. James's and Queen Anne's penchant for the masque could hardly escape the King's Company's notice. Shakespeare must have known what his contemporary and rival, Ben Jonson, was doing. The masque, accordingly, strongly influenced Shakespeare's last noncollaborative play (or at least the version of it presented in 1613), for he included a masque – the pageant of Ceres, Juno, and Iris, complete with music and dance – in Act IV to grace Ferdinand and Miranda's betrothal. He also used masque elements in the initial storm, in the disappearing banquet, and, not least, in Ariel's characterization. Thus, of all the possible literary genres that might have influenced *The Tempest*, the Jacobean court masque seems the most likely candidate. If so, Caliban may be an antimasque figure. His conspiracy to overthrow Prospero clearly parodies the twelve-year-old usurpation against Prospero, as well as Sebastian and Antonio's plans against Alonso. Moreover, wild men were used in Elizabethan spectacles and Jacobean masques. Caliban's promise in Act V to "be wise hereafter, / And seek for grace" may indeed parallel earlier wild men's yielding to Elizabeth's "civility"; or it may reflect the Jacobean antimasquer's co-optation into a final dance of universal celestial harmony. Shakespeare's political sensibilities are not at issue. What we cannot fathom is the extent to which political concerns were figured into *The Tempest*'s plot and characters. Similarly, we find no convincing clue to Caliban's origins in the many (sometimes fanciful) explanations of his name's etymology.

The gypsy "cauliban" seems to us more plausible than the Caribbean "cannibal," for reasons we discussed in Chapter 2, but we stop short of advocacy. The etymological issue is simply unresolved.

A definitive answer to the ancient "intentionalist" question is, then, impossible; the plausible answers are bewilderingly numerous. But we suggest – tentatively and at risk of appearing to accept all explanations simultaneously – that Shakespeare did not mean Caliban to symbolize any particular person, group, or quality, but rather a general *unruliness* in society and in nature. He seems to us to blend the (largely pejorative) Jacobean attitudes toward gypsies, conspirators, and other rambunctious elements in English society with similarly suspicious attitudes toward the Irish, the American Indians, and the Africans, all of whom inhabited the outer fringes of England's expanding world and whom the English hoped eventually to redeem from "savagery" to "civility." At the same time, the ubiquitous wild-man motif suggested civility gone astray – bestial, treacherous, rapacious, yet capable, in the end, of suing for grace. Why Shakespeare named this eclectic character (if such he was) "Caliban" remains a mystery, but an original name for an original composite creature makes perfect sense.

II

The broad outlines of Caliban's three-and-three-quarter-century odyssey through the briers and thorns of interpretation and adaptation are, we trust, evident in the foregoing chapters. We offer here an overview that integrates the various artistic media through which Caliban has passed. The odyssey is perhaps most poignantly epitomized by the seriatim (but not sequential) privileging of the three operative words in the cast of characters: "savage and deformed slave." Whereas seventeenth- and eighteenth-century interpretations of Caliban emphasized "deformed," and nineteenth- and early-twentieth-century interpretations focused on "savage," for the past forty years the emphasis has been overwhelmingly on the final word: Caliban as American or African or some other "slave," either literally in bondage or bound by cultural chains of language and custom.

To recapitulate more fully, our chapters on literary, theatrical, and artistic representations suggest that widespread concern in the seventeenth and eighteenth centuries over distinctions between crucial opposites – humans and beasts, civility and savagery, innocence and corruption, order and anarchy – made Caliban (judging from the few early clues and the more abundant later evidence) a representative brute, a "monster" not only in the eyes of Trinculo and Stephano but also in the more general sense of human nature at its most bizarre. *The Tempest* comes from an era fascinated by monsters; they rear their ugly heads in exploration literature, of course, and in almost every other literary genre, as well as in pageantry, art, iconography, and the theatre. Caliban, accordingly, was played, interpreted, and depicted in his first century and a half as a barely human grotesque; only the details of his deformity distinguished one version from another. Even if Shakespeare himself hoped for an ambivalent reaction to Caliban – both abhorrence and empathy (as later readings of the text insist, and we also believe) – for almost two centuries the overwhelming critical, artistic, and theatrical image of Caliban was singularly unflattering: He had no redeeming virtues of thought or action, nor even, as the extensive critical discussions of the time make clear, of speech – despite the beauty that modern readers find in his lines.

A significant shift in European and American sentiments in the late eighteenth century finally produced a more admirable monster. If in the earlier interpretations Caliban was scarcely human, in the romanticism of the late eighteenth and early nineteenth centuries he was, by and large, scarcely animal. Despite the persistence of some bestial attributes on stage, some references to bestial characteristics in the critical literature, and an occasional artistic rendition that emphasized an animal shape, Caliban was now more of a savage than a monster. Even when the powerful influence of Darwinian evolutionism turned Caliban into the missing link, his amphibian or – alternatively – apish characteristics were muted, transient, benign. This appears to have been the case in all creative media; stage, illustration, and critical commentary generally concurred in portraying Caliban as a redeemable savage.

That loose consensus dissolved on the eve of the twentieth century. For the first time, Caliban's odyssey took multiple paths. Whereas stage representations remained generally on the course laid out by the preceding century's travels, critical commentary and socioliterary appropriation moved in other, quite opposite, directions. The critical commentary, inspired by an Anglo-American social, political, and intellectual rapprochement and led by the intrepid Sidney Lee, struck out for the North American continent, where *The Tempest* became a play about early English colonization, and Caliban became the local aborigine. At almost the same moment, the sociopolitical branch of *Tempest* appropriation veered southwest, across the Atlantic and into Central America (initially in Nicaragua), then to the South American mainland (especially Uruguay), and on to the Caribbean islands; in all regions of Latin America the motive force was fear of Anglo-American military and cultural imperialism. Thus Caliban, on this leg of the journey, shared with his incarnation to the northward an identification with the United States, but whereas Anglo-American literary critics saw him as the original and usually admirable inhabitant of the land that would someday become the United States, Latin American appropriators found in Caliban the current and quite despicable Uncle Sam. The three Calibans – on stage, in critical studies, and in sociopolitical discourse – kept on their separate, simultaneous paths for almost half a century. Yet they had in common with each other and with the preceding century a sense that Caliban was primarily a savage – whether Beerbohm Tree's primitive man or Sidney Lee's American aborigine or José Enrique Rodó's North American boor.

All that changed in midcentury. Since World War II, preoccupation with global and ideological concerns has refocused views of Caliban once again. Inaugurated by Mannoni's revolutionary reassessment in *Prospero and Caliban*, and fed by the breakup of the colonial empires, the decline of western imperialism, the cold war, and later the revulsion against United States military efforts in Vietnam, Caliban-as-colonial-victim dominated the interpretive paradigm throughout the Third World and even within the Anglo-American orbit. Caliban on stage, on film, in criticism, in poetry, and in art became more often than not the embodiment of imperialism's victims – sometimes tragic, sometimes defiant, sometimes victorious, but almost always resentful of his bondage and usually the play's true hero.

Concomitant with new sympathy for Caliban's dispossession, his resentment of his master, and his desire for freedom has been a deprivileging of Prospero. No longer the eighteenth-century all-wise magus, an Enlightenment *philosophe* in control of his world, Prospero has become an irascible, fallible man, perhaps a bungler, surely a tyrant. Caliban is his temporarily conquered slave, an indigenous native whose oppression the audience must resent and whose yearning for liberty it must respect; Prospero, not Caliban, draws hisses. That, surely, has been the dominant reading, staging, and painting of *The Tempest* from the 1950s until very recently.

III

If Caliban's current image is once again a bit cloudy, his future is even less clear. Stage characterizations seem to be drifting toward "dissensus": He still is often a colonial victim, very often played by a black actor; yet other wide-ranging interpretations have recently been presented, and forthcoming productions are likely to defy easy categorization. Similarly, scholarly interpretation continues to emphasize Caliban's victimization and Prospero's tyrannical and exploitive qualities – especially in new-historicist readings of early-seventeenth-century historical and literary contexts – yet other interpretive schemes retain their vitality and popularity. Sparked by Stephen Orgel's work on the Jacobean court masque, as well as Jonathan Goldberg's study of James I, literary critics will continue to find royal resonances in the play. But how that will affect Caliban is difficult to say. Caliban may be interpreted as one member in a regal allegory or the representative of indigenous populations of the New World. Or he may be analyzed in terms of his opposition to Ariel in psychoanalytic studies of the artist's imagination, or as one pole in a modern psychomachia.

In the realm of sociopolitical discourse, and even in critical commentary and artistic representation, Caliban's symbolization of exploited Third World natives seems to be waning. Half a century ago, Caliban emblemized white imperialists, an image its adherents probably expected would last indefinitely. But that role was built on shifting sand. Until the 1950s, most metaphoric uses of Caliban had elitist roots and less than universal support. Such intellectual giants as Ernest Renan and José Enrique Rodó faced criticism from

the outset regarding their symbolic strategies for Caliban; Leonard
Barnes's association of Caliban with Dutch Afrikaners was a cry
in the wilderness; and Mannoni, despite the profound influence of
his paradigm, aroused vehement rebuttals. By contrast, Caliban's
current role of rebellious and resilient survivor of western imperialism appears to be widely accepted and deeply felt throughout
the Third World. The new Caliban was sired by spokesmen of
indigenous cultures and has been nourished by a generation of
readers who find in Shakespeare's savage a poignant – if often
ambivalent – symbol of their own experience and aspirations.

And yet, as Rob Nixon has suggested, the high tide of Caliban's
Third World role probably has passed, for *The Tempest*'s applicability
has built-in limitations for readers and viewers in the recently liberated nations. The play ends with Caliban once again in command
of his island; what he does with his new freedom is beyond the
metaphor. At the moment of national liberation, newly freed people
often strengthened their own identities by verbally thrashing their
former masters; now that political and cultural identities have been
substantially reconstructed, spokespersons for the new nations (or,
in most cases, the old nations free again) focus on the more pressing concerns of economic and political stability; preindependence
Caliban is irrelevant. Adding to *The Tempest*'s limitations as an on-
going anticolonial metaphor, as Nixon points out, is its exclusively
male identification; it has no role for female spokespersons.[2] And as
we related in Chapter 6, many African writers and some Caribbean
writers are highly ambivalent about an English imperialist's play,
however useful it may be in certain situations. "[T]here can be no
political liberation," asserts the Senegalese poet-statesman Léopold
Senghor, "without cultural liberation."[3] Accordingly, indigenous

2 Rob Nixon, "Caribbean and African Appropriations of *The Tempest*," *Critical Inquiry*,
  XIII (1987): 576–78. Cf. Diana Brydon, "Re-Writing *The Tempest*," *World Literature
  Written in English*, XXIII (1984): 75–88, which argues (as we discussed in Chapter 6)
  that Miranda has been an important symbol for English-Canadian writers. That
  seems to be a special situation, one of the few instances of a "colonial" setting that
  is not also "Third World."
3 Léopold Sédar Senghor, quoted in Ali A. Mazrui and Michael Tidy, *Nationalism and
  New States in Africa: From about 1935 to the Present* (London: Heinemann, 1984),
  p. 298.

cultures probably will, in the long run, find indigenous symbols more meaningful and enduring. They are unlikely to reverse the metaphor (as Mannoni did so dramatically in 1950); they are very likely to discard it.

Whether or not there is an abatement in the use of Caliban as colonial metaphor, *The Tempest*'s popularity continues, especially on the stage. During 1988, a visitor to England could see three different professional productions; in December 1989 the play was staged in both New York and Washington, D.C. Schoolteachers and their pupils love the play for its fantasy, its dream of strange creatures and faraway places, regardless of changing fashions in theatrical interpretation. And *The Tempest*'s popularity on stage is almost certain to stimulate further criticism and adaptation. Professional scholars will surely plumb the play for ideas about Shakespeare and his art and will forge new versions of the Caliban paradigm.

When they do, they will have three and a half centuries of critical discourse to ponder – the odyssey we have described in the preceding pages. Although our focus has been on Caliban, the complicated and changing relationship between Prospero and Caliban we have described is a reminder that the interpretation of any one character in a Shakespearean drama influences our understanding of the whole. Scholars and directors are not likely to revert to the stern Prospero of the eighteenth century. Caliban has been unleashed from his abject servitude and will not be incarcerated again. Rather, we predict a continuing softening of the binary opposition between Prospero the master and Caliban the slave. As a result of the twentieth-century appropriation of Caliban as a symbolic figure, both characters have been humanized. Prospero no longer knows all the answers; he suffers doubts and fears and bears much of the blame for discord in Milan and on the island. Caliban, too, harbors human longings in addition to his rage; his desire for freedom, long overlooked by *Tempest* critics, is unlikely ever to be ignored again.

We have offered the reader many *Tempests*, sometimes conflicting *Tempests*, and many Calibans, often conflicting. That has been Caliban's fate. Had Shakespeare described him more fully, of course, there would be less ground for contention but also less food for thought. Caliban's odyssey promises to continue unabated, unpredictable. And it promises, too, to remain "rich and strange," for, paradoxically, Caliban is simultaneously one of Shakespeare's most ambiguous and most memorable characters.

Index

285

Index

243, 247–8; as Asian, 139–40n55, 161, 169; as Australian/New Zealander, 169, 257; as Canadian, 170–1, 257–8; as cannibal, 26–32, 47–8, 141, 163–4, 278; as conspirator, 18–19, 43, 48, 52–4, 82, 139, 207; as fish, 12–14, 158, 237, 256; as harlequin, 78–80, 210, 276; as human, 10–12, 226–7, 228–9, 233, 243–7, 279; as Irishman, 54, 141–2, 276, 278; as monster, xxii, 14, 25, 76–8, 116–17, 133, 205, 256, 260–1, 276, 279; as savage, 7–9, 11, 105, 278, 279–80; as slave, 9, 25, 105–8, 133, 156–7, 162, 191, 264, 278, 280–1; as tortoise, 13–14, 176, 223; as wild man, 70–1, 79, 80, 83, 100, 134, 137, 139, 141, 182, 213, 274, 276–7

Caliban's etymology, 26–36, 163, 277–8
Caliban's language, 95–100, 156, 165–9, 264–5
Caliban's parentage, 15
Caliban's stage costume, 180–96 passim, 206–7, 213, 220, 276
Calibia, 32–3
Cassavetes, John, 211–12
Cawley, Robert Ralston, 52, 128–9, 274
Césaire, Aimé, 156, 162
Chambers, E. K., 34
Cheney, Donald, 74
Chodowiecki, Daniel Nicolaus, 222–4
civility: Caliban's lack of, 50, 71, 85, 105, 137–8, 278; as uncharacteristic of European wild man, 63–5, 67–9, 71–4; Jacobean concept of, xxii, 8–9, 137–8, 142, 278
Clark, John Pepper, 166–7
Clarke, Warren, 208
Cobb, Noel, 61–2
Cohen, Walter, 49
Cohn, Ruby, 112
Coleridge, Samuel Taylor, 103–4, 178, 221, 233
colonial interpretations: Caliban as imperialist, 147–53, 158–9, 280; Caliban as victim, 48–50, 128–9, 132–8, 140–2, 155–7, 164–71, 191–5, 197–8, 210–12, 274, 280–3; causes, xiv–xv, 117, 118–19, 124–31, 132–3, 144–7, 150–5, 159–64, 280; *see also*

Caliban: as African, as American Indian, as Asian, as Australian/New Zealander, as Irishman, as slave
Columbus, Christopher, xv, 27–8, 37, 134
commedia dell'arte, 78–80, 276
Cook, Dutton, 183
Cooke, William, 177
Cooper, John Gilbert, 98
Craig, Edward Gordon, 185–6
Cranch, Christopher Pearse, 112
Crane, Walter, 240–3
Crosse, Gordon, 188
Cruikshank, Isaac Robert, 234
culture, definition of, xvii

Daly, Augustin, 186–7
Dance, James (alias James Love), 177–8
Darío, Rubén, 131n29, 147–8, 152
Darwinian interpretations, xxii, 100, 109–14, 116–17, 121, 184–9, 203, 238–43, 279
Davenant, William, 91–3, 94, 173–7, 180, 275
Davie, Donald, 261–2
Davies, Anthony, 208
Dekker, Thomas, 35
Del Castillo-Morante, Mark, 195
Dickason, Olive Patricia, 139
Donne, John, 75
Dorsinville, Max, xxi, 170–1
Dotrice, Roy, 190
Downes, John 175–6
Drayton, Michael, 90
Dryden, John, 90–3, 94, 173–7, 180, 275–6
Dudley, Robert (Lord Leicester), 66
Duffett, Thomas, 93–4

Eden, Richard, 37, 50, 51, 119
Edwards, Edward, 220, 221
Edwards, Philip, 276
Egan, Robert, 81
Eliot, T. S., 252
Elizabeth I of England, 65–7, 71, 82
Elizabeth of Bohemia, 4, 5
Elze, Theodor, 32–3, 51
Emery, John, 179
Erickson, Peter, 195

Index

Index

Index

Phelps, Samuel, 181
Phillpotts, J. S., 51, 120
Pigafetta, Antonio, 37–8, 43, 119–20, 134, 138
Pinciss, G. M., 135
Pitcher, John, 59
Pliny, 75, 119
Pocahontas, 43–4
poetry, Caliban: in early twentieth century, 113; in eighteenth century, 98; in nineteenth century, 109–10, 112
Ponce, Aníbal, 155
Porter, Joseph A., xivn12
Powell, Jocelyn, 91
Power, Tyrone, 186–7
Primaleon of Greece, 78
Prospero, 4, 6, 7, 80–1, 114–15, 154, 191, 206; as educator, 18, 148; as imperialist, 132–3, 141, 156–7, 159–62, 164–71, 210–12; as magician, 5, 82, 180–1, 183, 227–8; relation of, to Ariel, 16; relation of, to Caliban, 9–13, 15, 196–7, 270, 283
Prospero's/Caliban's island, location of, 32, 120, 123–4, 132, 136n45, 142, 197
Prudentius, 61
psychomachia, 61, 281

Quilley, Denis, 192

Raleigh, Sir Walter, 76
Raleigh, Walter Alexander, 122–3, 127
Randall, Dale B. J., 34
Ray, Sibnarayan, 169
Reid, Alexander, 259–60
Renan, Ernest, 111–12, 148–9, 281–2
Retzsch, Friedrich August Moritz, 235–7
Reynolds, Joshua, 224, 226, 228
Rezeptionsästhetik, xi
Rich, Richard, 41
Rignold, George, 183
Ringwald, Molly, 211–12
Roberts, Jeanne Addison, 191
Rodó, José Enrique, 131n29, 147–55, 281–2
romantic interpretations, xxii, 102–5, 180–3, 220–1, 228, 279
Roosevelt, Theodore, 150, 151–2
Rosten, Norman, 260–1

Rothwell, Kenneth S., 203
Rowe, Nicholas, 95–6, 216
Rowse, A. L., 136
Rozewicz, Tadeusz, 262
Ryder, John, 183
Rymer, Thomas, 95, 276

Sanchez, Jaime, 192
Sarandon, Susan, 211–12
savage (salvage), meaning of, in Shakespeare's time, 7–9; *see also* Caliban as savage
Schaefer, George, 206–8
Schlegal, Augustus William, 103, 120
Schmidgall, Gary, 52–3, 73n45, 78
Sea Venture, 38–9, 40, 41, 42, 43
Sebastian, 18, 72, 84, 102
Selden, John, 95, 96, 98, 99
Senghor, Léopold Sédar, 282
Seoane, Manuel, 153
Service, Robert, 257–8
Shadwell, Thomas, 93–4, 174–6
Shakespeare, William: *All's Well That Ends Well*, 45; *Antony and Cleopatra*, xiii, 36, 180; *As You Like It*, 36, 83; *Comedy of Errors*, 6; *Coriolanus*, 30; *Cymbeline*, 84, 85n75; *Hamlet*, xiii, xv; *Henry IV, Part 2*, 216; *Henry V*, 180, 199; *Henry VI, Part 3*, 30; *Henry VIII*, 45, 229; *Julius Caesar*, xix, 139; *King Lear*, 202; *Love's Labour's Lost*, 26; *Macbeth*, xiii, xv, 61, 200; *The Merchant of Venice*, xiii, 83, 177, 275; *A Midsummer Night's Dream*, 45, 84, 119; *Much Ado About Nothing*, 26, 83, 262; *Othello*, xiii, xivn11, 30, 33, 36, 45, 61, 76, 106, 107, 231, 275; *Pericles*, 84; *Richard III*, xix, 24, 177, 189, 202; *Romeo and Juliet*, xivn12, 24, 26, 36, 200; *The Taming of the Shrew*, xiii, xix; *Timon of Athens*, 180; *Twelfth Night*, xix, 26, 83, 180; *Two Gentlemen of Verona*, 229; *The Winter's Tale*, 26, 84, 202
Shakespeare Gallery, 220, 225–31, 234
Shakespeare Jubilee (1769), 100–1, 225
Sheehan, Bernard, 137–8
Sill, Richard, 118
Simon, Robin, 217–18
Skura, Meredith Anne, 83n71, 142–3

289

Index

Smirke, Robert, 228–9, 233
Smith, Captain John, 41, 43
Smith, John Christopher, 176
Smith, John Orrin, 234–5
Smythe, Sir Thomas, 39, 41
Somers, Sir George, 39, 43
Sorelius, Gunnar, 92n6
Sparacino, Dennis N., 79–80
Spenser, Edmund, 57, 69, 71–5, 119, 277
Spevack, Marvin, 7
Srigley, Michael, 73n45, 82
Steevens, George, 15, 30, 99, 225
Stephano, 78, 79, 81, 135, 196; in
  adaptations and appropriations, 92,
  101–2, 105, 174, 212; in art, 220, 229,
  234; in critical commentary, 48–50,
  104, 123, 137; in performance, 182, 183,
  187, 191, 197, 207; in Shakespeare's
  text, 7, 9, 12–13, 14, 18–19, 45
Stoll, Elmer Edgar, 129
Stothard, Thomas, 229–31
Stow, Percy, 201
Strachey, William, 24, 39–40, 43, 132
Suchet, David, 192–3
Sutherland, Ronald, 170
Sycorax, 141; in adaptations and
  appropriations, 102, 108–9, 175, 176,
  190–1, 210; in Shakespeare's text, 15,
  16, 51–2, 82; and worship of Setebos,
  38

Takaki, Ronald T., 139–40n55
Tatspaugh, Patricia E., 197
Tayler, Edward, 72
Taylor, Gary, xi–xii, xvi
Tempest, The, editions of: eighteenth-
  century, 30, 95, 96, 98–100, 225; First
  Folio, 3, 4, 7, 10, 12, 41, 81, 90, 92, 131,
  176, 217, 275; nineteenth-century, 30,
  232; *see also* Furness, Horace Howard
Thanhouser, Edwin, 201–2
Theobald, Lewis, 96
Thevet, André, 46, 50, 274
Thompson, Edward, 100
Tonkin, Humphrey, 74
Topsell, Edward, 76
Tree, Herbert Beerbohm, 10n19, 187–8,
  201, 208
Trinculo, 78, 79, 81, 135, 158, 196, 218; in
  adaptations and appropriations, 92,

101–2, 105, 173, 174, 175, 176, 210,
212; in art, 220, 229, 234; in critical
commentary, 48–50, 104, 137; in
performance, 182, 183, 185, 197, 207; in
Shakespeare's text, 7n10, 9, 12–13, 14,
18–19, 43, 45

Ulrici, Hermann, 237
Untermeyer, Louis, 255–6
Urban, Charles, 201
Urban, Raymond A., 60–1
Vaughan, Henry, 95, 96, 98, 99
Velz, John, 193
Virgil, 58–60
Virginia colony, 5, 38–43, 54, 121, 123,
  125, 129, 132

Wain, John, 169
Waldron, Francis Godophin, 100–2
Walker, Rudolph, 192, 197
Warburton, William, 96, 98
Ward, Adolphus William, 120, 127–8
Warton, Joseph, 97–8
Webster, John, 180
Webster, Margaret, 189
Weiss, Theodore, 267–70
Wheeler, Alfred A., 113
Whetstone, George, 68
White, Hayden, 57, 60, 62–3
White, John, 44, 138, 275
wild man, 57–8, 60, 62–75, 274; *see also*
  Caliban as wild man
Wilde, Oscar, 112–13, 241
Williams, Arnold, 74
Williams, Heathcote, 209, 210
Wilson, Daniel, 110–11, 184, 238, 243
Wimsatt, W. K., xix
Winter, William, 187
Wittkower, Rudolph, 75
Woodroffe, Paul Vincent, 243
Wright, Joseph, 226
Wright, Louis B., 40

Yates, Frances, 82
Young, David, 79

Zabus, Chantal, 171
Zeeveld, Gordon, 136
Zeffirelli, Franco, 200
Zimbalist, Efrem, Jr., 213